HYPERLOCAL

HYPERLOCAL

Place Governance in a Fragmented World

Edited by
JENNIFER S. VEY
NATE STORRING

BROOKINGS INSTITUTION PRESS
Washington, D.C.

The Brookings Institution is a private nonprofit organization devoted to research, education, and publication on important issues of domestic and foreign policy. Its principal purpose is to bring the highest quality independent research and analysis to bear on current and emerging policy problems. Interpretations or conclusions in Brookings publications should be understood to be solely those of the authors.

Library of Congress Cataloging-in-Publication data has been applied for.

ISBN 9780815739579 (pbk)
ISBN 9780815739586 (ebook)

9 8 7 6 5 4 3 2 1

Typeset in Janson Text LTStd

Composition by Westchester Publishing Services

Contents

Preface

JENNIFER S. VEY AND NATE STORRING

When the teams at Project for Public Spaces and the Brookings Institution first began working together in 2015, we experienced something of a clash of cultures. Project for Public Spaces traces its origins back to the 1970s work of public space researcher William H. Whyte, and it still carries that focus on street-level observations of human behavior today. Meanwhile, since its founding in 1916, the Brookings Institution has largely focused on issues of national public policy, though this partnership included veterans of what is now Brookings Metro, a place-focused program established in 1996.

One characteristic episode early on in our collaboration revolved around the word *hub*. We had been talking past each other for fifteen minutes or so because the policy wonks in the room thought an "innovation hub" must be a cluster of businesses, research institutions, and intermediary organizations within a regional economy, while the placemaking wonks thought an "innovation hub" was a physical space where entrepreneurs and researchers could collaborate and socialize. As it turns out, both concepts had value to our investigation on innovation districts—the central focus of our collaboration at the time—but only once we learned how to blast through our own intellectual silos.

The two of us didn't know it then, but those early philosophical debates about the gap between the scale of human interaction and the scale of a metro area would become the productive tension, the reciprocating engine, that would ultimately power this book. Indeed, our organizations' work together has continued over these past several years with projects big and small, but the idea of the "hub" as a place within a region where people, jobs, and physical assets cluster and connect with one another has been the unifier—the "hyperlocal" scale at which our respective knowledge and interests converge. Through both research and practice, our organizations collect, co-design, and communicate strategies to strengthen hyperlocal economic ecosystems, built environments, and social well-being. We share a theory of change that strong *places* are the foundation of prosperous, equitable, and resilient *cities and regions*.

Yet as much as the "where" has sustained our organizations' collaboration, it's the "who" within the where that has motivated it. We care about places because we care about the people in them—as residents, workers, business owners, and community leaders. People and the places they inhabit are always entwined in virtuous and vicious cycles of making and unmaking, always shaping one another. Many call these processes "community building" or "placemaking." In this volume, we use the more expansive term "place governance" to draw attention both to the *scale* at which these processes occur and the underappreciated role of *stewardship* in guiding them. In any case, the cycles are always in motion—with or without resources, formal organizations, and regulation.

So it has always been. But in an economic landscape marked by stark inequalities of income, race, and geography, our civic infrastructure has become both more fragile and more vital. Now more than ever there is an urgent need to reexamine how community stakeholders come together to exert agency—governance—over their places. As we explore in this volume, there are innumerable place governance organizations operating in communities around the world— overlapping in some communities, barely existent in others, and serving purposes both good and perverse. Yet there exists very little systematic research and documentation on these organizations' varying structures or the governance ecosystems in which they relate to one another.

Hyperlocal aims to fill this gap. The volume offers a set of eight chapters exploring the role of place governance; the evolving tensions, challenges, and opportunities associated with place governance; and recommendations for creating, reforming, and sustaining place governance structures that benefit more people and places. It addresses place governance in a range of forms—from public-private business improvement districts (BIDs) to public community boards to private neighborhood associations—and across an array of land-use contexts, including urban, suburban, and rural areas.

We hope *Hyperlocal* will find its way into the hands of practitioners and scholars alike. The leaders of place governance organizations will find here one of the few interdisciplinary, intersectoral treatments of their field. The essays in this book explore what a diversity of organization types can learn from one another, their relative strengths and weaknesses, and innovative practices—wherever we may find them.

Likewise, the insights in the book will be useful to those who oversee, support, or engage with place governance organizations, from city agencies to real estate developers to anchor institutions to foundations. The authors delve into the brass tacks of issues like governance structure, enabling legislation, and resource allocation. While these may seem esoteric, obscure, or even immovable forces of nature, we think readers will find that they may, in fact, be some of the most powerful levers of change in the field of place governance.

On the academic side, *Hyperlocal* may find use in a wide variety of fields. The early chapters provide a concise overview of the history and current state of place governance, one of the most important developments in American urban affairs, urban studies, urban geography, and political science of the late twentieth and early twenty-first centuries. The remaining chapters offer plenty of specific case studies, data, and analysis to spark debate among students and teachers of city planning, nonprofit and public management, public policy, law, and other disciplines.

Perhaps the most productive conversations around this book, though, will happen at the intersection of these readerships. This book is the result of a lively discourse among practitioners and scholars, place managers and city planners, historians and nonprofit leaders, data geeks, and writers. We hope *Hyperlocal* is only the beginning of this conversation, because working across organizations, fields, sectors, and cultures is the only way to move place governance forward in today's increasingly fragmented cities and regions.

Acknowledgments

The editors are enormously grateful to the many people who gave their time and knowledge to make this volume possible.

First and foremost, we want to thank the authors, without whom we'd have no book—or at least not such a good one (and we say this without bias). Their tremendous insight and expertise are evident not only in their individual chapters, but throughout the whole of the volume that they collectively helped shape. A special shout out to Tracy Hadden Loh, who convinced us that our wild idea about "some sort of report series on place governance" was small thinking and that what the field *really* needed was the full-on book now before you.

The quality and value of the book is in large part due to the amazing group of scholars and practitioners who reviewed early chapter drafts and attended workshop sessions to discuss their virtues and weaknesses. They include: Natalie Avery (The Javera Group); Matt Bergheiser (University City District, Philadelphia); Steve Coe (The Centre for Conscious Design); Margaret Crawford (University of California, Berkeley); Richardson Dilworth (Drexel University); Zahra

Ebrahim (Monumental); Kevin Finn (Strategies to End Homelessness, Inc.); Carola Hein (Delft University of Technology); Samantha Jackson (Downtown Mesa Association); Wonhyung Lee (University at Albany–State University of New York); Ricardo León (Metro West Community Development Organization, Cleveland); Setha Low (The City University of New York); Steve McGovern (Haverford College); Stephen Miller (University of Idaho, College of Law); Göktuğ Morçöl (Penn State Harrisburg); Sara Rankin (Seattle University School of Law); Mary Rocco (Barnard College, Columbia University); Jefferey Sellers (University of Southern California); Richard C. Schragger (University of Virginia); André Sorensen (University of Toronto Scarborough); Robert P. Stoker (George Washington University); and Laura Wolf-Powers (City University of New York).

Huge thanks go to Phil Myrick and Meg Walker, former CEO and Senior Vice President, respectively, of Project for Public Spaces, who helped get this project off the ground and to Cailean Kok (Project for Public Spaces) and Joanne Kim and Hanna Love (Brookings), who did background research, helped identify chapter authors, and managed various tasks as the book was getting underway. We are also grateful to Brookings Institution Press and the Brookings Metro communications team, who together were responsible for the volume's editorial quality and ensuring that people are made aware that it is out in the world. Without them the book would be the proverbial tree falling in the forest (and one full of typos at that).

Finally, we acknowledge with enormous gratitude Bob and Anne Bass, both for their generous support of PPS and Brookings, but also for playing matchmaker between our organizations seven-odd years ago. The intellectual journey we've been on together since then is reflected in these pages.

ONE

Introduction

Defining Place, Defining a Field

TRACY HADDEN LOH

JENNIFER S. VEY

P lace has always mattered to people and the economy, in ways that are constantly evolving.

In the nineteenth century, America's cities grew to become not only centers of commerce and trade but also powerhouses of invention and industry. Within these cities, the various needs of manufacturers, artisans, retailers, and other businesses determined where and how they clustered, giving rise to the growth of downtowns, industrial districts, and surrounding enclaves of worker housing. The demands for place dramatically changed during the twentieth century, however. The advent of the automobile, coupled with new infrastructure investments, new housing and land-use policies, and changing demands of industry, led to the movement of people and jobs from central cities to greener, and whiter, suburban pastures—while leaving many, predominantly Black and brown, urban communities in economic and fiscal decline.[1]

But these patterns are not static. As with past innovations, the digital revolution is disrupting growth and development patterns. The new economic geography that is emerging is one of polycentric megaregions, where jobs, people, and amenities concentrate at key nodes in both historic urban cores and suburbs.[2] Older cities and regions have had limited success in consolidating governments to encompass this new reality, leading to a fragmented landscape replete with city centers, mature and emerging suburbs, exurbs, and rural towns, often with different jurisdictional boundaries.[3] Yet larger or more consolidated regions are not necessarily more efficient or effective at providing services or managing resources.[4] Indeed, Jane Jacobs once described a region as "an area safely larger than the last one to whose problems we found no solution."[5] There is simply an inevitable mismatch between the boundaries of our formal government units, the scale of different markets, and the way we actually live our lives.[6]

One consequence of this fragmentation is sustained and growing place-based inequality. Even as many downtowns, waterfronts, and innovation districts have in recent decades seen significant revitalization and reinvestment, concentrated poverty and racial segregation remain persistent in neighborhoods across the regional landscape.[7] Traditional units of government are less able than ever to understand and, ultimately, help meet the needs of places within a region and network them together efficiently and equitably.

These uneven patterns of economic growth and governance require a shift in the way places are governed and managed—one that acknowledges the changing socioeconomic realities of place and the pressing need to bring inclusive economic growth and prosperity to more people and places. Making this shift successfully could unleash a new era of inclusive American growth. Perhaps sensing this, many residents, philanthropies, and businesses have responded by attempting to do this work themselves, organizing at the hyperlocal level new forms of governance to improve places' economic competitiveness or advance social equity, among other goals.[8]

This chapter introduces and offers specific definitions for *place*, *placemaking*, and *place governance* to explain exactly what is meant by "the hyperlocal level," and make available to the reader and our co-authors a consistent, shared vocabulary. Next comes a review of the literature relating place governance to the issues of segregation and inequality and the role place governance has in addressing, or exacerbating, them. Finally, the chapter foreshadows the explorations of various dimensions of place governance offered in chapters 2 through 8 of this volume.

What Is Place?

Where is the hyperlocal level? To answer this question, we begin from John Agnew's three-part definition of *place* as a "meaningful location."[9] All places consist of:

- Location (macro)
- Locale (objective)
- Sense of place (subjective)

Location refers to the context within which the place is situated—for example, the location of a ship is in the ocean or a port, or the location of a neighborhood is in a city, and so on. Proceeding from this idea that some larger ecosystem is the setting of a place, for the purposes of this book, the location is a metropolitan area, or "region," containing one or more primary cities, suburbs, and rural areas that are related and connected to one another by daily labor flows. As such, *places* must be smaller than regions. These "hyperlocal" places are within, or sometimes straddle, the areas bounded by legal jurisdictions recognized by state constitutions (for example, counties, cities, townships, parishes, boroughs, etc.).

Locale refers to the "material setting for social relations." We know and recognize neighborhoods as the locales surrounding our homes. However, as noted by Emily Talen, the historical typology of this "spatial unit that people relate to" also includes locales defined by specific anchors or "clusters of related land uses" beyond housing, such as community, recreation, consumption, institutional, infrastructure, or economic assets.[10] These clusters, or "activity centers," also are places with unique governance challenges.[11] The scope of this book, and our definition of place, is inclusive of both residential neighborhoods and activity centers. We are investigating here the relationships—civic structures—we create to manage assets and negotiate needs within these places.

Sense of place refers to "the subjective and emotional attachment people have to a place." A shared sense of place can be thought of as a legible meaning for the place based on a "reading" of its collective assets. This sense is critical—it is the primary source of the legitimacy, reach, and leverage of any attempt at place governance. By combining this meaning with the previously specified location and locale, we arrive at a concise definition of *place* for the purposes of this book:

Place: A neighborhood or activity center, within or cutting across a local government unit, composed of a meaningful collection of assets in proximity to one another.

What Is Placemaking?

Because of the importance of sense of place to the very definition of place, governance actors have a stake in shaping who is and is not included in the place, as it is the interpretation, feelings, and desires of included people that determine a place's identity. However, David Harvey notes that, in today's fragmented and uneven metropolitan context, "ideals of urban identity, citizenship and belonging . . . become much harder to sustain."[12] The cultivation of a sense of place by place governance actors also often has a cyclical character: A shared sense of place creates the foundation for place governance among a group of insiders, and place governance aims to further define that sense of place for that group. Ultimately, despite the "mushiness" implied by the subjectivity and negotiability of sense of place, it grows from a personal judgment that gives it a powerful, authentic core that matters to people and drives concrete action.

Actions that establish, shift, enrich, or complicate a place's identity are part of defining a place. While in the original anthropological sense *placemaking* as a term referred to the acts of settlement, construction, and dwelling by everyday people, the term has been adopted by the design, urban planning, and place management professions to describe actions that "make our places meaningful," including both "daily acts of renovating, maintaining, and representing" and "special . . . one-time events" like a celebration or the opening of a new facility.[13] Placemaking today describes both a distinct professional practice as well as an activity that everybody does, but with a crucial distinction: A professional class engaging in these activities without the participation of the people who use a place is appropriative place-taking, not placemaking.

Placemaking: Daily and special acts to make a place useful and meaningful.

Placemaking includes an enormous range of activities at many scales. Each one is a "framing action" in that "every time we decide to do something, we are simultaneously deciding not to do something else. . . . Placemaking thus includes and excludes people in every intervention . . . [and] privilege[s] ways of working at the expense of alternative methods."[14] It is this very process of filtering and refinement that adds specificity and meaning to a place, while also "constructing community" by setting boundaries on who and what is included and represented—and who and what is excluded.[15] In the act of placemaking, individuals or groups are projecting preferences or desires about what they want a place to be, expressing their sense of place, and ultimately claiming and exerting a sort of power.

There are many disciplines that want to change places, often motivated by ambitious objectives such as racial equity, environmental justice, or wealth building. In fact, both experts and advocates have long been aware that, because place influences so many different outcomes for people, there is a need for a more expansive kind of placemaking that acts not just on what a place is but also how it works in relation to other places and in its regional context. Individual, often siloed, approaches from the economic development and community development fields, the smart growth movement, and the placemaking movement have had limited traction and success at achieving this kind of change on their own. A "transformative placemaking" approach—as defined by the Brookings Bass Center for Transformative Placemaking—aims to encompass insights, methods, and goals from all these domains.[16]

Transformative placemaking: An integrated framework and practice for realizing a holistic set of economic, physical, social, and civic outcomes for places.

What Is Place Governance?

Broadly, the concept of governance refers to a shift from twentieth-century government structures, in which the public sector exerted full control, to a hybrid structure in which governmental and nongovernmental actors collaborate and share control and influence.[17] The acts of collaboration and sharing are definitional here. Governance is the difference between people and/or organizations acting (or reacting) in isolation and, instead, co-creating with one another. When applied to the act of governing urban places, place governance often manifests as a collaboration among public sector actors (state and local governments), private sector actors (retailers and business owners), civic sector actors (foundations and nonprofits), and citizens (residents and users) to co-govern a specific location through a narrow or wide span of design, maintenance, programming, and service delivery activities.[18]

Governance is a capacious concept that covers an extremely broad range of actors and actions. People in proximity organize to create place governance structures to fill gaps that arise from the treatment of places strictly as mutually exclusive collections of public and private property. Governance acknowledges the reality of places as emergent entities that are not fully public but are clearly not private either. The aggregate dynamics of places, which include both positive and negative spillovers resulting from the complex mix of commercial, residential, recreational, and myriad other activities that are constantly changing within them, suggest a simple yet specific definition of place governance.

Place governance: The collaboration of actors across sectors to make decisions that help shape the economic, physical, and/or social dynamics of a specific place.

Today, there are uncounted thousands—likely tens of thousands—of place governance structures in the United States and around the globe. What all these structures have in common is that they use a specific geographic grounding to situate their work, which may be called "place-based," "place-rooted," or "place-conscious."[19] These structures may be made up of one or more organizations operating in a single or overlapping geography, including private civic or business institutions, such as a neighborhood association or a chamber of commerce; community-based nonprofit organizations; public-private entities such as business improvement districts (BIDs); or formal public entities like New York City's community boards, Los Angeles's

FIGURE 1-1. Common Examples of Place Governance Organizations on a Spectrum from Private to Public

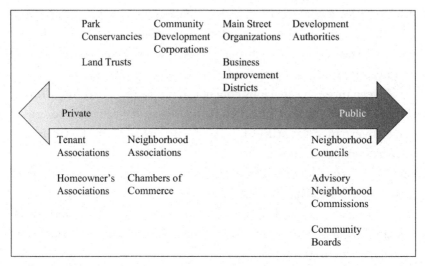

Source: Authors' analysis.

neighborhood councils, or the District of Columbia's advisory neighborhood commissions. Figure 1-1 summarizes these forms on a spectrum from private to public.

Place governance organizations have a huge range of missions and capacity. At one end of the range is place management, the targeted delivery of services, beautification, and programming in particular areas—such as a park or public plaza—shown to require special funding and maintenance outside of what the public sector can or should provide.[20] Activities and services could include neighborhood watches, community cleanups, events, or the deployment of "clean and safe" teams. However, this type of normative place management may appear from one perspective as stewardship and from another as policing, erasure, or sanitization of people, cultures, behaviors, or values that are not preferred by a dominant group. In response to this critique, numerous scholars and practitioners have advanced the concept of "placekeeping," proposing a practice dedicated to "the active care and maintenance of a place and its social fabric by the people who live and work there."[21] This implies both a bigger timescale and a more holistic sense of what is valued and how returns are measured, "not just preserving the facade of the building but also keeping the cultural memories associated with a locale alive, keeping the tree once planted in the memory of a loved one lost in a war and keeping the tenants who have raised their family in an apartment."[22]

Near the other end of the range of place governance activities is place production, the literal building or development of places. Historically undertaken in the United States primarily by the private sector and occasionally by the public sector, new organizational forms are attempting to combine the motivations and accountability frameworks of the public and private sectors in public-private partnerships (PPPs). Public-private partnerships have long functioned as quasi-institutional venues for reworking state-market relations at the local level, including the widespread privatizing of core public sector management and social service delivery.[23] At their best, effective PPPs allow public governments to gain from business know-how, such as brokering deals and financing, and allow businesses to profit from normalized ties to government, through, for example, buy-in from agencies and quicker turnaround from regulatory bureaucracies. Through collaborative, interdisciplinary, networked leadership, cities are able to "think like a system and act like an entrepreneur."[24] Figure 1-2 frames this range of activities as a cumulative ladder of place governance.

Does Place Governance Contribute to or Combat Place-Based Inequities?

As with any shift in power and control, place governance is controversial. Proponents argue it is an efficient, effective approach for tackling place-based challenges and promoting economic development without the hinderances of governmental bureaucracy—and a way to make improvements to places that governments cannot, will not, or should

FIGURE 1-2. The Cumulative Ladder of Place Governance

ACTIVITY What does the organization do?	MOTIVATION Why?
Advocacy / Strategy / Vision	POSITION PLACE
Development Projects	PRODUCE PLACE
Retention/ Recruitment (e.g., of businesses or residents)	ACTIVATE PLACE
Beautification	INVEST IN PLACE
Branding and Marketing	TEACH PLACE
Events	CELEBRATE AND SHARE PLACE
Maintenance "Clean and Safe"	CLAIM PLACE

Source: Adapted by authors from James Yanchula, "Finding One's Place in the Place Management Spectrum," *Journal of Place Management and Development* 1, no. 1 (2008).

not undertake.[25] Aside from efficiency, they contend, place governance can be used to promote equity because it restructures resources toward places with serious challenges and redistributes them on the basis of locational need rather than arbitrary circumstance.[26] They point out that place-focused organizations are uniquely positioned to bridge the gap between economic development and social justice by making a case for inclusive growth, ideally by ensuring that local stakeholders have voice and agency in proactively determining desired outcomes for their place and the strategies and investments needed to achieve them.[27] Such entities also provide an organized structure through which stakeholders can vet and react to proposed investments from public or private sector actors (for example, real estate developers) while providing those actors with an organized group with whom to work to coordinate public input.

However, it also is possible that place governance represents additional fragmentation of an already fragmented local government landscape. Critics argue, for example, that this new form of governance formalizes another phase of decline of the public sector, where any success of private sector management in delivering municipal services delegitimizes local governmental authority.[28] The privatization of public services and the creation of hyperlocal funding sources to do so can represent a form of hoarding that serves narrow interests, diverts dollars from under-resourced neighborhoods, and creates wealth-based disparities in the provision of public services.[29] As noted by Harvey, it simply may be the latest attempt of "the neoliberal project over the last thirty years . . . towards privatizing . . . control" over capital surpluses.[30]

A second, related, critique is that place governance potentially can create "spillover effects" in which place-based challenges (such as housing affordability, crime, and homelessness) simply are displaced between two neighborhoods rather than addressed holistically for the well-being of entire cities or regions.[31]

Finally, most place governance organizations are siloed to serve a specific constituency within a place, such as homeowners or renters, landowners, or business tenants. Emily Talen contends that this restricts participation and thus legitimacy, leaving place governance "in constant search of authenticity" and "easily challenged as inefficient and backward."[32]

A major challenge in understanding the field of place governance, or carrying out a critically reflective practice as a member of it, is that the devil is in the details. The benefits and critiques enumerated here both can be true of a given organization or place at the same time. Just as every place is unique, so, too, is every place governance arrangement. The same emergent quality of place that defines and motivates place governance also complicates any effort to generalize about it.

That said, questions of power and accountability clearly are central concerns of a just place governance practice.[33] Who has the power? Who

are organizations accountable to? How can accountability be operation-
alized, measured, and monitored? Proponents argue that place governance organizations are politically accountable as long as they provide
annual reports, audits, and reauthorization requirements, yet others are
not so sure given the methodological difficulties in isolating the effects
of governance to specific management practices and the dearth of consistent, formal accountability structures.[34] As a whole, the field still lacks
a comprehensive understanding of the kinds of metrics place governance
organizations regularly track (or even should track) and how often and
in what ways they share them to ensure accountability.

There also is a pressing need for place governance models that are
more inclusive across siloes of constituencies. Harvey warns that "the
right to the city, as it is now constituted, is too narrowly confined, restricted in most cases to a small political and economic elite who are
in a position to shape cities more and more after their own desires."[35]
Place governance could represent a mechanism to organize more expansive and inclusive movements to gain control of capital and democ-
ratize the right to the city—or the exact opposite.

John R. Logan and Harvey Molotch discuss this polarization in
terms of the conflict between "use" and "exchange" values in places.
They distinguish individuals and groups for whom place is primarily
precious in terms of use value (that is, as the venue for life) from "place
entrepreneurs," for whom place has an exchange value as a commod-
ity. In their terms, the question is whether place governance is a
system for organizing inequality or for harnessing a finer balance
between a place's exchange and use value.[36]

In short, while place governance holds significant potential to give
stakeholders a structure through which to share their vision and ideas,
voice their concerns, advocate for investments, and codesign plans and
strategies with others both inside and outside their place, scholars
and practitioners have raised concerns about its impact on the public
sector, wealth-based inequities, neighborhood spillover effects, and
the well-being of vulnerable populations and citizens at large. More
research is needed on how place governance organizations remain

accountable to society and track outcomes to ensure such negative effects are not proliferated.

Understanding Place Governance:
Challenges, Opportunities, and Models for the Future

The intersecting crises of 2020 and beyond—including the coronavirus pandemic, social revolt over police brutality, climate catastrophes, and an economic recession—revealed that the current structure of many place governance organizations may limit their ability to meet the changing needs of places. For example, organizations dependent on revenue from events that were incompatible with stay-at-home orders and social distancing found themselves without the resources to fully respond to the distress of the workers, residents, and businesses in their places. Similarly, downtown organizations that derive their revenue from property assessments dominated by top-dollar office real estate are still confronting the fact that many post-pandemic adaptations will likely result in reduced assessments—and that their boards often are dominated by actors invested in the status quo. Meanwhile, new place-based collaborations, such as the movement for mutual aid, have sparked and flourished in response to the crises but have not yet gained recognition as formal place governance entities—and it may be they never will.

This is a timely moment to connect the healing of people and places—but the place governance field will need to adapt to these changing realities to do so. This may mean redrawing boundaries, sharing control in new ways and with new actors, and creating formal and informal mechanisms to build trust and innovate new models. The purpose of this volume is to explore these issues over seven chapters, covering the challenges and opportunities of place governance as well as models and innovations that could help today's organizations evolve to more effectively serve more people in more communities.

Place governance in the United States did not spring into being in the civil rights era, or as a contemporary craft of neoliberal policymakers. There have always been common-pool resources—"the commons"—and a need to manage them. Place governance as a mechanism for formalizing and managing aspects of American civic life has its roots in the colonial period, and modern place governance organizations have many precedents. In chapter 2, author Alexander von Hoffman provides a delightful and thorough history of American place governance as an undertaking of both elites and everyday citizens. His able telling illuminates for readers how we arrived at the place governance we see today, which is critical to understanding how it could and should evolve.

While they may exist in a similar legal framework, all place governance organizations do not serve the same mission or stakeholders. Each organization uniquely fits within a broader jurisdictional geography and governmental context and represents a particular attempt at collaboration between a mix of actors from different sectors, both within and across the places they govern. In chapter 3, legal scholar Sheila R. Foster dissects four distinct models of place governance with differing mixes of private, public, and community leadership and involvement to examine who governs, what is at stake, and how tensions and trade-offs are negotiated in each case.

At this point, it is already clear that different place governance models are suited to differing ends. In chapter 4, Juliet Musso uses a case study from Los Angeles to examine three kinds of place governance structures—BIDs, neighborhood councils, and community land trusts—exploring how each possesses different dimensions of power that influence how, how well, and to whose advantage they govern the places in their purview.

With authorizing legislation in all fifty states and the District of Columbia, BIDs have become a relatively ubiquitous form of place governance. However, there is considerable variation in the size, structure, and function of BIDs between states and, even, neighborhoods. In chapter 5, author Jill Simone Gross zooms in on this type of place governance structure to interrogate who benefits from place governance, who is accountable for its oversight, and why some BIDs become "community builders" while others become community "breakers" or "erasers."

Perhaps no social challenge embodies inequity and exclusion more than homelessness, and organizations that manage common spaces often are on the frontline of this complex issue. In chapter 6, authors Elena Madison and Joy Moses provide an overview of homelessness in the United States and explain why people experiencing homelessness are concentrated in particular public spaces. The authors discuss how conventional place governance models often are, at best, limited in their success in supporting unsheltered people or, at worst, employ practices openly hostile to them. Finally, the chapter surfaces promising practices from the field to better address the needs of people and places challenged by homelessness.

There is nothing particularly American about the mandate or the models for stewardship of place. In fact, place governance is an organic construct in communities all over the world, and many innovations in place governance, such as BIDs, originated and evolved beyond U.S. borders. In chapter 7, through a comparative study of governance efforts in Seoul, Rotterdam, Porto Alegre, Berlin, and other cities around the globe, author Nancy Kwak's analysis yields critical insights into how to thread the needle of inclusive growth at the place level.

Last, in chapter 8, authors Tracy Hadden Loh and Nate Storring synthesize key lessons for readers that resonate across the individual chapters, supplementing them with insights distilled from interviews with contemporary U.S. place governance leaders. The authors spotlight best practices for accountability as well as efforts to bring place governance to more people and places through new financing, organizing, and ownership models. They conclude with an attempt to grapple with the inherent messiness of place governance with a call for a polycentric approach to understanding, stewarding, and improving our urban landscape.

This is a pivotal moment to document the current state of place governance. Every structure can be used for ill or good. So how do we maximize the potential to yield positive impacts and minimize the risk of harm?

This volume aims to help answer these questions by deeply exploring both the tensions and opportunities of governing places in an increasingly fragmented, and inequitable, economic landscape. In so doing, we hope to provoke new thinking about how, why, and for whom place governance matters, and highlight practices and models for creating more connected, vibrant, and inclusive communities.

NOTES

1. D. W. Rowlands and Tracy Hadden Loh, "Reinvesting in Urban Cores Can Revitalize Entire Regions," Brookings Institution, June 2, 2021, www .brookings.edu/research/reinvesting-in-urban-cores-can-revitalize-entire -regions/.

2. Chad Shearer, Jennifer S. Vey, and Joanne Kim, "Where Jobs Are Concentrating and Why It Matters to Cities and Regions," Brookings Institution, June 18, 2019, www.brookings.edu/research/where-jobs-are-concentrating -why-it-matters-to-cities-and-regions/.

3. Per table 2.1, on page 74 of David Rusk, *Cities Without Suburbs: A Census 2010 Perspective* (Washington: Woodrow Wilson Center Press, 2013), 42 percent of the top 137 major metro areas in the United States are zero- or low-elasticity, meaning they have expanded their boundaries (or consolidated with neighboring or surrounding jurisdictions) very little since 1950.

4. Elinor Ostrom, "Beyond Markets and States: Polycentric Governance of Complex Economic Systems," *American Economic Review* 100 (June 2010), p. 32.

5. Jane Jacobs, *The Death and Life of Great American Cities* (New York: Vintage Books, 1961), p. 410.

6. Ibid. Also discussed in further detail in Tracy Hadden Loh and Annelies Goger, "In the Age of American 'Megaregions,' We Must Rethink Governance across Jurisdictions," Brookings Institution, May 7, 2020, www.brookings.edu /research/in-the-age-of-american-megaregions-we-must-rethink-governance -across-jurisdictions/.

7. Joanne Kim and Tracy Hadden Loh, "How We Define 'Need' for Place-Based Policy Reveals Where Poverty and Race Intersect," Brookings Institution, September 22, 2020, www.brookings.edu/research/how-we-define-need -for-place-based-policy-reveals-where-poverty-and-race-intersect/.

8. Jacobs, *The Death and Life of Great American Cities*, p. 418.

9. John A. Agnew, *Place and Politics: The Geographical Mediation of State and Society* (London: Routledge, 1987), p. 5.

10. Emily Talen, *Neighborhood* (Oxford University Press, 2018), pp. 1, 13.

11. Tracy Hadden Loh and Hanna Love, "Why 'Activity Centers' Are the Building Blocks of Inclusive Regional Economies," Brookings Institution, March 8, 2021, www.brookings.edu/research/the-future-of-the-inclusive-economy-is-in-activity-centers/.

12. David Harvey, "The Right to the City," *New Left Review* 53 (Sept./Oct. 2008), pp. 23–40.

13. Lynda H. Schneekloth and Robert G. Shibley, *Placemaking: The Art and Practice of Building Communities* (New York: John Wiley & Sons, Inc., 1995), p. 1.

14. Lynda H. Schneekloth and Robert G. Shibley, "The Practice of Place-making," *Architecture & Behaviour* 9 (1993), p. 139.

15. Jeremy R. Levine, *Constructing Community* (Princeton University Press, 2021), pp. 16–18.

16. Jennifer S. Vey and Hanna Love, "Transformative Placemaking: A Framework to Create Connected, Vibrant, and Inclusive Communities," Brookings Institution, November 19, 2019, www.brookings.edu/research/transformative-placemaking-a-framework-to-create-connected-vibrant-and-inclusive-communities/.

17. Nicola Dempsey and Mel Burton, "Defining Place-Keeping: The Long-Term Management of Public Spaces," *Urban Forestry & Urban Greening* 11 (January 2011), pp. 11–20.

18. Hadi Zamanifard, Tooran Alizadeh, and Caryl Bosman, "Towards a Framework of Public Space Governance," *Cities* 78 (August 2018), pp. 155–65.

19. Susan E. Clarke, "Local Place-Based Collaborative Governance: Comparing State-Centric and Society-Centered Models," *Urban Affairs Review* 53 (April 2016), pp. 578–602; Deborah Markley and others, "A New Domain for Place-Rooted Foundations: Economic Development Philanthropy," *Foundation Review* 8 (September 2016), pp. 92–105; Margery Austin Turner, "A Place-Conscious Approach Can Strengthen Integrated Strategies in Poor Neighborhoods," Brookings Institution, August 10, 2015, www.brookings.edu/research/a-place-conscious-approach-can-strengthen-integrated-strategies-in-poor-neighborhoods/.

20. Peter Walsh, "Improving Governments' Response to Local Communities—Is Place Management an Answer?," *Australian Journal of Public Administration* 60 (June 2001), pp. 3–12.

21. Citizen Artist Salon, "Creative Placemaking, Placekeeping, and Cultural Strategies to Resist Displacement," March 8, 2016, https://usdac.us

/blogac/2017/12/11/creative-placemaking-placekeeping-and-cultural-strategies
-to-resist-displacement.

22. Roberto Bedoya, "Spatial Justice: Rasquachification, Race, and the City," *Creative Time Reports*, September 15, 2014, https://creativetimereports.org/2014/09/15/spatial-justice-rasquachification-race-and-the-city/.

23. Brett T. Goldstein and Christopher Mele, "Governance within Public-Private Partnerships and the Politics of Urban Development," *Space and Polity* 20 (March 2016), pp. 194–211.

24. Bruce Katz and Jeremy Nowak, *The New Localism* (Brookings Institution Press, 2018), chapter 4.

25. Göktuğ Morçöl and James F. Wolf, "Understanding Business Improvement Districts: A New Governance Framework," *Public Administration Review* 70 (November 2010), pp. 906–13.

26. Walsh, "Improving Governments' Response to Local Communities," pp. 3–12.

27. International Downtown Association (IDA), "Inclusive Places: Prioritizing Inclusion and Equity in the Urban Place Management Field," 2018. https://downtown.org/publications/.

28. Lorlene Hoyt and Devika Gopal-Agge, "The Business Improvement District Model: A Balanced Review of Contemporary Debates," *Geography Compass* 1 (July 2007), pp. 946–58.

29. Zamanifard and others, "Towards a Framework of Public Space Governance"; Morçöl and Wolf, "Understanding Business Improvement Districts"; Hoyt and Gopal-Agge, "The Business Improvement District Model"; Alice Mathers, Nicola Dempsey, and Julie Frøik Molin, "Place-Keeping in Action: Evaluating the Capacity of Green Space Partnerships in England," *Landscape and Urban Planning* 139 (July 2015), pp. 126–36.

30. Harvey, "The Right to the City."

31. Walsh, "Improving Governments' Response to Local Communities"; Hoyt and Gopal-Agge, "The Business Improvement District Model."

32. Talen, *Neighborhood*, p. 173.

33. Morçöl and Wolf, "Understanding Business Improvement Districts."

34. Ibid.; Hoyt and Gopal-Agge, "The Business Improvement District Model."

35. Harvey, "The Right to the City."

36. John R. Logan and Harvey Molotch, *Urban Fortunes: The Political Economy of Place, 20th Anniversary Edition* (University of California Press, 2007), pp. 1, 13.

TWO

Improvising and Innovating

A History of Place Governance in North America

ALEXANDER VON HOFFMAN

Across the United States, dozens of coalitions, alliances, and partnerships of institutions, private businesses, government agencies, nonprofit organizations, and citizens create, govern, and foster activities within public and private spaces of all different sizes. It might seem that these governance models arose in recent decades to fill gaps in services that governments were not willing or able to provide. In fact, such arrangements have a long history in the towns and cities in North America. For almost 400 years, American placemakers and managers—elite and democratic, formal and informal—have adopted diverse forms of "public-private" arrangements to meet the needs and circumstances of a particular moment and locale.

This chapter chronicles the evolution of these arrangements and their role in shaping and managing communities—and specific projects and spaces within them—over time. For simplicity's sake, the chapter places these undertakings in two broad categories, *elite* and *democratic*. The term *elite* here refers generally to wealthy and powerful individuals and institutions. The term *democratic* describes those in the rest of society operating in organized groups, informal communities, or as individuals. Neither category is monolithic; each encompasses a variety of actors who, at times, have competed and clashed with one another.

Although the line between elite and democratic entities is not always distinct, projects that fall within each category typically have taken different approaches. The elite tradition of place governance often has exercised control through formal channels, while democratic forms of place governance often have been carried out in relatively informal ways. And elite placemaking and governance usually takes a top-down approach, while democratic efforts have tended to be bottom-up, although not in all cases.

In the late twentieth century, as cities matured and faced social and economic problems, both elite and democratic modes of place governance evolved. Each continued to respond in an ad hoc fashion to particular problems or needs, but with growing scale and complexity. Increasingly, the elite and democratic traditions merged or overlapped to create new, hybrid forms of urban placemaking and governance. In recent years, these hybrid arrangements have demonstrated innovative ways to revive the social and economic life of cities. They hold potential for wider use, but it is an open question whether the fragmented examples of place governance today can replicate and grow into a viable system for the common good.

Placemaking and Governance in Early America

From the earliest days of European settlement, the urban places of North America were surprisingly diverse. Mercantile in character, these sea and river ports were busy sites of trade, industry, and, in some cases, government, and their residents held a wide variety of oc-cupations and social ranks. In a developing society with the imperial government an ocean away, public officials and private inhabitants had to devise ways to share responsibilities for governing these small but complex places.

Colonial Elite

During the colonial and early republican eras, small government bodies of the growing towns and cities of North America were re-sponsible for public affairs and facilities. Given rudimentary forms of governance, members of the community expected the elite—merchants, professionals such as lawyers and ministers, and prosper-ous artisans and manufacturers, all of whom were almost always white males—to shoulder its large responsibilities. The inhabitants of colonial towns accepted this top-down form of governance because loyalties ran vertically within clans, trades, occupations, and churches. Furthermore, the material success of the towns, which is to say local trade and employment, depended on the productivity of the better-off residents—especially merchants. Conversely, town improvements helped the elite succeed. As individuals, and sometimes in commit-tees, wealthy citizens funded—and profited from—large-scale proj-ects such as town halls, market buildings, and wharf improvements.

The history of the New Haven Green demonstrates the early min-gling and evolution of public and private arrangements in the elite style of governing places. When the English colonists founded the town of New Haven in 1638, the largest landholders or "proprietors" purchased the land on which it sits. Over time, the proprietors, in co-operation with town officials, distributed farm lots to newcomers but retained their ownership of "the market place," the square at the cen-ter of the settlement's original nine-square grid. For a century and a half, the proprietors worked with town officials to manage the square as a site for community institutions, including a school, a prison, and three churches, one of whose successors sits there even now. The part-nership proved enduring. In the nineteenth century, the town and a committee of the proprietors used donations from private citizens to convert the marketplace to a public park, the New Haven Green, which the city of New Haven and the Proprietors' Committee jointly manage to this day.[1]

In many colonial elite-supported public-private projects, individuals provided capital and the corporate entity of the town acquired and maintained a facility that advantaged both the elite and the community at large. In Boston, for example, the merchant Robert Keayne, who died in 1656, bequeathed a large sum to the town to construct a two-story wood frame townhouse containing a marketplace on the first floor and meeting rooms for courts and town officials, an armory, and a library on the floor above. Here, merchants met daily to exchange prices and information about transatlantic trade shipping, which redounded to the benefit of the town's artisans, shipbuilders, and sailors. In 1743, after the commerce and official business of Boston had outgrown the building, another prosperous merchant, Peter Faneuil, built and gave the town a new brick market building, complete with town offices and meeting hall, which later came to be known as the "cradle of liberty."[2]

Beyond accepting gifts, colonial towns contrived partnerships that promoted the private gain of individuals in exchange for making and managing places for the use of the public—an early American ancestor of incentive zoning for developers. From the 1720s, officials of the corporation of the city of New York granted waterlots under the East River to wealthy individuals, usually the owners of adjacent valuable riverfront land. The grants gave the purchasers the right to charge rents on any docks, wharves, piers, or slips they built—a lucrative plum in the bustling seaport. But the corporation, which retained the right to take back unproductive grants, required grantees to build and maintain for the use of the public and the city two streets or wharves adjacent to their waterlot, as well as additional public spaces, such as a public slip to be used by deep water ships, from which all revenues derived from their use would pass to the city. As a result of enlisting private landowners, the relatively small government of New York was able to contract out the construction and management of filled land, piers, and port facilities at little expense.³

Although the colonial forms of elite place governance resulted from the particular historic conditions—the limited capacity of governments and close-knit deferential societies—they set a precedent for nineteenth- and twentieth-century top-down place governance, in which economically and socially elite members controlled and managed private and civic urban projects.

The Colonial Demos

If the elite were largely responsible for financing and managing spaces and facilities in colonial towns, the general populace also had a say in the governance of urban places.

Town residents of all ranks not only expressed their wishes through formal means, such as petitions and voting in town councils and meetings, but also exercised authority through informal, but no less accepted, means. By performing traditional harassment rituals—such as midnight charivari visits accompanied by a cacophony of pots, pans, and drums— crowds, sometimes called mobs, enforced community morals against transgressors ranging from wife abusers to merchants charging exorbitant prices. Sometimes crowd actions represented a portion of the community, such as when seamen protested British press gangs forcing sailors to enlist in the navy. At other times, crowds included a cross section of the population, as in the many incidents opposing British officials' mercantile policies during the eighteenth century.⁴

Democratic participation was built into the governance of colonial society. To impose order or stop crime, a colonial sheriff would raise "the hue and cry" and deputize a *posse comitatus* of nearby inhabitants. When mobs protested grievances, historian Pauline Maier points out, that could likely involve recruiting members of the very crowd that was demonstrating. In an era of limited government, the line between public and private governance could be indistinguishable.⁵

The colonial towns were hardly unified, however, and their residents often contested their governance, including the places and methods of food distribution. Members of the elite—leading merchants and officials—favored regulated food markets, in which town officials assigned stalls to food purveyors, rang the bell to open and close the market, and certified the weights of goods sold there. In eighteenth-century Boston, nevertheless, many townspeople preferred to patronize unregulated hucksters—many of whom were African American—who sold produce, poultry, and meat on the town streets.

Despite merchant-class complaints of hucksters forestalling the market, hundreds of Bostonians fervently opposed the markets. In the 1730s, they boycotted them, voting in town meetings to prevent their operations by banning the market bells and use of paper money. One night in 1737, a crowd dressed as clergymen demolished Boston's central market and sawed off the pillars of another market building in the North End neighborhood. Several years later, when Peter Faneuil first announced his gift of a public market, anti-market townspeople voted against it *en masse* in the town meeting, while persons unknown tore down the butcher stalls around it. In the end, Bostonians accepted both the market and street vendors, choosing elite as well as democratic forms of food distribution and the governance of the places where it occurred.[6]

Place Governance and Urban Growth in the Nineteenth Century

During the nineteenth and early twentieth centuries, the number and size of cities in the United States grew dramatically, stimulating and stimulated by tremendous increases in population, economic activity, technology, communications, and modes and speed of transportation. As urban territories expanded, Americans employed new methods of making and administering new places, institutions, and communities.

Rise of the Private Elite

During the nineteenth century, increasing demand for housing and the rising wealth of many merchants, manufacturers, attorneys, and other well-positioned professionals gave rise to residential urban land development—literally making places—for the pleasure of the elite. Consortiums of monied "gentlemen" investors developed homes for the wealthy with private or semi-public landscaped spaces. The property owners at such posh addresses as Tontine Crescent (1795) and Louisburg Square (1847) in Boston, and Bowling Green (1786–1825) in New York City were given exclusive access to the adjacent parks and responsibility for their upkeep (unless the developer retained control). Seeing the development of affluent neighborhoods as a sign of progress, city officials approved the creation of private parks under the control of nearby property owners. In New York City, the government adjusted property tax rates to discourage building in Gramercy Park (1831) and paid for construction of an ornamental fence at Union Square (1834–1839).[7]

Foreshadowing present-day state-sponsored luxury development, from the 1860s, the Commonwealth of Massachusetts implemented a plan to create an elegant Back Bay residential district in Boston out of the tidal flats and basin of the Charles River. When it sold lots to private investors, the Back Bay Commission adopted the usual method of creating and maintaining exclusive residential enclaves by appending restrictive covenants to the deeds of the properties that, for example, prohibited commercial stables and manufacturing and required building set-back distances from the street.[8]

In the years after the United States achieved independence, wealthy, high-born citizens directly governed American cities as mayors and aldermen, and in those roles continued to use private actors to create and maintain public places. In the 1820s, Mayor Josiah Quincy initiated the next stage in the evolution of Boston's main market area with an ambitious scheme to expand wholesale and retail market facilities near Faneuil Hall. In 1826, the city government built the central building at Quincy Market with its own funds, but sold lots on either side of the building to individuals who agreed to construct large granite warehouse buildings according to the city's criteria.[9]

In the nineteenth century, reformers and citizens called for the establishment of public recreational spaces and institutions, which were run by elites with the intention of cultivating the taste and intelligence of the general population. Beginning in 1831, when the Massachusetts Horticultural Society, an association of wealthy male owners of large estates, created Mt. Auburn Cemetery in Cambridge, Massachusetts, affluent citizens of towns and cities across the United States established and administered landscaped burial grounds known as "rural cemeteries." Most rural cemeteries were private institutions, but all welcomed members of the public, who flocked to them by the thousands.[10] Rural cemeteries soon gave way to public parks, which educated and well-to-do advocates typically managed through special function boards and commissions structured to keep the projects out of local politics and, if possible, patronage. In Chicago, three distinct park districts—each run by its own board whose blue-blood members were appointed by the governor of Illinois—planned and maintained thousands of acres of public parks and tens of miles of parkways.[11]

Similarly, the institutions of public libraries, housed in impressive, centrally located edifices and supplemented by neighborhood branches, fell under one form or another of elite governance. In cities such as Baltimore and Pittsburgh, rich philanthropists funded libraries. In Philadelphia, Milwaukee, and San Francisco, city governments footed the bill.[12]

The Public at Large

The ordinary residents of nineteenth-century American cities, no less than the elite, controlled public spaces, sometimes in formally sanctioned ways and other times informally or through extra-legal activities. Some of those who visited rural cemeteries came, as intended by the directors, to be elevated by the verdant scenery and impressive monuments. But others used the burial grounds to picnic, gambol, and—if the cemetery regulations are an indication—shoot firearms. In the late nineteenth and early twentieth centuries, working- and middle-class city dwellers transformed parks from the quiet, passive-recreation spaces envisioned by landscape architect Frederick Law Olmsted and his followers into hives of activity. Tens of thousands gathered to take in baseball matches in the parks and vacant lots, while untold numbers gathered in public landscaped grounds to play tennis, pedal on bicycles, court lovers, and, in the case of so-called tramps, smoke pipes and sleep.[13]

Working-class residents of nineteenth-century cities shared the governance of their neighborhoods with the municipal government, whose authority by modern standards was thin. On the streets, a lively array of city dwellers commanded the spaces for their own purposes. Largely oblivious to established authority, gangs of working-class youth played, partied, stole, and fought. Shoeshine boys snapped their rags, boy and girl newsies hawked newspapers, and people of all ages peddled flowers, foods, pots, rags, and various household services, not least of which was the sharpening of knives and scissors. A demimonde of gamblers, pickpockets, and thieves operated freely and were even sometimes vaunted as local celebrities.

While the men of working-class neighborhoods frequented the "poor man's club," as the local saloon was described, women presided on the house stoops and sidewalks over female communities based on mutual help. In the latter nineteenth century, centrally organized police departments regulated such neighborhoods to a degree. Yet even then, patrolmen walking their beats alone largely accommodated the demands and wishes of local citizens.[14]

In the absence of government regulations, small-scale entrepreneurs took it upon themselves to run their businesses. In some cases, they united in formal or informal trade associations to manage specialized places of commerce. In the 1880s, for example, New York City's retail florists and flower peddlers organized and regulated their own wholesale flower mart at an all-night restaurant near the East River loading docks, then collectively decided to relocate inland to 26th Street and 6th Avenue, where they formed the New York Cut Flower Association to conduct operations.[15]

The diverse members of urban society often contested its governance, however, and particularly in the commercial realm. On New York's immigrant lower East Side, the main thoroughfares served as market districts where crowds purchased necessities at first-floor tenement shops and pushcarts that lined the streets. The ethnic shop and pushcart owners were regulated formally by city inspectors but informally by their customers, a fact demonstrated in the early 1900s by violent boycotts that forced butchers to lower the price of kosher meat. Labor disputes in urban factories, shops, docks, and trainyards were frequent and, often, violent, and in early-twentieth-century New York, tenants fought "the great rent wars" to control the conditions and payments of the apartments they inhabited.[16]

Over the course of the nineteenth century, a proliferating array of private institutions and voluntary associations created and managed urban spaces for their members' activities. Prominent citizens of the "nation of joiners," affluent Americans established, patronized, and managed hospitals, universities, genealogical societies, art museums, symphonies, and exclusive social clubs. As a rule, the governance of these private organizations and institutions took a corporate form, in which a small group of trustees or a board of directors set the overall direction, one or more managers actively oversaw operations and staff, and a large body of members participated to a greater or lesser degree. Upper-class white males controlled and governed many of these institutions and the places they occupied, including, for example, the exclusive clubs devoted to yachting, tennis, and other sports.[17]

Indeed, men and women of all incomes and ethnicities organized and enrolled in innumerable churches, trade unions, athletic clubs, political organizations, and associations of all stripes, where they applied Robert's Rules of Order to their proceedings. While many white Protestant men enrolled in fraternal lodges—such as the Freemasons and the International Order of Odd Fellows—African American men formed lodges of the Prince Hall Masons, Catholics joined the Knights of Columbus, and Irish Americans organized local chapters of the Ancient Order of Hibernians. Women were equally active. They were the most numerous members of churches and social work organizations such as settlement houses, formed independent auxiliaries to male organizations, and established thousands of social, literary, and reform clubs, including women's abolition, labor, and suffrage organizations.[18]

All the organizations required spaces—including large buildings, halls of varying sizes, single rooms, and playing fields—which they owned or rented to carry on their activities, many of which were open to the public. In the late twentieth century, however, participation in this dense web of voluntary associations declined, a phenomenon evoked by Robert Putnam's memorable phrase "bowling alone." As a result, once busy places lost their patrons. The waning of traditional organizational life would give rise in the twenty-first century to a quest for ways to renew communities through novel forms of place-making and governance.[19]

Complexities of Place in the Twentieth-Century City

During the late nineteenth century and much of the twentieth century, American cities boomed. Technological innovations spurred growth in the scale of commerce and industry and the urban spaces devoted to them. The expanding economy attracted both capital and people to cities, which, in turn, spurred further growth. Within these growing urban environments, the early forms of mixed, ad hoc, and informal means of place governance persisted, but both elite and democratic actors increasingly used formal and legal mechanisms to organize and manage urban places.

Elite Private Developers

Perhaps the most striking spatial feature of big cities in their heyday was the central business district, typically known as "downtown," which was largely the domain of elite entrepreneurs and investors. It was comprised of a set of loosely bounded subdistricts devoted to finance—especially banking and insurance—wholesale commerce, law offices, retail shopping, theaters, manufacturing, and publishing. Although exotic and palatial department stores and magnificent vaudeville theaters were the main attraction for the public at large, much of the downtown landscape was devoted to office buildings, which, thanks to elevators and steel girder and column construction, grew ever higher.[20]

Albeit with government officials' approval and cooperation, private entities financed, developed, owned, and largely controlled the downtown spaces. In the early twentieth century, local businessmen, in consultation with urban planners, maintained the main shopping corridors to give them a modern look free of clutter such as overhead electric wires, unsightly store signs, and unpainted trash cans. At the same time, as the historian Alison Isenberg shows, the arrangements and varied experiences of downtowns reflected the inequities of American urban society.[21]

Nonetheless, in the first part of the century, large-scale private development in the elite mode created some impressive commercial spaces. Perhaps the best known is Rockefeller Center, built in midtown Manhattan during the 1930s. John D. Rockefeller Jr. developed the Art Deco complex as a media and entertainment headquarters complete with ice-skating rink and managed through the family firm, Rockefeller Center Inc. Rockefeller Center is still considered one of New York City's premier public places, one that millions of people, including tourists, visit every year.[22]

Decades later, downtown businesses devised a model of small place governance known as Privately Owned Public Spaces (POPS), which revived the tradition dating from the colonial period of inducing the elite to make and govern places for the benefit of the community. Prodded by government land-use regulations and incentives, business corporations in the nation's largest cities created and managed plazas, squares, and mini-parks adjacent to high-rise buildings. This caught on after the enactment of a New York City 1961 zoning regulation that allowed developers to add extra floors on office and apartment buildings if they created public plazas in their developments.

In the years that followed, developers dotted the downtowns of American cities with small open spaces that private corporations sponsored and the public frequented to greater or lesser extent. Probably the best-known example is Liberty Plaza Park, developed in 1968 in New York's financial district by U.S. Steel and later renamed Zuccotti Park after the chair of the new owners, Brookfield Office Properties. The park gained national fame in 2011 when it was temporarily transformed into a protest site by members of the Occupy Wall Street movement.

In the 1980s, William H. Whyte extensively surveyed and analyzed the characteristics and use patterns of POPS in North American cities. He found that the most popular spaces were located along well-traveled routes, possessed design elements—for example, furniture, sculptures, water features—that attracted people and encouraged them to linger, and were programmed intelligently, such as, for example, by allowing street vendors. Whyte concluded that unsuccessful POPS not only lacked such traits but also suffered from fragmented authority over their regulation and management that often led to lack of maintenance.[23]

Outside the city centers, private developers accommodated the outward movement of the upper middle class by providing new kinds of residential places. The practice of creating planned subdivisions began in the mid-nineteenth century, reaching a crescendo in the 1890s when Edward Bouton developed Roland Park, Maryland, a Baltimore suburb that was later annexed to the city. At Roland Park, Bouton combined the use of landscaping, detailed restrictions on the construction of buildings, and assessment on owners to pay for the upkeep of public-common areas.

Starting in 1906, Kansas City developer J. C. Nichols created arguably the first and most influential modern planned suburb, the Country Club District, adjoining the Kansas City Country Club. With its carefully planned elements, such as landscaping and minimum cost requirements for home builders, Nichols advertised the sprawling district's properties with the slogan, "1,000 acres, restricted." If the most visible achievement was Country Club Plaza, the nation's first shopping center oriented to the automobile, perhaps its most significant was the use of private homeowner associations for long-term governance. In 1914, Nichols began organizing associations of fee-paying property owners responsible for maintaining sewers, streetlights, and signs; the landscaping of public grounds; collecting garbage; and fire protection. In other words, the homeowner associations did, according to the historian William Worley, "everything a city government would normally do."[24]

Despite the innovations, Bouton, Nichols, and other developers of "high class residential properties" practiced racial and religious discrimination by refusing to sell building lots or houses to African Americans, Jews, and Catholics. Some high-end developers like Nichols used restrictive covenants explicitly to prohibit owners from selling their homes to African Americans. Other developers used indirect means to the same end. At Shaker Heights, a planned suburb of Cleveland, Ohio, the Van Sweringen brothers embedded discrimination in the governance structure by giving the majority of twenty-one abutting owners the right to reject a prospective buyer. In the postwar years, developers of less expensive developments, such as William Levitt, adopted similar discriminatory practices to ensure white-only, and in some cases gentile-only, residential places. In 1948, racially restrictive covenants were declared unconstitutional, and in 1968, the Fair Housing Act banned discrimination in real estate transactions, yet their poisonous legacy lives on in segregated communities, intolerant homeowners' associations, and exclusive zoning and environmental regulations.[25]

Democratic Communities—Ethnic and Artistic

If elite developers and property owners exerted more control over expensive urban spaces, members of diverse population groups created and oversaw their own communities in less formal and democratic fashion.

As urban populations continued to swell, immigrant and African American neighborhoods evolved into vibrant mixed-income communities. Most large cities contained Little Italy and Chinatown neighborhoods, but in other cities, depending on the immigrant flows, one could find Little Tokyos, Germanies, Swedens, Polands, Serbias, and Mexicos, among other nationalities. Discrimination by whites encouraged the growth of "Black belts," in which African Americans concentrated in greater numbers, densities, and durations than did immigrant groups in their respective neighborhoods. Although private and public racial discrimination limited both the physical and economic mobility of their residents, neighborhoods such as New York's Harlem, Bronzeville in Chicago, and South Central Los Angeles were vital centers of African American culture, community, and entrepreneurship.

Like earlier democratic models of place governance, a combination of agents managed the affairs and public spaces of ethnic and racial neighborhoods. Community leaders—those elected and those recognized by common consent—negotiated with the city government over the terms of their businesses and use of space. In Chicago, for example, the popular Bud Billiken parade and picnic, begun in 1929 to celebrate pride and unity among African American children, was conceived and run by representatives of the *Chicago Defender,* the preeminent African American newspaper, the president of the National Negro Council, and the superintendent of the city of Chicago's South Park Board.

At the same time, the police and government officials tolerated, often in exchange for bribes, the operation of vice businesses— gambling, prostitution, illegal sales of alcohol and narcotics—in ethnic and, particularly, African American neighborhoods. In such neighborhoods, well-recognized bookmakers moved about the streets openly, taking bets on lottery games known as "policy" and "the numbers." The illegal, untaxed lotteries were effectively public activities that provided a source of employment and banking services for African Americans cut off from the mainstream economy.[26]

Sometimes the rulers of the people's places ignored formal authority altogether. Chinatowns, for example, functioned surprisingly independently of officialdom. In these immigrant communities, commercial signs, posters, and verbal communications in the Cantonese (Guangzhou) language were unintelligible to English-only speakers, including police as well as tourists. In the absence of official oversight, merchant associations, criminal organizations known as Tongs, and committees of respected elder citizens governed with relatively little interference from city officials.

In contrast to such ethnic neighborhoods, a novel type of urban place, the artists' colony, was, at first, too individualistic to engage in self-governance. Starting in the late 1800s, artists, writers, political left-wing rebels, lesbians, gays, and others seeking a "bohemian" environment settled on the fringes of working-class ethnic neighborhoods, particularly those with old, picturesque architecture. While the poorer bohemians moved to tenements or dilapidated houses, off-beat members of the upper and middle classes, along with a few adventurous developers, "remodeled" old houses. The first wave of such resettlements redefined such places as New York's Greenwich Village, Georgetown in Washington, DC, the New Orleans French Quarter, and Boston's Beacon Hill into artists' quarters.[27]

Such communities, however, often lacked a means of governance to protect their character, which depended on impecunious bohemians, off-beat shopkeepers, and low-end developers operating in a slack real estate market. As a result, when more affluent people followed the artists into the artist colonies to enjoy the ambience, rents quickly rose. As early as 1921, the area around Washington Square in Greenwich Village had become too expensive for artists, who were forced to seek homes in other parts of the Village and New York City.[28]

With this experience in mind, in the latter twentieth century, artists and their allies sought government assistance to control the destiny of their neighborhoods. In the early 1960s, artists living in SoHo, the Lower Manhattan area of loft factories and historic cast iron buildings south of Houston Street, fought off threats of displace-

ment. Led by the SoHo Artists Tenants Association, they successfully lobbied city and state governments to allow artists to inhabit
industrial and commercial buildings and to designate SoHo as a historic preservation district, protecting it from demolition or external
alterations. Although eventually market demand in SoHo pushed real
estate values to exorbitant levels, in cities across the United States, artists and artistic entrepreneurs followed suit by working with government to maintain their artist colonies.[29]

The Authorities of the Technocratic Elite

At the same time they created new suburban and inner-city spaces,
Americans strove to modernize American cities with what can be categorized as a technocratic-elite model of place governance.

The public corporation or authority, originated as a device by
which government officials used special assessments and revenue
bonds to pay for large public works, dramatically expanded the scale
of elite-dominated place governance. The first public corporations,
such as the Port Authority of New York and New Jersey (1921) and
the Metropolitan Water District of Southern California (1927),
were established to develop and manage industrial rail and dock
areas and infrastructure projects. The popularity of tax exempt special purpose bonds gave rise to state building authorities, first created
in Pennsylvania, which borrowed to construct facilities, such as ar-
mories, hospitals, administration buildings, exhibition halls, convention centers, and even sports stadiums, then leased them back to a
state-sponsored agency to operate.[30] Where once commissions ruled,
public authorities now reigned.

Like the elite-style park, library, and infrastructure commissions,
public authorities were, and still are, decidedly undemocratic forms
of place governance. In most cases, appointed (not elected) board
members hired an executive director, who hired and supervised the
staff. Located outside the main body of government, the authorities
were relatively insulated from political influence. New York's great
powerbroker Robert Moses, for example, operated with impunity from

his positions as chair or president of numerous park, bridge, parkway, and slum clearance commissions and authorities—holding as many as nine such positions concurrently. Despite opposition from citizens and high officials, Moses transformed and managed great swaths of the city—including highways, parks, housing projects, the New York Coliseum convention center, and the Lincoln Center for the Performing Arts—even as his projects destroyed the homes of countless numbers of New Yorkers.[31]

In the 1930s, during the New Deal, public authorities first took on explicitly social purposes. The primary goal of the nation's public housing program, enacted in 1937, was to eliminate slums and replace them with planned rental apartment complexes for low-income working people. In the 1930s and 1940s, state after state enabled the creation of municipal public housing authorities with the power to clear and rebuild "blighted" areas and manage the new housing projects. Funded by revenue bonds and federal grants and loans, housing authorities acquired land, cleared it, reconfigured it to form isolated superblocks, and constructed apartment buildings and row houses, which they maintained with rent revenue received from the tenants.

Despite their social purpose, public housing authorities were top-down organizations, comprised of business executives, real estate developers, political operatives, social workers, and representatives of labor and African American constituencies, who generally lived outside the districts they ruled. Not surprisingly, given the elite and largely white membership of their boards, public housing authorities proved unsympathetic to slumdwellers. They freely demolished working-class housing and stores without much thought to the communities they served or the people they displaced, few of whom met the requirements to reside in public housing. Almost as a rule, housing authority officials let the apartments on a basis of racial segregation, even on sites that had previously been integrated. The housing authorities imposed a paternalistic regime on tenants, excluding them from decisionmaking, subjecting their apartments to inspection, and imposing petty regulations upon them.

In the postwar era, the job of replacing dilapidated districts shifted from public housing authorities to urban redevelopment or "urban renewal" authorities, setting off an explosive growth in the scope of government-sponsored placemaking—and destruction. Starting in the 1940s, state legislatures authorized such authorities to use the power of eminent domain to acquire areas deemed "blighted," clear the sites, and, in a return to public-private arrangements, sell them to private entities to develop, control, and manage thereafter. Title I of the U.S. Housing Act of 1949 injected federal funds into the process, authorizing loans to the authorities to acquire tracts and grants to cover two-thirds of the difference between the cost of land and its reuse value. In addition, local governments discounted the taxes for private developers. After the Supreme Court affirmed in 1954 that eminent domain for slum clearance and private development constituted a public benefit, the urban renewal program took off.[32]

Like the public housing authorities, urban renewal agencies were top-down elite organizations that implemented placemaking and governance projects ostensibly for a public purpose. Often, the new authorities worked with business-civic consortiums, such as the Allegheny Conference on Community Development that spearheaded the Pittsburgh Renaissance, which transformed a riverfront warehouse district into the glitzy Gateway Center office complex, among other projects. Redevelopment took many forms, including public and private housing, office buildings, industrial facilities, sports stadiums, and even parking lots. Yet the business and political elites on the authorities so often implemented schemes that destroyed working-class communities and homes of people of color that critics derided the program as "Negro Removal."

Government officials and civic leaders soon discovered the potential of using public authorities for large-scale economic development and city booster projects without the urban renewal rationale of "blight." As tools of local "growth machines," public authorities made or remade urban places and transferred them to private entities to manage and profit from. Increasingly, cities instituted public-private

nonprofit "development" corporations, to encourage physical and economic growth. The city of Baltimore pioneered this movement in
the 1950s when private corporations led an effort to redevelop Baltimore's Inner Harbor by establishing a private company, the Charles
Center-Inner Harbor Management, Inc., whose sole business was its
contract with the municipal government.[33]

Expanding this kind of public sector–led placemaking and governance, in 1958, the Philadelphia city government and Chamber of
Commerce created the Philadelphia Industrial Development Corporation (PIDC), a public-private economic development organization.
In 1960, the PIDC broke ground on a new factory for Whitman's
Chocolates, which dissuaded the company from relocating out of the
city. From there, PIDC began creating and managing large suburban-
style industrial parks and industrial districts along major corridors.
Within a few years, "PIDC was operating in virtually every section
of the city, buying, improving, and selling land in new industrial parks;
investing in infrastructure; and issuing industrial revenue bonds to
finance the retention of an important piece of the manufacturing and
industrial economy and job base."[34]

The economic development corporations spun off and collaborated with specialized entities to assist in making development-
related places, which they either ran themselves or sold or leased to
private parties. Since its creation in 1978, for example, the Economic Growth Corporation of Detroit has helped execute several
lavish downtown projects, including a sports arena, luxury housing,
and a twenty-two-block residential complex surrounding the world
headquarters of the General Motors Corporation. With an executive committee comprised mainly of business executives, it collaborated with other agencies, such as the Economic Development
Corporation of the city of Detroit, the Detroit Downtown Development Authority, and the Detroit Brownfield Redevelopment Authority. Such high-end public-private placemaking and governance
schemes, however impressive, failed to stem Detroit's massive population loss.[35]

The Hybridization of Place Governance
in the Late Twentieth Century

In the latter twentieth century, new, decentralized, democratic, and incremental modes of reviving, remaking, and managing urban places differed sharply from technocratic elite use of public authorities. The forms of place governance that resulted were hybrids, in which individual citizens and grassroots organizations received support, financial and otherwise, from elite institutions and local government.

Hot Spots and Markets

During the Cold War, arts districts and renovated marketplaces sprouted in American cities, nurtured by individuals, entrepreneurs, and government officials working together in an ad hoc fashion. In St. Louis, in the 1950s, off-beat entrepreneurs moved into a once-fashionable corner of the business district located on the city's racial dividing line. There, they set up funky antique shops, jazz clubs, and gay bars and, over the years, attracted everyone from beatniks to suburbanites. In 1961, the St. Louis Board of Aldermen took notice and renamed the heart of the area Gaslight Square, which inspired the local utility company to install gas streetlights there. Tourists of all sorts swarmed through Gaslight Square and artsy nightlife districts in many other cities—in Kansas City's River Quay, in Chicago's Old Town, and, in New York, the original arts district, Greenwich Village—until they became victims of their own success, with rising rents, loud rock-and-roll halls, and criminal activity stealing much of their original charm or killing them off altogether.[36]

Another kind of urban place that evoked the past while offering present-day attractions were renovated marketplaces, which, like the art districts, were products of efforts of enterprising individuals and government officials. In Omaha, Nebraska, in 1963, local lawyer Samuel Mercer inherited some properties in Old Market, a declining wholesale meat, dairy, and produce mart that city leaders threatened to demolish. Mercer quietly began purchasing brick and cast iron market buildings and, in 1970, he and kindred spirits sympathetic to the old architecture began renting them out to stores, restaurants, and clubs. By the 1980s, the surprising juxtaposition of wholesale businesses—including meatpacking—with trendy dining in largely unchanged warehouse buildings created one of the premier tourist attractions in Omaha.[37] While owners of old hotels, warehouses, and factories tapped state and federal tax credits to rehab their properties, the city of Omaha embraced Mercer's vision, designating Old Market as a landmark heritage district and insisting that any construction or alterations maintain the scale and character of this "thoroughly enjoyable and honest place."[38]

Seattle's historic Pike Place Market, the popular farmers and seafood market located downtown above the waterfront, developed a uniquely mixed form of place governance. When the government planned to raze the market in favor of high-rise office and apartment buildings, local partisans of the market forced a referendum, and in November 1971 Seattle's citizens overwhelmingly voted to save the market. After the city's historical commission proved unable to keep the enterprise afloat, Seattle's city government set up the Pike Place Market Preservation and Development Authority to manage the market, but this public authority was a far cry from the imperial agencies of Robert Moses. With the goal of creating an authentically Seattle-style offbeat place, the authority's first director hunted for foundation grants and federal funds to purchase and restore the market buildings, which he rented at below-market rates to farmers, fishmongers, and unconventional shop owners. In addition, the Pike Place Market Foundation, established in 1982, raised money for social services, such as a medical clinic and food bank, as well as repairs and improvements to the market's historic buildings. In the end, a governance collaboration of a public authority and a philanthropic foundation ensured the success of the city's wildly popular iconic site.[39]

Inevitably the success of renovated marketplaces led to more commercial, well-financed, and elite-controlled marketplace developments. In yet another chapter in the history of Boston's wholesale markets, a public-private collaboration converted Quincy Market, built in 1826 but then in decay, into a prototype of adaptive reuse of buildings. Boston's redevelopment authority acquired and prepared the site, and the Rouse Company, a private real estate firm, paid rent to develop and manage the property. When it opened in 1976 without a national chain store or what experts considered adequate parking its success was considered a long shot. In the hope of attracting visitors, Rouse officials invited street entertainers to perform, decorated the site with balloons, and disguised vacant storefronts by placing artisans' pushcarts in front of them. Faneuil Hall Marketplace proved to be a success beyond its promoters' wildest dreams: In its first year of business, it attracted 10 million visitors and generated total sales three times that of sales at Boston stores. In the 1980s, the Rouse Company copied the "festival marketplace" formula at Baltimore's Harborplace and New York City's South Street Seaport, and other developers created marketplaces and shopping malls in urban and industrial locales all over North America.[40]

Like some public development projects, arts districts and renovated marketplaces contributed to the overall economic prosperity of the cities in which they were located and, by extension, to their citizens. In contrast to urban renewal authorities, they usually revived existing locales without sweeping displacement of residents or store owners. Although not purely democratic, the public-private partnerships that ran arts districts and marketplaces were bottom-up in that they owed their existence to visionary individuals, willing vendors, and enthusiastic consumers. Yet their success spawned expensive, highly commercial projects that lacked the imagination and freshness of the originals.

Community-Based Place Governance

From the 1960s, the nonprofit community development movement generated new democratic forms of urban placemaking and governance. The movement grew out of the efforts of working-class and low-income neighborhoods to fend off threats such as urban renewal and highway projects, waste transfer stations, and disinvestment. Moving beyond protest, citizens formed local organizations that would revitalize urban neighborhoods and improve the lives of their inhabitants. To one degree or another, community development groups combined the passion for social justice from the civil rights movement, the political tactics of the community organization field, and financial and management skills from the world of business. By the end of the twentieth century, thousands of community development corporations (CDCs) and similar nonprofit organizations, such as "community-based housing organizations," were operating businesses, providing social services, and managing housing developments in urban neighborhoods.[41]

In the final decades of the twentieth century, the number of CDCs and nonprofit housing organizations multiplied, reaching a peak sometime around the year 2000. They received crucial financial assistance from federal programs, such as the Community Development Block Grant and Section 8 housing programs, and grants and loans from national financial intermediaries and foundations.[42] In addition, numerous state and city governments supported community development groups with financial incentives, technical assistance, land acquisition, and building and use permits.

The trial-and-error approach to managing their neighborhoods led CDCs to develop and manage federally subsidized low-income housing. From the start, community development groups tackled a wide range of projects, including attracting heavy industry, commercial real estate development, operating stores, and providing social services. Despite occasional victories, such as convincing IBM to set up an assembly plant in Bedford-Stuyvesant, the efforts to industrialize the inner city turned out to be impractical. Moreover, many of the early CDCs that invested in risky and low-margin small businesses, such as local supermarkets, failed. In contrast to other types of investment, the costs, financing, and returns—from development and management fees—of subsidized housing were relatively predictable. Besides penciling out, housing developments anchored the population in stable, pleasant-looking environments, which, in turn, advertised the neighborhoods as attractive places in which to live and invest. Community development leaders continued to pursue a range of activities but found that subsidized low-income housing provided the most feasible line of business.

A far cry from public housing, community-development housing was attuned to working-class consumers' desires. In Boston, two well-organized community groups of low-income and minority residents produced and managed entire housing subdivisions for low-income and moderate-income people. Between 1972 and 1982, in the city's South End, the predominantly Puerto Rican Emergency Tenants Council (later *Inquilinos Boricuas en Accion*) blocked the city's urban renewal plan and, instead, developed Villa Victoria, acclaimed for its urban design of townhouses, mid- and high-rise apartment buildings, landscapes, and open recreational spaces, where more than 3,000 low- and moderate-income people lived. In Lower Roxbury, where government-sponsored urban renewal had cleared hundreds of homes of poor African Americans, Hispanic Americans, and Cape Verdeans, the Madison Park Development Corporation rebuilt the neighborhood with 263 townhouse apartments and two mid-rise apartment buildings of about 130 units each. Both groups manage their housing developments, as well as provide a variety of social services to the working-class and low-income residents.[43]

Most nonprofit community development organizations could reasonably claim to be bottom-up, community-based organizations. True, the executive director of a CDC was generally a professional from outside the neighborhood and, often, so were the staff specialists in real estate development, social services, finance, and so on. Yet almost all had headquarters in the neighborhoods they served, most had residents on their boards of directors (and, in some cases, staff), and the most effective groups organized well-attended annual meetings and neighborhood events at which they surveyed residents to set their priorities. Moreover, without substantial community support, CDCs could not hope to gain approval from local government for their projects, which often included subsidized housing. The deeper problem for many CDCs was their small size and financial vulnerability—such as dependence upon government and philanthropic grants. This became painfully evident in the 2008 economic crisis when hundreds of CDCs went out of business.

On a larger scale, the Dudley Street Neighborhood Initiative (DSNI), located in the Roxbury section of Boston, demonstrates the potential for community-controlled place governance. In 1984, an alliance of local social service agencies, CDCs, and churches founded the DSNI to fight off a proposal by Boston's redevelopment agency to blanket an area of approximately one and a half square miles with office towers and luxury hotels. At a series of well-attended community workshops organized by the DSNI, local residents created a master plan for developing an "urban village" of houses, parks, and shops. After adroit political maneuvers that won the support of Boston's mayor, Raymond Flynn, in 1988, the DSNI wrestled the power of eminent domain from the city and took over supervision of the development of the neighborhood's many acres of vacant lots. With formal control over its service area—alone among nonprofit community groups—and a serious commitment to community organizing, DSNI helped residents of Roxbury not only to plan but also to implement their own agenda for their neighborhood.[44] (For more on DSNI, see chapter 3 of this volume.)

Modern Greenspace Governance

While some citizens banded together to revitalize their neighborhoods, others were organizing to save and maintain parks. In the 1970s, city governments responded to slumping tax revenues by cutting budgets, including for public parks. As the conditions of the parks deteriorated, citizens, many of whom were inspired by the historic preservation movement and passionate about urban green spaces campaigned to restore the parks. When lobbying city officials proved to be in vain, in the 1980s, private citizens organized "conservancies" and "friends of the park" groups that donated funds and volunteered their labor to clean and maintain their parks.

In New York City, the Central Park Conservancy, an organization of private citizens, many of them quite wealthy, took up the cause of the famous greenspace designed by the great landscape architect Frederick Law Olmsted. In 1980, after Mayor Edward Koch agreed to share the administration of Central Park, the conservancy took responsibility for restoring the park and supervising park department employees. By 1990, it was providing more than half the park's budget.[45]

The conservancy model of greenspace management took hold in dozens of cities across the United States. The public-private park partnerships varied, from citizen organizations that volunteered labor to those that helped finance and manage the parks directly. Most focused on a single park, but some, as in Louisville and Memphis, became stewards for several or all of a city's park system—a tall order.[46]

As citizen organizations, the conservancies were democratic, but only in a certain sense. Like public meetings of local governments and grassroots efforts in general, they were comprised of the people who had the time and motivation to show up. In cases such as the Central Park Conservancy, many of the motivated citizens were elites, who have been criticized for using their wealth and prestige to impose their vision of park landscape and uses on the public. Indeed, supporters of parks often clashed with one another over the proper approach to restoration and functions—debates over Forest Park in St. Louis and Piedmont Park in Atlanta delayed the creation of working partnerships for years.[47]

Yet it was possible for independent grassroots organizations to share governance of public parks. In 1974, community activists in Boston founded the Franklin Park Coalition as a kind of guerilla movement to save one of Olmsted's finest urban landscapes, Franklin Park, located near a predominantly African American neighborhood. Although at first the activists harshly criticized the parks department for allowing the greenspace to become a dumping ground, they took on the task of organizing events and volunteer conservation efforts at the park in collaboration with the department. The Franklin Park Coalition, whose board is comprised entirely of neighborhood residents, continued to advocate for the park and its neighbors and is, even today, fighting to convince the city government to protect the park grounds from a proposed homeless housing and social services project by moving the facilities to a different but nearby site in their neighborhood.[48]

Special Districts Redux

While the community development movement allowed citizen residents to shape and manage places and services in their neighborhoods, city leaders sought new ways to revive and run downtowns and neighborhoods. In the face of foundering fiscal conditions, local government officials joined with business executives to create novel financing and governance arrangements in the elite public-private tradition.

In the 1970s, municipal officials began creating Tax Increment Financing (TIF) districts to bankroll redevelopment, infrastructure, and economic development projects in downtowns, industrial areas, and residential neighborhoods. By the early 1990s, more than half the American cities with populations of more than 100,000 had exploited the TIF method (and many continue to do so today). The city of Chicago created TIF districts in every section of the city.[49] To pay for improvement projects, local governments issued bonds based on an anticipated increase in tax revenues and financed the project with money raised from the bonds. If and when property values and taxes rose, the city repaid the bondholders, after which the TIF expired.[50]

Projects financed by the TIF method successfully repaid their bonds most often in industrial and commercial areas. In 1977, for example, the city of Minneapolis partnered with Oxford Properties, a large Canadian real estate firm, to redevelop several blocks of old downtown commercial buildings. Using $50 million of tax increment bonds, Minneapolis acquired, cleared, and prepared the site and transferred it at no cost to Oxford. The developer built a department store, corporate headquarters, chain hotel, and indoor retail mall, which generated tax revenues that not only repaid the bonds but also supported other city programs.[51] In residential neighborhoods, in contrast, TIFs generally paid for themselves only in places that were gentrifying or relatively stable, not in highly disinvested low-income communities.

Unlike TIFs, a type of special assessment district—known variously as a business improvement district (BID), a business improvement area, or a community improvement district—created a permanent place-based governance structure. It began life as a way for local government officials, community organizations, and boosters such as businesspersons and real estate professionals to upgrade commercial areas without having to raise general taxes. In 1970, Toronto organized the first BID in North America; five years later, New Orleans created the first BID in the United States, and in the following decades, the idea took off. By 2000, there were more than 1,000 improvement districts in the United States and Canada, and their numbers have continued to grow.[52]

Enabled by state legislation, local governments create BIDs, and supervisory boards, mainly comprised of local business and property owners, administer them. In contrast to other special assessment districts, BIDs control their own funds, most of which come from an additional property tax assessed above the normal tax rate on properties within their jurisdiction. They use their revenues to perform many functions, but most often to collect garbage, maintain and beautify streets and sidewalks, and organize safety patrols. These activities supplement, but do not replace, normal city services.[53]

BIDs come in all sizes, as do their budgets, which range from less than $10,000 to millions of dollars. The largest and most visible BIDs, such as the Times Square and Grand Central districts in New York City, are located downtown and run by large corporations. But BIDs also took root in the neighborhoods. In New York City in the early 1990s, there were BIDs in the Russian and Asian immigrant neighborhood of Brighton Beach, along a main street in a Puerto Rican neighborhood in Brooklyn, and at the 165th Street Mall, a discount store shopping center in a Black middle-class neighborhood in Queens.[54]

As the number of BIDs have grown, they have become rooted in the matrix of public, private, and public-private institutions that govern places in local communities. In Philadelphia in the 2000s, the city government instigated the formation of a BID in the sports complex area to build new stadiums, and the Philadelphia Industrial Development Corporation and the Greater Philadelphia Chamber of Commerce started a BID to revitalize the working-class Port Richmond neighborhood. Community development corporations and a state senator's sponsored charitable nonprofit, Citizens' Alliance for Better Neighborhoods, supported and coordinated with local BIDs to provide services and improvements to their areas.[55]

BIDs are place-based but not formally democratic, for which they have been frequently criticized. (For more detailed discussion, see chapter 5 of this volume.) Like elite place governance in early America, BIDs are dominated by local propertied interests. Some BID governing boards include all local businesses as well as residents, but others do not. Yet their priorities reflect the area in which they are located, and many neighborhood BIDs coordinate programs and projects with CDCs or other local entities. Moreover, even the most inclusive BIDs are affected by broader patterns of place-based inequality. BIDs in low-income communities can raise only a fraction of the tax revenues that affluent commercial districts can generate; thus, they often are less active than wealthier BIDs.[56]

Nationally, the BID came to be seen as a useful tool for urban revitalization. For example, Main Street America is a national nonprofit that, since 1980, has assisted towns and cities to preserve and revive their historic downtowns and commercial areas. Along with local business associations and CDCs, BIDs make up many of the members of its network of accredited groups.[57]

The Rise of Megaprojects

With new tools for place governance, during the last decades of the twentieth century city and state government agencies engaged in ever grander development schemes, reaching the scale of megaprojects.

The trend began in the late 1970s when city governments took advantage of federal redevelopment funds to promote large-scale private projects. For example, in the face of declining population and employment the governments of Detroit and Baltimore each received more than $100 million of federal urban development funds.[58] The city of Detroit used its funding to produce high-rise corporate and luxury-residence towers along the Detroit River, while the city of Baltimore redeveloped the Inner Harbor with an array of public and private projects, including the Rouse Company's Harborplace.[59]

From the 1980s, the public-private high-finance mode of large-scale urban development took off. In cities across the country, public-private redevelopment schemes generated thousands of downtown offices, hotels, and mixed-use complexes. In the 1990s and 2000s, local governments approved and assisted the construction of dozens of ever-larger downtown convention centers, more than a hundred sports stadiums—most of which lost money—and even casinos, which despite their questionable morality provided strapped municipalities with revenue. Public authorities of one sort or another often organized the planning, choice of developer, and sale for mixed-use projects, and built and ran sports stadiums, convention halls, and parking garages. The financing for the projects included tax-exempt bonds for redevelopment projects and government-owned facilities, TIFs, and BIDs.[60]

At the same time, cities fostered the public-private development of theme park entertainment complexes. These "urban entertainment destinations" are the highly commercial offspring of informal entertainment neighborhoods and controlled tourist entertainment areas, such as Las Vegas's giant resort-casinos and New York City's Times Square. In response to the city of Houston's request for proposals in 1997, the developer David Cordish produced Bayou Place, a $23 million complex of theaters, concert hall, restaurants, and bars. In 2003, the Cordish Company converted a giant industrial building in Baltimore's Inner Harbor to Power Plant Live!, a collection of chain and locally owned restaurants, nightclubs, and bars, and then built similar complexes in Louisville, Kansas City, and Philadelphia. Typically, a city government or authority planned and supervised the creation of an entertainment district, which a private developer, and perhaps a media or entertainment firm, developed, owned, and managed.[61]

The scale of public-private place development has reached enormous proportions. Twenty-three years after the San Francisco Redevelopment Agency approved a plan by the major l, the Mission Bay project had transformed a 300-acre site of former railroad yards on the San Francisco waterfront into a mixed-use neighborhood. Government provided hundreds of millions of dollars in financing, including TIF bonds, and infrastructure, while the private sector invested and built projects worth more than $4.5 billion. By 2020, Mission Bay contained 6,400 units of housing, 6.5 million square feet of commercial office and biotech lab space—including the University of California at San Francisco (UCSF) Medical Center, Children's Hospital, and a bio-tech research campus—285,000 square feet of retail space in numerous buildings, and a 250-room hotel. Most of the properties were sold to private end users or builders, but the city of San Francisco built a police station and public library adjacent to the central part of the development.[62]

The open spaces at Mission Bay illustrate the complex and novel ways the megaproject mingled private and public governance. Some open spaces, such as Koret Quad, a sculpture garden in a pine tree grove on the UCSF campus, are privately owned but accessible to the public. Many more, including a playground, dog park, and ten-acre esplanade along Mission Creek, are under public domain, but not the San Francisco Recreation and Park Department. Instead, the San Francisco Office of Community Investment and Infrastructure (the redevelopment agency's successor) controls the entire Mission Bay Parks system. That office, in turn, has contracted with a private company that specializes in managing public spaces to operate Mission Bay Parks. The company not only maintains the grounds but also coordinates their uses with Mission Bay's residents, building managers, businesses, and private institutions, and organizes large events, ranging from Easter Egg hunts to jazz concerts, to which the public is invited.[63]

In some megaprojects, the partnership between wealthy individuals and high government officials smacked of insider dealing. The development of Pacific Park, located near downtown Brooklyn on a twenty-two-acre site of residences, stores, and light industry, was particularly controversial. With little regard for the residents and property owners of the area, the state and city governments pushed through a plan for fifteen high-rise buildings—which would loom over the nearby brownstone neighborhood—and the Barclays Center, a sports arena to house the New Jersey Nets basketball team owned by the project's developer, Bruce Ratner. The lead state entity, Empire State Development Corporation, pledged $200 million in direct subsidies to Forest City Ratner Companies and used the power of eminent domain to acquire the land, which included occupied homes. In addition, the city of New York put up $105 million and granted the stadium a thirty-year tax exemption. To dampen opposition, Ratner agreed to set aside contracts and construction jobs for women and minorities and provide 2,250 affordable apartments, yet many local residents and organization continued to contest the project, delaying it for several years.[64]

In contrast, some recent elite-style mixed-use projects explicitly adopted civic as well as profit-making goals. For example, in 2002 major educational, health, and cultural institutions in St. Louis created a nonprofit developer, the Cortex Innovation Community, to oversee the development of a 200-acre technology district. The developer's mission was to generate tech jobs, increase the city's tax revenues, and create a socially diverse neighborhood. The city government enthusiastically approved a TIF that enabled Cortex to create and maintain the district's streetscapes, sidewalks, lighting, and Cortex Commons, a public park. The investment paid off. By 2019, the Cortex district had grown to become a major research and development center, where about 370 companies and institutions tenants employed almost 5,800 workers.[65]

Large-scale public-private projects are by definition led and administered by elites in a top-down manner. Often, as in the case of sports stadia, government officials hope the project will attract tourists and increase local businesses and so give financial incentives to developers, but they exercise little control over the project. In some mixed-use developments, however, a methodical planning process, which can be contentious, may enable the public at large to extract concessions or "community benefit agreements" from developers in the form of hiring practices, affordable housing, or social services.

A New Era of Community-Oriented Place Governance

While the scale, scope, and number of elite-style mixed-use projects increased in the first decades of the twenty-first century, a plethora of place-based efforts combined old and new practices to remake, revive, and maintain public places. Citizens, institutional leaders, and government officials built on past practices of economic development, community development, arts districts, and park conservancies to carry out civic efforts ranging from single projects to city-wide campaigns. Some efforts aimed to improve the planning and development of downtowns, others to steward natural resources, and others to revitalize neighborhoods.

Increasingly, philanthropic foundations have become partners, if sometimes as silent financiers, in placemaking and governance. In 2016, for example, four national foundations organized the Reimagining the Civic Commons to support coalitions in multiple cities aimed at renewing and managing public spaces in ways that advanced social, economic, and environmental goals.

One of those coalitions is the nonprofit Memphis River Parks Partnership. Like public-private park conservancies, the partnership manages, maintains, operates, and runs events in five riverfront districts comprising 250 acres of parkland with numerous rental and performance facilities. Yet, like a community development organization, it has a strong democratic orientation. Its board is made up of leaders of local businesses and institutions, and the partnership consults the public extensively, such as in 2017 when it surveyed more than 4,000 Memphians about a plan to restore natural ecology of the riverfront and make it part of downtown and neighborhood life.[66]

In 2009, the District of Columbia's decision to replace the city's 11th Street Bridge set off a particularly expansive place-based campaign. The city's planning department proposed to build a park on the bridge and adjacent riverfront with spaces and facilities that would serve all Washingtonians, especially neighboring low-income residents, who were invited to help choose the park's design. This inspired a local nonprofit group, aptly named Building Bridges Across the River, to conduct an intensive community engagement drive for "equitable development" within a one-mile radius of the bridge. Numerous collaborations with the district, local CDCs, and a workforce center, among other groups, produced a cascade of programs and transformed spaces—job training and placement, first-time home-purchase classes, a community land trust for affordable housing, community gardens, public art installations, and festivals to celebrate African American culture and the Anacostia River environment—well before construction had begun on the bridge that started it all.[67]

In the twenty-first century, one can find an almost endless variety of place governance alliances in North American cities. Their approaches vary from relatively top-down to high levels of community engagement. Although each effort must be measured on its own merits, it has become accepted practice for elite institutions, government agencies, community organizations, and individual citizens to collaborate on managing urban spaces for civic purposes.

Conclusion

The history of place governance reveals that, since the settlement of Europeans in North America, both elite and ordinary citizens have shaped and managed public and semi-public spaces in towns and cities. In the process, they developed a broad array of open spaces, business districts, main streets, commercial areas, and residential neighborhoods. The efforts utilized diverse forms of public-private collaborations to realize and manage a wide range of economic, recreational, welfare, and cultural activities. Governments have played a large role, frequently helping implement elite projects but also, in various ways, assisting more democratic types of placemaking and governance.

Both the elite and democratic modes of place governance had their advantages and weaknesses. At their best, elite modes brought financial resources and professional skills to the problems of making and running places in ways that benefitted the city at large. At their worst, they became too centralized and insular, and exacerbated inequalities of class or race. The directors of top-down large-scale schemes, from public housing to megaprojects, were too often oblivious to the needs and wishes of the people they were supposed to serve and, even, the public at large. Rooted in communities, in contrast, successful democratic forms of place governance identified local needs and celebrated local cultures. Yet many represented only segments of their communities or lacked stable structures that could sustain places over time.

In recent years, the elite and democratic traditions have merged to create hybrid forms of urban placemaking and governance to revitalize urban economies, knit together communities socially, and provide recreational and educational spaces. The result is a patchwork quilt of entities and financial devices, the success of which depends on the vision, ingenuity, and persistence of local actors, be they entrepreneurs, citizens, or government officials. The challenge will be to encourage highly engaged citizens and enterprising leaders to extend these methods to cities, neighborhoods, and sectors where they have not yet emerged.

It will be worth the effort. In devising partnerships to fill their needs, Americans throughout their history have worked out flexible and creative approaches to place governance that responded to local circumstances and desires in ways no single entity or program could hope to match.

NOTES

1. Henry Taylor Blake, *Chronicles of New Haven Green* (New Haven: The Tuttle, Morehouse & Taylor Press, 1898), pp. 9, 12–13, 21, 25–27, 42 (note 7), passim; David Holahan, "The New Haven Green: City's Center of Public Life on Private Property," *Hartford Courant Magazine*, April 21, 2016.

2. Bernard Bailyn, *The New England Merchants in the Seventeenth Century* (New York: Harper & Row, 1955), pp. 97–98; Walter Muir Whitehill, *Boston: A Topographical History*. 3rd edition (Harvard University Press, 2000), pp. 41–42; Lawrence W. Kennedy, *Planning the City upon a Hill* (University of Massachusetts Press, 1992), p. 19.

3. Rachelle Alterman, "Land-Use Regulations and Property Values: The 'Windfalls Capture' Idea Revisited," in *Oxford Handbook on Urban Economics and Planning*, edited by Nancy Brooks, Kieran Donaghy, and Gerrit-Jan Knapp (Oxford University Press, 2012), pp. 755–86; Hendrik Hartog, *Public Property and Private Power: The Corporation of the City of New York in American Law, 1730–1870* (Cornell University Press, 1983), pp. 44–59.

4. Thomas P. Slaughter, "Crowds in Eighteenth-Century America: Reflections and New Directions," *Pennsylvania Magazine of History and Biography* 115, no. 1 (January 1991), pp. 3–34; Pauline Maier, *From Resistance to Revolution* (New York: W. W. Norton & Company, 1991), pp. 3–26; Jesse Lemisch, "Jack Tar in the Streets: Merchant Seamen in the Politics of Revolutionary America," *William and Mary Quarterly* 25 (1968), pp. 371–407; Paul A. Gilje, *The Road to Mobocracy: Popular Disorder in New York City, 1763–1834* (University of North Carolina Press, 1987).

5. Maier, *From Resistance to Revolution*, pp. 16–19.

6. Gary B. Nash, *The Urban Crucible: Social Change, Political Consciousness, and the Origins of the American Revolution* (Harvard University Press, 1979), pp. 129–34.

7. Walter Muir Whitehill, *Boston: A Topographical History*. 3rd edition (Harvard University Press, 2000), pp. 52–54, 63; Kennedy, *Planning the City upon a Hill*, p. 34; Elizabeth Blackmar, *Manhattan for Rent, 1785–1850* (Cornell University Press, 1989) ("gentlemen"), pp. 79, 99–100, 164–66; "Bowling Green Fence," New York City Landmarks Preservation Commission, July 14, 1970.

8. Nancy Seasholes, *Gaining Ground: A History of Landmaking in Boston* (MIT Press, 2003), pp. 186–96; Bainbridge Bunting, *Houses of the Back Bay an Architectural History, 1840–1917* (Harvard University Press, 1967), pp. 251–53, 391. In St. Louis, house subdividers built and sold the infrastructure to homeowners, who then maintained their own streets, sewers, and water pipes. David T. Beito and Bruce Smith, "The Formation of

Urban Infrastructure through Nongovernmental Planning: The Private Places of St. Louis, 1869–1920," *Journal of Urban History* 16, no. 3 (1990), pp. 263–303.

9. Seasholes, *Gaining Ground*, pp. 50–53; Kennedy, *Planning the City Upon a Hill*, pp. 48–49.

10. Blanche Linden-Ward, *Silent City on a Hill: Landscapes of Memory and Boston's Mount Auburn Cemetery* (Ohio State University Press, 1989); David Schuyler, *The New Urban Landscape: The Redefinition of City Form in Nineteenth-Century America* (Johns Hopkins University Press, 1986); David Charles Sloane, *The Last Great Necessity: Cemeteries in American History* (Johns Hopkins University Press, 1991).

11. Jon C. Teaford, *The Unheralded Triumph: City Government in America, 1870–1900* (Johns Hopkins University Press, 1984), pp. 66–72.

12. Teaford, *The Unheralded Triumph*, pp. 72–75; Enoch Pratt Free Library, "History of the Library," www.prattlibrary.org/about-us/history.

13. Roy Rosenzweig and Elizabeth Blackmar, *The Park and the People: A History of Central Park* (Cornell University Press, 1992), pp. 307–28; Alexander von Hoffman, "'Of Greater Lasting Consequence,' Frederick Law Olmsted and the Fate of Franklin Park, Boston," *Journal of the Society of Architectural Historians* 47 (December 1988), pp. 339–50.

14. Perry Duis, *The Saloon: Public Drinking in Chicago and Boston, 1880–1920* (University of Illinois Press, 1983); Jon M. Kingsdale, "The 'Poor Man's Club' Social Functions of the Urban Working-Class Saloon," *American Quarterly* 25 (October 1973), pp. 472–89; Christine Stansell, *City of Women: Sex and Class in New York, 1789–1860* (University of Illinois Press, 1987), pp. 56–58; Christopher Thale, "The Informal World of Police Patrol: New York City in the Early Twentieth Century," *Journal of Urban History* 33, no. 2 (January 2007), pp. 183–216; Alexander von Hoffman, "An Officer of the Neighborhood: A Boston Patrolman on the Beat in 1895," *Journal of Social History*, 26, no. 2 (Winter 1992), pp. 309–30.

15. Jane Jacobs, "Flowers Come to Town," in *Vital Little Plans*, edited by Samuel Zipp and Nathan Storring (New York: Random House, 2016), pp. 18–19.

16. Paula E. Hyman, "Immigrant Women and Consumer Protest: The New York City Kosher Meat Boycott of 1902," *American Jewish History* 70 (1980), pp. 91–105; Robert M. Fogelson, *The Great Rent Wars: New York, 1917–1929* (Yale University Press, 2013).

17. Stephen A. Reiss, *City Games, The Evolution of American Urban Society and the Rise of Sports* (University of Illinois Press, 1989), pp. 25–26; Stephen Hardy, *How Boston Played: Sport, Recreation, and Community, 1865–1915* (North-

eastern University Press, 1982), pp. 131–32, 139–42; The Country Club, Constitution, By-Laws and List of Members (Boston, 1910).

18. Arthur Schlesinger, "Biography of a Nation of Joiners," *American Historical Review* 50, no. 1 (October 1944), pp. 1–25; Alexander von Hoffman, *Local Attachments: The Making of an American Urban Neighborhood, 1850 to 1920* (Johns Hopkins University Press: 1994); Ann Firor Scott, *Natural Allies: Women's Associations in American History* (University of Illinois Press, 1992); Jane Cunningham Croly, *The History of the Woman's Club Movement in America* (New York: H. G. Allen & Co., 1898).

19. Robert D. Putnam, *Bowling Alone: The Collapse and Revival of American Community* (New York: Simon & Schuster, 2000).

20. Gunter Barth, *City People: The Rise of Modern City Culture in Nineteenth-Century America* (Oxford University Press, 1980); Robert M. Fogelson, *Downtown: Its Rise and Fall, 1880–1950* (Yale University Press, 2001).

21. Alison Isenberg, *Downtown America: A History of the Place and the People Who Made It* (University of Chicago Press: 2004).

22. Carol Krinsky, "Rockefeller Center," *Encyclopedia of New York City*, Kenneth T. Jackson editor (Yale University Press, 1995), p. 1015; Wikipedia, "Rockefeller Center," https://en.wikipedia.org/wiki/Rockefeller_Center #History.

23. William H. Whyte, *City: Rediscovering the Center* (New York: Doubleday, 1988); Project for Public Spaces, www.pps.org/.

24. William S. Worley, *J. C. Nichols and the Shaping of Kansas City: Innovation in Planned Residential Communities* (University of Missouri Press, 1990), p. 166, passim.

25. By 1919, Nichols had decided he would sell to Jews. Worley, *J. C. Nichols and the Shaping of Kansas City*, pp. 144–53; Virginia P. Dawson, "Protection from Undesirable Neighbors: The Use of Deed Restrictions in Shaker Heights, Ohio," *Journal of Planning History* 18, no. 2 (2019), pp. 116–36; Paige Glotzer, "Exclusion in Arcadia: How Suburban Developers Circulated Ideas about Discrimination, 1890–1950," *Journal of Urban History* 41 (May 2015), pp. 479–94; Marie-Alice L'Heureux, "The Creative Class, Urban Boosters, and Race: Shaping Urban Revitalization in Kansas City, Missouri," *Journal of Urban History* 41, no. 2 (March 2015), pp. 252–54; Kevin Fox Gotham, *Race, Real Estate, and Uneven Development: The Kansas City Experience, 1900–2000* (State University of New York Press, 2002); Bernard J. Frieden, *The Environmental Protection Hustle* (MIT Press, 1979); Evan McKenzie, *Privatopia: Homeowner Associations and the Rise of Residential Private Government* (Yale University Press, 1994).

26. Bud Billiken Parade, http://budbillikenparade.com/history.htm; Matthew Vaz, "'We Intend to Run It': Racial Politics, Illegal Gambling, and the

Rise of Government Lotteries in the United States, 1960–1985," *Journal of American History* 101, no. 1 (June 2014), pp. 71–96; Shane White, Stephen Garton, Stephen Robertson, and Graham White, *Playing the Numbers: Gambling in Harlem between the Wars* (Harvard University Press, 2010), pp. 211–12.

27. Dennis Gale, *The Misunderstood History of Gentrification* (Temple University Press, 2021); Steve Shipp, *American Art Colonies, 1850–1930: A Historical Guide to America's Original Art Colonies and their Artists* (Westport, CT: Greenwood Press, 1996); Joanna Levin, *Bohemia in America, 1858–1920* (Stanford University Press, 2010).

28. Andrew Scott Dolkart, *The Row House Reborn: Architecture and Neighborhoods in New York City, 1908–1929* (John Hopkins University Press, 2009), pp. 122–36, 169–73, passim.

29. Mary Beth Betts, editor, "SoHo—Cast-Iron Historic District Extension Designation Report," New York City Landmarks Preservation Commission (May 11, 2010), p. 17; Sharon Zukin, *Loft Living: Culture and Capital in Urban Change* (Johns Hopkins University Press, 1982, new edition 2014); Stephen Petrus, "From Gritty to Chic: The Transformation of New York City's SoHo, 1962–1976," *New York History* 84, no. 1 (Winter 2003), pp. 50–87; William Eckstein, "An Evaluation of New York Loft Conversion Law," *Fordham Urban Law Journal* 10, no. 3 (Fall 1981), p. 512, note 8; West Loop Community Organization, http://westloop.org/about/history/; City of Los Angeles, Adaptive Reuse Ordinance, http://preservation.lacity.org/incentives/adaptive-reuse-ordinance.

30. Gail Radford, *The Rise of the Public Authority* (University of Chicago Press, 2013), pp. 86, 130–32; Jameson W. Doig, *Empire on the Hudson: Entrepreneurial Vision and Political Power at the Port of New York Authority* (Columbia University Press, 2001).

31. Robert Caro, *The Power Broker: Robert Moses and the Fall of New York* (New York: Random House, 1974); Christopher Gray, "The Coliseum; The 'Hybrid Pseudo-Modern' on Columbus Circle, *New York Times*, April 26, 1987; McCormick Place Chicago, "History," www.mccormickplace.com/about/history; Heywood T. Sanders, *Convention Center Follies: Politics, Power, and Public Investment in American Cities* (University of Pennsylvania Press, 2013).

32. Jon Teaford, *The Rough Road to Renaissance—Urban Revitalization in America, 1940–1985* (Johns Hopkins University Press, 1990); Wendell E. Pritchett, "The Public Menace of Blight: Urban Renewal and the Private Uses of Eminent Domain," *Yale Law and & Policy Review* 21, no. 1 (2003), pp. 1–52; James Q. Wilson, *Urban Renewal: The Record and the Controversy*. (MIT Press, 1966).

33. John R. Logan and Harvey L. Molotch, *Urban Fortunes: The Political Economy of Place* (University of California Press, 1987); Martin L. Millspaugh, "The Inner Harbor Story," *Urban Land* (April 2003), pp. 36–41.

34. Philadelphia Industrial Development Corporation, "60 Years of Driving Growth to Every Corner of Philadelphia," www.pidcphila.com/images /uploads/resource_library/pidc-history-lores.pdf, p. 12; International Economic Development Council, "Forty Years of Urban Economic Development: A Retrospective" (Washington, DC: 2008), p. 83.

35. Leda McIntyre Hall and Melvin F. Hall, "Detroit's Urban Regime: Composition and Consequence," *Mid-American Review of Sociology* 17, no. 2 (1993), pp. 23–24, 27–28; Detroit Economic Growth Corporation, www.degc .org/public-authorities/.

36. Isenberg, *Downtown America*, pp. 273–83; Tim O'Neil, "Gaslight Square in St. Louis Burned Brightly but Briefly in the 1960s," *St. Louis Post-Dispatch*, March 24, 2013; Paul Delaney, "Violence Destroys a Boom in Kansas City's Old Section, *New York Times*, April 19, 1977; Stephanie Harrington, "How to Reform without Really Going Square," *Village Voice*, June 9, 1966; Stephen Petrus, "Greenwich Village Fights the Heroin Epidemic, 1958–1963," Gotham Center for New York City History, December 21, 2016, www.gothamcenter .org/blog/greenwich-village-fights-the-heroin-epidemic-1958-1963.

37. Leo Adam Biga, "Sam Mercer: The Old Market's Godfather," *Omaha Magazine*, April 25, 2013; Emerson Clarridge, "Sam Mercer, Old Market's Guiding Hand, Dies in France," *Omaha World-Herald*, February 15, 2013; Alison Isenberg, *Downtown America*, pp. 293–94; The Old Market, http:// oldmarket.com/About_Us.

38. City of Omaha Landmarks Heritage Preservation Commission, Application for Landmark Heritage District Designation for Old Market and Wholesale District, September 1984; City Council of the City of Omaha, Ordinance 30574, An Ordinance to Designate the Old Market and Wholesale District . . . as a Landmark Heritage District . . . passed January 22, 1985; Tax Incentive Program Projects in Douglas County, www.nebraskahistory.org /histpres/tax/douglas.htm; City of Omaha Department of Urban Planning, Old Market and Wholesale District Guidelines, 2009, p. 1.

39. Bernard J. Frieden, and Lynne B. Sagalyn, *Downtown, Inc.: How America Rebuilds Cities* (MIT Press, 1989), pp. 115–19; Public Market Center, Pike's Place Market, "PDA Council Members," www.pikeplacemarket.org/pda -council-committees; Berk Associates, "Pike Place Market Preservation and Development Authority: A Business, Economic and Public Policy Assessment of the PDA's Properties," (2004), pp. 7–10, https://s3.amazonaws.com/aws -website-ppsimages-na05y/pdf/pike_place_economic_impact_study.pdf; Pike

PlaceMarketFoundation,"Mission+History,"www.pikeplacemarketfoundation
.org/about-us/history/.

40. John Quincy Jr., *Quincy's Market: a Boston Landmark* (Northeastern University Press, 2003), pp. 136–217; Frieden and Sagalyn, *Downtown, Inc.*, pp. 1–7, 107–15.

41. Robert O. Zdenek, *Taking Hold: The Growth and Support of Community Development Corporations* (Washington: National Congress for Community Economic Development, 1990), cited in Julia Sass Rubin, *Financing Low Income Communities: Models, Obstacles and Future Directions* (New York: Russell Sage Foundation, 2007), p. 2.

42. The most important are NeighborWorks America, the Local Initiatives Support Corporation (LISC), and Enterprise Community Partners.

43. Mario Luis Small, *Villa Victoria: The Transformation of Social Capital in a Boston Barrio* (University of Chicago Press, 2007); Eric Hangen and Jeanne Pinado, Madison Park Development Corporation Case Study (Roxbury, MA: Madison Park Development Corporation, 2006), http://70.32.105.171/sites /default/files/MPDC%20Case%20Study.pdf.

44. Peter Medoff and Holly Sklar, *Streets of Hope: The Fall and Rise of an Urban Neighborhood* (Boston: South End Press, 1994); Dudley Street Neighborhood Initiative, "From the Bottom Up: The Dudley Street Neighborhood Initiative Strategy for Sustainable Economic Development (December 1997); Dudley Street Neighborhood Initiative, www.dsni.org.

45. Roy Rosenzweig and Elizabeth Blackmar, *The Park and the People: A History of Central Park* (Cornell University Press, 1992), pp. 506–23.

46. Olmsted Parks Conservancy, www.olmstedparks.org/; Memphis River Parks Partnership, www.memphisriverparks.org/parks.

47. Peter Harnik and Abby Martin, Public Spaces/Private Money: The Triumphs and Pitfalls of Urban Park Conservancies, Center for City Park Excellence, The Trust for Public Land, 2015, www.tpl.org/public-spacesprivate -money; Michael Murray, "Private Management of Public Spaces: Nonprofit Organizations and Urban Parks," *Harvard Environmental Law Review* 34 (2010), pp. 179–255.

48. Richard Heath, "What I've Learned From 40 Years of Community Organizing," *Jamaica Plain News*, May 9, 2015; Franklin Park Coalition, www .franklinparkcoalition.org/.

49. Richard Briffault, "The Most Popular Tool: Tax Increment Financing and the Political Economy of Local Government," *University of Chicago Law Review* 77: 1 (2010), p. 69; Alex Schwartz, "Rebuilding Downtown: A Case Study of Minneapolis," in *Urban Revitalization: Policies and Programs*, edited by Fritz W. Wagner, Timothy E. Joder, and Anthony J. Mumphrey (Thou-

sand Oaks: Sage Publications, 1995), pp. 190–91; Minnesota State Planning Agency, Office of Local and Urban Affairs, "Minneapolis St. Paul Study: Municipal Expenditures: Redevelopment," 1978, p. 2.

50. Briffault, "The Most Popular Tool," pp. 65–68.

51. Iric Nathanson, *Minneapolis in the Twentieth Century: The Growth of an American City* (St. Paul: Minnesota Historical Society Press, 2010), pp. 176–78; Minnesota State Planning Agency, "Minneapolis St. Paul Study, Municipal Expenditures," pp. 23–24, 59–78.

52. Richard Briffault, "Government for Our Time—Business Improvement Districts and Urban Governance," *Columbia Law Review* 99, no. 2 (March 1999), pp. 365–477; Janet Rothenberg Pack, "BIDs, DIDs, SIDs, SADs: Private Governments in Urban America," *Brookings Review* 10, no. 4 (Fall 1992), pp. 18–21; Richard Briffault, "The Business Improvement District Comes of Age," *Drexel Law Review* 3, no. 1 (Fall 2010), pp. 19–33; Göktug Morçöl and Ulf Zimmermann, "Metropolitan Governance and Business Improvement Districts," *International Journal of Public Administration*, 29, no. 1–3 (2006), pp. 5–29.

53. Briffault, "Government for Our Time," pp. 399–409.

54. Pack, "BIDs, DIDs, SIDs, SAD," pp. 18, 21.

55. Briffault, "The Business Improvement District Comes of Age," pp. 24–28.

56. Ibid., pp. 28–32.

57. See Main Street America, www.mainstreet.org/home; https://downtownhelena.com/main-street-america/; see also www.mainstreet.org/mainstreetamerica/mainstreetawards/gamsa/2017/westchester; https://kingdriveis.com/mainstreet/.

58. The funding came from the Urban Development Action Grants program (1977–1988).

59. Leda McIntyre Hall and Melvin F. Hall, "Detroit's Urban Regime: Composition and Consequence," *Mid-American Review of Sociology* 17, no. 2 (1993), p. 27; June Manning Thomas, *Redevelopment and Race: Planning a Finer City in Postwar Detroit* (Johns Hopkins University Press, 1997), p. 157; International Economic Development Council, "Forty Years of Urban Economic Development," p. 61.

60. Sanders, *Convention Center Follies*, p. ix; Judith Grant Long, *Public-Private Partnerships for Major League Sports Facilities* (New York and London: Routledge, 2012).

61. John Hannigan, "Urban Entertainment Destination," Ray Hutchison, editor, *Encyclopedia of Urban Studies* (Thousand Oaks, CA: Sage Publishing, 2010).

62. Mission Bay Development Group, Mission Bay, www.mbaydevelopment .com/mission-bay-new; www.mbaydevelopment.com/mission-bay-case-study-.

63. Mission Bay Parks, https://missionbayparks.com/public-parks/); MJM Management Group, "Mission Bay Parks Case Study," https://mjmmg.com /mission-bay-park-case-study/.

64. As of this writing, about 800 of the affordable units had been built. "A Guide to the Major Megaprojects Transforming New York," *Curbed New York*, October 23, 2019, https://ny.curbed.com/maps/nyc-new-development-hudson -yards-wtc-megaprojects; Pacific Park Brooklyn, https://pacificparkbrooklyn .com/; "Ceremonial Groundbreaking for Barclays Center at Atlantic Yards in Brooklyn," *Business Wire*, March 11, 2010; Carolyn Thompson, "Discourses of Community Contestation: The Fight Over the Atlantic Yards in Brooklyn, New York," *Urban Geography* 32, no. 8 (2011), pp. 1189–207; "Pacific Park, Brooklyn," entry, https://en.wikipedia.org/wiki/Pacific_Park,_Brooklyn.

65. Washington University in St. Louis, Saint Louis University, University of Missouri—St. Louis, BJC Healthcare, and the Missouri Botanical Garden founded Cortex with "the mission of building a community of technology entrepreneurs and innovation companies that will transform the regional St. Louis economy." Cortex Innovation Community, "Cortex Innovation Community Impact Report, 2002–2018, Executive Summary," https://cortexstl.blob.core.windows.net/media/1485/cortex_impactreport _brochure_v2.pdf, p. 2.

66. Memphis River Parks, www.memphisriverparks.org/about/; Jon W. Sparks, "Revising the Riverfront," *Memphis: The City Magazine*, March 6, 2019, https://memphismagazine.com/features/revising-the-riverfront/.

67. 11th Street Bridge Park, https://bbardc.org/the-park/; Alexander von Hoffman, "The Ingredients of Equitable Development Planning: A Cross-Case Analysis of Equitable Development Planning and CDFIs," Joint Center for Housing Studies of Harvard University 2019.

THREE

Who Governs? Public, Private, Community, Civic, and Knowledge Actors in Place Governance

SHEILA R. FOSTER

At the heart of placemaking practice is collaboration between people, interests, and stakeholders to make or remake the places they share.[1] This is true for place governance, as well, though it is arguably more expansive in both scope and scale. Although the term *placemaking* often is associated with public spaces, *place governance* encompasses decisions about public *and* private spaces in a given geography, as well as abandoned or forfeited land and structures and other spaces "in transition." The diversity of these spaces and places—in both physical character and function—means that a complex and diverse set of actors is likely to have a role in place governance activities.

Place governance is part of a shift over the last few decades from "government to governance," involving a decentralization of state power and authority over the provision of local goods and services and revitalization of the places where we live, work, and play.[2] In this shift, the state enables and empowers a diverse cast of characters in different ways, often playing a critical role in helping form new collaborative and institutional structures that can transform urban (and rural) places. For all the potential benefits of these arrangements, though, there are inherent risks in bringing together actors who may be very differently situated on these landscapes, and the type of actors driving place governance efforts invariably influences which populations ultimately fare better or worse from placemaking activities.

Consider three specific examples of place governance with different constellations of actors at different scales in the urban environment.

University City District (UCD), established in 1996 in Philadelphia, is a partnership of anchor institutions, small businesses, local nonprofits, and neighborhood associations that largely operates as a coordinating body and financing vehicle for a variety of place-based economic development initiatives in West Philadelphia.[3] UCD was founded by leaders from neighborhood nonprofit organizations, including the three largest institutions of higher education in the area—the University of Pennsylvania, Drexel University, and the University of the Sciences. UCD's emergence was in response to the reality of Philadelphia's severe budget constraints in the 1990s, leaving the city unable to adequately address property abandonment, declining infrastructure, crime, and poverty in surrounding neighborhoods.[4]

Today, UCD engages in a range of activities, including bringing life to commercial corridors, connecting low-income residents to employment, promoting job growth, and fostering innovation and entrepreneurship. UCD also has spearheaded several successful projects transforming public spaces in the district—including improving streetscapes, creating parklets, expanding pedestrian plazas, and supporting community gardening efforts.[5] UCD derives its power from its designation as a special services district (SSD) modeled in part on a neighboring business improvement district except that, instead of imposing a special assessment on commercial property owners in the area, it depends on voluntary contributions from a variety of institutional and community partners.[6] All partners are represented on the board, which is elected, but the area's universities and hospitals have been its primary funders and leaders.[7]

The nonprofit Dudley Street Neighborhood Association was formed to oversee the process of revitalizing Nubian Square (formerly Dudley Square), one of the poorest areas of Boston at the time, in the late 1980s to early 1990s.[8] After cleaning up many of the vacant lots that littered its neighborhood, DSNI embarked on an ambitious plan to create an "urban village" that would develop the neighborhood without resulting in any displacement of the existing residents. Neighborhood residents worked with city and state officials to acquire, through eminent domain, fifteen acres of privately owned, tax-defaulted vacant lots and fifteen acres of city-owned vacant lots in an area once called the Dudley Triangle. The once vacant land has been transformed into an urban village of more than 225 new affordable homes, a 10,000-square-foot community greenhouse on the site of a former auto body shop, two acres of community farms, playgrounds, gardens, commercial space, and other amenities.[9]

DSNI set up a nonprofit community land trust (CLT) that would hold and secure the land for long-term affordability. The CLT is organized and run so that each cultural-ethnic grouping present in the newly dubbed Nubian Square community gets an equal voice. The elected board has thirty-five seats with twenty reserved for an equal number of representatives of the four main ethnic groups inside the community.[10] The remaining fifteen seats are split between community development organizations, local religious organizations, nonprofit partner organizations, and small businesses in the community. Today, DSNI is the lead collaborator for comprehensive community development initiatives in Nubian Square to revitalize the neighborhood and increase economic opportunity through workforce development and entrepreneurship.

NeighborSpace in Chicago is an independent, nonprofit land trust that preserves urban land throughout the city of Chicago for community gardens and open space.[11] Created in 1996 by a consortium of three government entities—the city of Chicago, the Chicago Park District, and the Forest Preserve District of Cook County—NeighborSpace now oversees 115 land-based sites located in thirty-three wards across the city, many of which are involved in community gardening projects.[12] The idea for NeighborSpace was first conceived when city leaders became increasingly concerned about the lack of open space in Chicago and the number of vacant plots being bought by private developers. In 1994, the three substate government entities brought together community leaders, residents, and nonprofit organizations to brainstorm possible solutions to this ever-growing problem. NeighborSpace's primary goal is to preserve and protect community-managed open spaces, particularly in underserved areas. NeighborSpace is supported predominantly by public funding; 80 percent of its operating budget is directly subsidized by its three founding government agencies. NeighborSpace operates as a higher-level authority and is not involved in the day-to-day management of the land plots. The real oversight of day-to-day affairs is handled by residents and groups of gardeners in the community where the spaces are located who act as stewards over the land.

These three examples illustrate the various ways place governance has taken root in many cities. These place-based, multi-actor, multi-sector collaborative arrangements can drive economic development and catalyze the transformation of underutilized land, public spaces, parks, and other public amenities. By relying on resources from the private and nonprofit sectors, and leveraging the assets of local institutions and communities, place governance also creates new classes of stakeholders and stewards of this revitalization. Instead of simply reacting to city planners, these stakeholders can play a more proactive role by offering their own vision of development, against which individual projects can be considered and vetted. Moreover, decentralizing the provision of municipal services offers the promise of a decisionmaking process more responsive to residents' needs and nimbler in meeting those needs. Place governance also might operate to preserve and even strengthen the social viability of neighborhoods through existing community-based associations, like DSNI, that exhibit strong social ties and networks.

At the same time, there are several potential costs and dangers that accompany these kinds of arrangements. In the first place, they can create a fractured and privatized urban landscape that exacerbates the uneven distribution of local services and amenities. For example, corporate-dominated institutions that manage a large central city neighborhood are often engaged in a very wide range of services and enjoy a broad grant of authority to render and expand their services. They can become, in effect, "cities within cities" administering their services in largely unaccountable ways, with little oversight by local government and with substantial budgets that allow them to self-govern much like a private neighborhood.[13] Moreover, depending on the actors involved and how their roles are allocated, decisions taken by place-based institutions with significant influence over neighborhood activities can lack accountability to the broader public or to public interests. This raises the specter of a powerful alignment of neighborhood interests able to successfully oppose policies or land-use reforms in a way that imposes costs on—or strips opportunity from—less powerful interests in the city. Policies to increase and distribute affordable housing units, limit parking, or diversify the location of homeless shelters or other locally unwanted but necessary land uses often conflict with strong neighborhood preferences for a particular kind of development.

Of course, the upsides and risks of place governance arrangements can vary dramatically, as these examples suggest. When place governance arrangements include a range of interests and stakeholders—such as nonprofits, community associations, public officials or agencies, residents, and neighborhood businesses—on their boards, it is more likely that a broader development vision will emerge and benefits will be more widespread. And attracting and utilizing public funding and private donations can give rise to greater accountability to public interests without crowding out the often necessary role of private capital in urban economic development.

These tensions and trade-offs are present in almost all place governance arrangements and will be explored in this chapter through the lens of several such arrangements, which include a narrow set of actors on one end of the spectrum to a broad and inclusive set of actors on the other. The range of typologies includes private governance, public-private partnerships, public-community governance, and public-private-community (plus) partnerships. The diversity of these structures, even within the same part of the spectrum, resists easy conclusions about their desirability absent a full assessment of each within a particular context, which is beyond the scope here. However, the chapter does make general observations about the potential benefits and costs of different place-based governance arrangements, the types of actors initiating and shaping these arrangements, and the kind of authority they are given or obtain over the places they govern.

Private Governance

At one end of the place governance spectrum is private governance of shared public and private spaces. Private governance is most often carried out through a formal or informal association of property-owning individuals or homeowners living in a common development or neighborhood. The quintessential examples are common interest communities (CICs) or common interest developments (CIDs). CICs and CIDs include homeowners and condominium associations, cooperatives, and gated communities. These kinds of private housing communities have been increasing over the past few decades, since the 1960s, fueled by the federal government's subsidization of residential developments and the resulting mass exodus from cities to the suburbs. Today, nearly 60 percent of recently built single-family houses, and 80 percent of houses in new subdivisions, are part of a homeowners' association (HOA).[14]

Common interest communities are viewed as a market solution to a public goods problem.[15] Many individuals and households are able and willing to pay more to live in a CIC because they provide tailored sports and recreational amenities, building use restrictions, private surveillance and safety protocols, common ownership of shared streets or other infrastructure, and maintenance over and above what local governments provide.[16] But these communities can also struggle with the lack of external support, given that they rely almost entirely on the resources of residents, and are weakly regulated with little oversight from state and local governments.[17] Much like BIDs, CICs and CIDs are authorized to assess their property owners, provide services and amenities to their residents, and manage common property and shared community spaces. Legal scholar Greg Alexander refers to CICs and CIDs and related kinds of private property associations as "governance property" and notes that they are the "dominant mode of [property] ownership today."[18] In addition to holding easements or "rights of way" to common areas, individual home or unit owners also have some kind of property interest in everyone else's property due to mutually enforceable contractual "covenants" (promises) in the formal documents establishing the association.[19] Because interests of multiple owners can come into conflict, he observes, CICs and CIDs require internal mechanisms or governance norms and rules to regulate relations between owners or between interested parties.

The success of CICs and CIDs has spurred some academics to propose scaling these private residential communities to existing neighborhoods, or to urban blocks, effectively shifting zoning and other decisions from the local government to neighbors. Public policy professor Robert Nelson, for example, proposes legislation to allow a group of individual property owners in an existing neighborhood to petition the local or state government to form a private neighborhood association.[20] The petition would describe: "(a) the boundaries of the proposed private neighborhood; (b) the instruments of collective

governance intended for it; (c) the services the neighborhood association would perform; and (d) the estimated monthly assessment."[21] If the
application meets the legislative standards, the government would negotiate an agreement with the neighborhood group, specifying the
transfer of ownership of municipal streets, parks, swimming pools, tennis courts, and other existing public lands and facilities located within
the neighborhood as well as the degree to which the neighborhood private association would assume responsibility for various common services. Once the agreement is executed and a neighborhood election
held to approve the association, the legal responsibility for regulating
land use in the neighborhood is transferred to the property owners in
the association, and the municipal zoning authority for that neighborhood is abolished.[22] Similar proposals at smaller scales, either block or
street level, have been offered by Robert Ellickson and John Myers.[23]

Nelson's main argument for privatizing existing neighborhoods
rests largely on the rationale that the collective benefits and maintenance of this kind of governance far exceeds the collective costs—
except where there are clear extraterritorial effects of neighborhood
action.[24] Allowing privatization of the neighborhood would arguably
introduce more innovation and responsiveness from those who most
utilize and depend on its resources.[25] Placing control directly in the
hands of property owners allows them to bargain directly for, and purchase, improved services, resulting in more efficiency. In addition, he
notes, there are civic benefits that flow from private governance in existing neighborhoods. The neighborhood association would become
a vehicle to "establish and sustain a strong spirit of community in the
neighborhood, not usually found in neighborhoods without a formal
institutional status."[26] He also throws in a distributive justice-oriented
argument, namely that the least well-off residents ("inner city neighborhoods") stand to gain the most in terms of net increases in the level
of neighborhood amenities, aesthetics, and services from privatizing
their communities.[27]

The Nelson proposal may seem to be a far-fetched or extreme form
of private governance of urban residential neighborhoods. However,

it borrows much from BIDs, which grant decisionmaking authority to commercial property owners over shared neighborhood assets, common spaces, and service delivery.[28] Non-property-owning residents or businesses have few, if any, representatives on the governing boards of BIDs or in proposed residential versions of them, at least in the United States (chapters 4 and 5 contain a more extensive treatment of BIDs). Similarly, and unlike a local government, a private neighborhood association would not be subject to legal constraints such as the one-person, one-vote principle, thus leaving non-property-owning residents without a significant role in the management of their neighborhood.[29] There is no reason to believe property owners would want to give up the power to make neighborhood governance decisions, especially given that they will bear almost all the financial risks and rewards of those decisions given their investment in the neighborhood.[30]

A telling sign of the impulse of groups of private property owners to act in their own self-interest are the countless examples, even in politically progressive cities like San Francisco and New York, of homeowners resisting land-use changes and new development that would benefit their broader cities. These "not in my backyard"— NIMBY—residents push back against proposals that would increase the supply of housing in tight urban markets and, hence, the inclusion of a more economically diverse populace, if it means changing their neighborhoods. As one investigative reporter notes: "In Seattle, the neighbors don't want apartments for formerly homeless seniors nearby. In Los Angeles, they don't want more high-rises. In San Jose, Calif., they don't want tiny homes. In Phoenix, they don't want design that's not midcentury modern."[31] Undergirding this pushback by neighborhood residents is the conviction "that owning a parcel of land gives them a right to shape the world beyond its boundaries."[32]

Previously declining but now gentrifying neighborhoods have borrowed this strategy from their more affluent counterparts to shield themselves against the threat of displacement and the loss of the history and cultural fabric of predominantly minority communities. In

Philadelphia, for instance, a coalition of neighborhood groups in a working class, Black neighborhood populated by blocks of brick row-houses convinced the city council to give approval for an "overlay" district restricting the height and density of new construction.[33] The uptick in the use of special zones and districts could be viewed as a form of private governance in line with Robert Nelson's proposal discussed above.

But private governance arrangements need not lean toward exclusion or tighter control over new development. There are circumstances under which private property owners might be inclined to perceive value in creating opportunities for local interests—including renters—to collaborate and cooperate toward common goals, including new and denser development. Consider Buffalo's West Side Community Collaborative, formed by homeowners in a fifteen-block area in one of the most ethnically diverse neighborhoods in the state to create a zone designed to attract new residents and investment without displacing existing residents.[34] As recounted by Ron Oakerson and Jeremy Clifton, the collaborative was initially formed to implement a five-year revitalization plan but became a multilevel initiative to gain control of vacant properties that were either directly owned by the city or up for tax sale to address blight and disinvestment. Before the collaborative's formation, realtors avoided working in this diverse but economically depressed area with a high crime rate. Although the collaborative never established itself as a formal nonprofit organization, the group members managed to leverage their informal relationships with community organizations, state and municipal agencies, police, realtors, and bankers to increase homeownership by turning qualified tenants into property owners and to encourage mixed-income growth to support commercial development.

The collaborative strategy was to proceed block-by-block, creating a zone sufficiently insulated from crime and blight to attract new residents and new investment. On one block, for example, the collaborative used the state-created housing court to register housing code violations on dilapidated properties used by drug dealers and sex work-

ers. By aggressively monitoring inspection and enforcement of cita-
tions, the collaborative eventually was able to convince these property owners to sell their homes to a nonprofit housing agency, which
evicted the users conducting illegal activities, demolished two of the
unsalvageable homes, and invested $200,000 in repairs on the remain-
ing homes.[35] Existing homeowners and tenants responded by purchasing and renovating their own properties. The collaborative used
residents' collective lobbying power to ensure the city housing agency
sanctioned housing code violations and monitored ongoing compliance.[36] Even though ultimate authority still rested with the municipal government, the collaborative wielded coercive enforcement power
by coordinating voluntary monitoring activities among neighbors. According to the authors, the threat of legal sanction was sufficient to
get absentee landlords to cooperate with the collaborative and allowed
residents to self-organize and pursue their own projects at the block-
level within the larger structure of the collaborative.

Unfortunately, the housing court judge who facilitated the collaborative's work stepped down after ten years and was replaced by another judge with little interest in continuing to use the court to push
for neighborhood change in the same way.[37] By that time, however,
the collaborative itself was dissolving, viewing its initial mission as
successful and its efforts no longer necessary in a neighborhood that
had been in a downward spiral for decades but had rebounded and
started spiraling upward. The housing market had improved, crime
was significantly curtailed, vacant houses were seen as opportunities
rather than problems, and employment opportunities had increased
for residents.

Having sustained itself with almost no institutional funding for a
decade, the collaborative's achievements demonstrate that when private citizens form an association to coordinate their activities, whether
formal or informal, they are able to overcome collective action problems and improve the neighborhood commons. While this can be
more difficult in low-income neighborhoods with aging infrastructure
and housing stock, the collaborative's ten-year success proves that

the capacity of residents to self-organize depends less on their income or wealth and more on their ability to sustain mutual assurance among residents and cooperation by public authorities. In the collaborative's case, the presence of both factors allowed residents to self-organize and pursue their own projects at the block level within the larger organizational structure while leveraging the scale of their efforts when necessary to secure the cooperation of a city agency, housing court, or nonprofit developer. Although the collaborative is now defunct, it served its purpose by kick-starting a virtuous cycle of development on the West Side of Buffalo that continues to this day (see table 3-1).

Public-Private Partnerships

The decline of municipal revenue during periods of economic downturn often shifts the impetus for preservation of shared neighborhood and public spaces to private actors and specifically to the private sector. At this point, it is useful to distinguish, in the context of partnerships with public authorities, between private citizens and private industry. This section refers to public-private partnerships to encompass the latter, while the next section refers to public-community partnerships (PCPs) to encompass the former. Both kinds of private actors are important in place governance partnerships but for different reasons and with the potential for dramatically different impacts on placemaking.

Public-private partnerships have become the main means of managing parks and related public spaces in cities across the United States.[38] They do so through their operation as a BID, which typically manages spaces in the broader hyperlocal geography in which such spaces sit, or as a conservancy, an alliance, or a "friends of" group (although some versions of the "friends of" groups fall into the next category of public-community partnerships). Examples include

Friends of the High Line (New York, New York); Forest Park Forever (St. Louis, Missouri); Piedmont Park Conservancy (Atlanta, Georgia); Memorial Park Conservancy (Houston, Texas); Pittsburgh Parks Conservancy (Pittsburgh, Pennsylvania); and Golden Gate National Parks Conservancy (San Francisco, California).[39] These groups have the virtue of being able to avoid the red tape, bureaucracy, and inaction in which city parks departments often become mired; they are able to make decisions faster, raise funds, save money, and serve as effective advocates for urban parks.[40] But they also have been criticized for imposing many of the costs that attend to the (at least partial) privatization of any public good—that is, enabling gentrification, exacerbating ethnic and class tensions, and creating a two-tiered park system that disadvantages parks in less affluent neighborhoods.[41]

Many scholars credit BIDs and park conservancies with revitalizing core areas of major cities like New York City after the fiscal crisis of the 1970s and 1980s. A steep decline in city appropriations for parks devastated the entire urban park system, leaving many parks and recreational areas unsafe, unkempt, prone to criminal activity, and virtually abandoned by most users.[42] Park conservancies are nonprofit entities that co-manage large urban parks in partnership with the local government by collaborating on planning, design, and implementation of capital projects, as well as sharing responsibility for park maintenance and operations.[43] They typically raise significant amounts of money from private entities and, in some cases, share with the local government a portion of concession revenues.[44]

Although private involvement in the management of urban parks is a phenomenon stretching back to the early twentieth century, the rise of park conservancies in large cities like New York City represents a dramatic shift of public responsibilities to the private sector in managing them.[45] Neighbors who live near urban parks, as well as wealthy donors and residents, have long exerted some power over park management—providing donations, labor, advocacy efforts, and planning ideas—but these efforts often suffered from a lack of coordination and efficiencies of scale.[46] Agreements or partnerships between local governments and park conservancies serve an important coordinating and stabilizing function, enabling private and public actors to undertake together significant responsibility for urban park management.

The Central Park Conservancy (CPC) is the prototype for similar conservancies around the country. CPC was founded in 1980 by several local leaders and groups; initially established as the Central Park Task Force, it later incorporated itself as the nonprofit CPC with an original board of trustees consisting mostly of executives of leading corporations and financial institutions headquartered in New York.[47] In a groundbreaking power-sharing arrangement, the Central Park administrator was appointed by the mayor to serve as the chief executive officer of both the park and the CPC but reported to the park commissioner. The first Central Park administrator became the driving force behind the master plan for rebuilding Central Park and, ultimately, of the formation of the CPC itself.[48] Almost two decades after its founding, the CPC and the city of New York formalized their relationship by signing a renewable management agreement, transferring official management functions and day-to-day maintenance and operation of the park from the city to the CPC.[49]

Today, the CPC combines donations from individuals with corporate donations and government funding to fulfill its budgetary needs and build its endowments.[50] It is run by a board of trustees of up to fifty-five members, including city officials, representatives from nonprofit organizations, and private corporations, among other interests.[51] The board itself may appoint up to two "community" trustees representing the interests of the communities surrounding Central Park, and the mayor may appoint up to five board trustees.[52] As with most park conservancies, the park and all its assets continue to be public, in this case owned by the city of New York, and local officials retain the power to set policies regarding access to and use of the resource.[53] Moreover, a variety of public bodies have oversight over the conservancy's management decisions, including the Landmarks Preservation Commission, five community planning boards in the city, the Public

Design Commission, and the city council.[54] This multilayer oversight is probably not typical of other conservancies, however.

Park conservancies, much like BIDs, carry all the advantages of and are subject to the same critiques as other kinds of public-private partnerships. Efficiency in service delivery and augmentation of resources for public spaces are clear advantages. In the context of place governance, however, the most problematic feature of these partnerships relates to their size and scale, which drives the kinds of actors involved and determines what kind of capacity they have to shape entire neighborhoods. The larger the resource and the more complex it is, both in terms of its functionality and in terms of the heterogeneity of users and interests, the broader range of functions it is likely to be granted or assume. Jill Gross's work on BIDs, including her analysis in chapter 5 of this volume, is instructive on this issue. Specifically, her comparative study of BIDs in New York City found that the largest ("corporate"), medium ("main street"), and smallest ("community") BIDs each have very distinctive characteristics and functions that largely track their size.[55] Corporate BIDs, like large park conservancies, tend to have large boards of directors that include many members with professional expertise and the ability to raise significant funding toward service and capital improvements in the places they manage. Others have similarly noted that well-resourced BIDs are able to hire professional staff to plan future development; lobby for their district's interests with the city government; and undertake transformative initiatives that affect the appearance and quality of life in their districts.[56]

In contrast, Gross found that main street BIDs have small boards of directors, consist mainly of second-generation immigrant property owners with limited formal education, and have much less revenue intake.[57] Moreover, Gross found that "BIDs in low-income neighborhoods have less fiscal and human capital to apply to service provision than do those in high-income neighborhoods."[58] Likewise, large park conservancies also have come under scrutiny for being able to raise and dedicate private funds toward the improvement of larger, more prominent city parks while parks and playgrounds in poorer neigh-

borhoods are left underfunded and relatively unattended.[59] This suggests a system of different tiers of public-private "stewardship" of public spaces, depending on the demographics of those who live closest
to those places and the affluence of those who have a stake in them.[60]

In addition, given their influence over large public assets and spaces,
some worry about the accountability of powerful BIDs and park
conservancies to larger public values and interests.[61] Large park conservancies are inevitably involved in daily decisions about how
urban parks are used and by whom, even as they are subject to significant oversight. Similarly, large BIDs are subject to significant
local government monitoring; representatives of city officials often
sit on their managing boards, and a BID's recommendations for significant changes in land use or policy cannot be implemented without
approval by elected city officials.[62] It might be that the largest scale of
these institutions ultimately are more accountable to a broader array
of interests and can better check these exclusionary tendencies. Nevertheless, because the largest BIDs and major conservancies often
are given broad authority over public space management, some point
to instances in which they have exercised that authority to exclude
marginalized groups (for example, people experiencing homelessness) from those spaces.[63]

Public-Community Partnerships

Like public-private partnerships, public-community partnerships are
enabled by and accountable to local officials without privatizing
ownership of the underlying resources being stewarded. For example,
as Alexander von Hoffman noted in the previous chapter, community
development corporations have long received government support to
revitalize and develop low-income, underserved urban neighborhoods.
This support includes federal grants, financial incentives, technical
assistance, and land acquisition. Although quite diverse in form and
scope, CDCs have, over many decades, transformed low-income urban

neighborhoods by building affordable housing; revitalizing commercial corridors; running workforce and community development programs; and providing social services to their communities. It is notable that, unlike private developers, most CDCs maintain strong links to their communities by involving residents in their governance and development activities.[64] Typically, at least one-third of a CDC's board is composed of community residents. The number of CDCs has declined over the years, largely due to dwindling public and private funding, and CDCs have "increasingly turned to partnerships with other organizations and institutions as a way of stretching their resources and the scope of their activities."[65]

Today, place-based revitalization efforts in disinvested (and other) communities are often led by a variety of nonprofit community-based organizations (CBOs) largely driven by residents. The Dudley Street Neighborhood Initiative example in the chapter's opening section is illustrative of this kind of community-driven effort, enabled and facilitated by state actors. To create an "urban village" on thirty acres of vacant land, residents, CDCs, religious and civic organizations, and local businesses came together to form DSNI. To assemble the public and private land for the urban village, DSNI approached the Boston Redevelopment Authority and requested eminent domain authority, which was granted by the city of Boston. With the help of philanthropic and public funding, including a federal Housing and Urban Development (HUD) grant (secured with the help of the city), DSNI steered the development of the urban village and now governs it through a community land trust.

Vacant land and structures, like those in Nubian Square, are ubiquitous in many low-income communities and communities of color due in large part to "the legacy of racial segregation, redlining, and urban renewal, and more recently exacerbated by predatory lending, the ensuing mortgage foreclosure crisis, and new discriminatory practices in access to credit."[66] In many of these communities around the country, residents work to clear vacant lots, remove trash and drug paraphernalia, and cultivate trees, flowers, and vegetables to create community gardens and urban farms, among other improvements.[67] Gardeners collectively formulate their own rules of use and allocate resource units (for example, plots of land) and shared infrastructure (for example, water connection, greenhouse), often without a formal organizational structure. However, vacant lots are transformed into community gardens with the implicit, and often explicit, consent of the local government. Local governments provide long-term, renewable leases of these city-owned lots to community gardeners for a nominal fee, and provide small grants, technical support, and gardening tools.[68] As Nobel Prize winner Elinor Ostrom's work demonstrates, communities in close proximity to particular place-based assets are sometimes able to manage and govern these resources in sustainable ways, often working closely with public authorities.[69] As she found, these are often relatively homogenous communities that manage relatively small-scale resources. In part because of these characteristics, they are able to establish shared norms and create and enforce rules for the use of resources by those who depend most upon them.

Another example of public-community partnerships involving place governance is the result of residents who take care of underserved neighborhood parks, almost always aided by local government financial and technical support. Much like park conservancies, the era of urban decline in the 1980s and 1990s ushered in the emergence of smaller "friends of the park" groups—consisting of volunteers and neighborhood residents who live near these parks or are otherwise invested in their upkeep—that plan and raise support for restoration, maintenance, and preservation. Hundreds (if not thousands) of these groups all across the country have revitalized neighborhood public parks and filled the void left by the loss of most of their public operating funds and active local government management.[70] They also assist in community outreach and park programming, organize park cleanups and community events, build or donate simple infrastructure or facilities for community activities (for example, small pools, sand pits, etc.), and patrol the park as a way of deterring criminal and other undesirable activities.[71] While many of these groups are informal collections of volunteers, they often are incorporated as nonprofit membership organizations with a governing board of directors and bylaws. Parks departments often incentivize the formation of these "friends" organizations by offering them technical assistance, training, materials, and funding.[72] For example, New York's Partnerships for Parks, a joint venture between the New York City Parks Foundation and the New York City Department of Parks & Recreation, encourages the formation, and nurtures the development of, neighborhood parks groups across the city.[73]

A scaled-up version of this kind of public-community partnership is NeighborSpace in Chicago, described in the introduction to this chapter. NeighborSpace was inspired by the recognition that many community members were already working together, on an informal and ad hoc basis, to revive and preserve vacant or blighted land in their communities. Each year, local officials acquire vacant lots and then relinquish operational control of them to the land trust. The land trust then transfers most of that control to local gardeners and community groups. NeighborSpace handles land purchases; performs environmental assessments and title work; holds the titles, easements, or leases it acquires; provides liability insurance and legal defense; acts as the liaison between the government and the participating community groups; and works to secure a dedicated water line for every parcel of land it obtains. It also provides some guidance and other forms of support, "including a signage template, a list of gardeners' rights and responsibilities, and a tool lending library."

NeighborSpace is not involved in the day-to-day management of the land plots, which is left to the community and plot users in what is described as a "non-hierarchical" governance structure that prevents the centralization of power in the hands of any one individual or group. The rules of the land trust require collective governance over the acquired plots, which are prohibited from having a single lead gardener or overseer but must have multiple leaders overseeing its development, as well as community support and buy-in.

Like private governance and public-private partnerships, public-community partnerships have clear advantages and notable downsides. On the upside, public-community partnerships depend upon and foster collaborative relationships and social ties among neighborhood residents. They encourage residents to cooperatively work toward common neighborhood goals and to support the livelihood and well-being of their communities. These spaces keep their communities safe and healthy and address some of the economic and social disparities in many low-income communities of color, which disproportionately lack what these resources offer when well managed.

On the other hand, like public-private partnerships, these partnerships mark the retreat of the state from the direct provision of public goods and services. These goods and services are effectively outsourced with an often-limited monitoring role left to those public authorities over either community or private actors managing public resources. While residents typically do not exert the same economic or political power over local officials as private sector partners, particularly in low-income and minority communities often stewarding these resources, there are still legitimate concerns about accountability of nonstate actors over public resources. As legal scholar Robert Ellickson notes, a distinct danger is the ways in which "insider" group norms designed to maximize group welfare can do so at the expense, or exclusion, of nongroup members in small self-governing groups.[74]

While this is theoretically a concern, there seems little empirical evidence or anecdotal accounts that document this danger in the context of public-community partnerships. It might be that the lack of significant fundraising by these groups and their dependence on local government (including for permission to use the land itself) leaves them with very little decisionmaking authority over the resource. Even when these groups are given a great deal of operational autonomy, as in the case of the NeighborSpace gardeners, they remain directly accountable to the local authorities that control the governing board of the land trust. In this sense, NeighborSpace represents what Ostrom calls a "nested" place governance structure, involving self-organized small units or groups of users acting relatively autonomously but within a federated system that prevents the centralization of power in the hands of any one individual or one group and with strong oversight by public authorities.

Public-Private-Community (Plus) Partnerships

At the far end of the place governance spectrum are multistakeholder collaborative place governance arrangements that involve some mix of public officials, private sector actors, neighborhood civic organizations, residents, and, often, major anchor institutions typically operating at a large scale in the core of major cities. As with University City District in Philadelphia (discussed above), these sometimes take the form of "public-private-community partnerships" (PPCP), extending the framework of the public-private partnerships by integrating community-based actors—such as civic organizations and anchor institutions—into the governing partnership. Adding community-based actors to the traditional "P3" (public-private partnership) has given rise to "P4" and "P5" governance arrangements—"public-private-people partnerships" and "public-private-people-philanthropy partnerships," respectively—that expand the possibilities for transforming neighborhoods to meet a more diverse set of needs and interests.

Some scholars have argued that multistakeholder collaborations involving this multiplicity of actors hold the potential for more innovation. Christian Iaione and I refer to the "quintuple helix" of urban collaborative governance involving five main actors—public authorities, businesses, communities, civil society organizations (nonprofits), and knowledge institutions—building on the "triple helix" concept in innovation studies.[75] The basic idea behind the triple helix is that the potential for innovation in a knowledge society lies in the hybridization of elements from university, industry, and government to generate new institutional and social formats for the production, transfer, and application of knowledge.[76]

As applied to the urban context, these interactions create the conditions for an innovation system of urban economic development. The quintuple helix extends this idea even further, down to the community level. Moreover, different actors can have distinct responsibilities in these arrangements. Universities can play a bridging role between the public authority and the private sector on one side and local anchor social organizations (consisting of residents and communities) on the other side. Public authorities can encourage bottom-up solutions and experimentation, participation across different actors and sectors, and stronger civic engagement, and can incentivize opportunities for the co-design and co-creation of innovations that are oriented toward addressing huge place-based challenges like affordable housing or workforce development.

The rise of some kinds of "innovation districts" contain this potential in bringing together leading-edge anchor institutions and companies that cluster and connect with start-ups, business incubators, and accelerators.[77] This constellation of actors is well positioned to take advantage of what urban economists refer to as "agglomeration economies." Agglomeration economies result in the positive spillover effects of firm co-location and the attraction of knowledge or creative workers to these areas that offer the kinds of neighborhood amenities they seek. St. Louis's Cortex Innovation Community is one example of this model.[78] Cortex is the nonprofit developer responsible for managing a community that consists of 4.5 million square feet of mixed-use facilities, a light rail station, and new park space. Cortex emerged following successful redevelopment efforts in the Central West End neighborhood of St. Louis led by area hospitals affiliated with the Washington University School of Medicine (the hospital system would later become the BJC Healthcare).

An association of local anchor institutions organized early fundraising and planning efforts to get Cortex off the ground. Washington University, BJC Healthcare, University of Missouri-St. Louis, Saint Louis University, and the Missouri Botanical Gardens seeded the initial investment of $29 million, and Cortex was designated a "master developer" by the city, which granted it powers of eminent domain and the ability to provide tax abatements. A local ordinance passed in 2012, the same year the master plan was approved, enabled tax increment financing in the Cortex redevelopment area. Cortex's governing board includes representatives from the city of St. Louis, the St. Louis Development Corporation, three area universities, small and large private corporations, a nonprofit health care provider, and a nonprofit economic development corporation, among others.

Setting aside the innovation potential of multi-actor place governance arrangements, it is difficult to assess how well these collaborative arrangements function and for whose benefit. To get at this question, one useful distinction to make is between top-down and bottom-up place-based governance, and their relative strengths and weaknesses. Those initiated by large or corporate anchor institutions are top-down, while those that arise from community leaders or community-based groups are bottom-up. In a top-down approach, large or corporate anchor institutions initiate a project and then invite residents and community groups to participate in some fashion. In a bottom-up approach, those large actors follow the lead of community groups and provide support without taking over the project or initiative.[79]

Compare the Cortex Innovation District and UCD with Baltimore's Southwest Partnership (SWP). Cortex and UCD are both top-down place governance arrangements whereas, as we will see, SWP is more bottom-up. Recall that UCD is a "special services district" supported by volunteer donations and founded by established anchor institutions, including the neighborhood's universities and public hospitals, the postal service, and a community development corporation. The private sector's initial role was limited since few large private employers were based in the neighborhood before UCD's founding. Over time, however, the area's universities and hospitals have been its primary funders and leaders, supplemented by service fees, philanthropic grants, and tax credits.[80] UCD's governing board is primarily composed of the interests that fund it but also includes several community associations from the surrounding neighborhoods.

In contrast to both Cortex and UCD, SWP emerged out of a more bottom-up orientation. SWP was formed in 2012 as a community development nonprofit by representatives of seven Baltimore neighborhood community groups to create a master plan to guide neighborhood growth in Southwest Baltimore.[81] After the partnership was created, the seven neighborhood groups then invited to the partnership six area anchor institutions—including a major university, a science and technology development company, a local museum, and a local nonprofit health system—that had a strong presence in the area and resources to contribute. SWP's funding comes exclusively from anchor institutions, a local philanthropic foundation, and individual donations. Although each partner has a vote in the organization, the structure of the organization ensures that its activity will be resident driven. SWP's master plan was adopted by the city planning commission in 2015, which prioritizes its development activities on five physical areas and two social areas (housing and education and workforce development).

One example of the way SWP's priorities shape development is its agreement with the city of Baltimore to have the first right of purchase on tax sale properties in the neighborhoods represented by SWP. Rather than the city selling those properties to individual bidders, SWP is able to vet interested buyers to ensure their intended use for the property fits with the focus of the master plan—for example, the emphasis on encouraging homeownership. SWP also engages in numerous placemaking, workforce, and small business development activities. For example, its "Southwest Works" initiative provides residents with basic skills training, job matching services, and career counseling. And local associations and groups can apply for SWP grants of up to $5,000 for placemaking and beautification projects (for example, murals, lighting, signage, landscaping).

At first glance, these three examples—Cortex, UCD, and SWP—seem to have much more in common than what might distinguish them. Collaborative place governance, in both the bottom-up and top-down approaches, represents a balancing act between dependency on private funding and organizational autonomy. Moreover, their long-term sustainability depends on their ability to mobilize and sustain reciprocal resources (volunteering and donations) to support economic development and the delivery of district-level goods and services.

On closer inspection, however, there is a potential tension between top-down and bottom-up multi-actor governance arrangements. That tension lies in the balancing of interests between those constituencies tied to anchor institutions and funders (for example, students, faculty, hospital staff) and those interests who have limited direct representation but are just as impacted by its activities (for example, legacy residents, local businesses). In other words, it might matter which actors, and who they represent, decide what kinds of place-based investments generate the best returns to these different constituencies. Notwithstanding the diversity of interests involved in multi-actor and multisector arrangements, some worry that the "unitary" focus of local authorities on development of the urban core and the shift of the burden of that development to anchor institutions could result in the type of economic development that sustains an entire city while coming at the expense of a city's outlying, and often disenfranchised, neighborhoods.[82]

This raises the obvious question: Might different outcomes result if these place-based collaborative governance arrangements are driven from the bottom-up rather than the top-down? It is difficult to say, of course, in every place whether the answer is positive or negative. What we do know, however, can be instructive and should inform how new arrangements are put together.

Top-Down versus Bottom-Up Place Governance

One reasonable hypothesis, based on what we know, is that whether place-governance arrangements arise from a bottom-up or top-down orientation is likely to shape what kind of development, and for whom, these arrangements ultimately (most) benefit. Consider UCD, for instance, through this lens. On the one hand, UCD represents a break from the urban renewal-era of community-university relations (1950s and 1960s) that was characterized by anti-blight "slum clearance," with superficial or nonexistent efforts at engaging residents in development planning.[83] UCD is characteristic of a new era of university-led neighborhood reinvestment initiatives working in partnership with the surrounding community and focused on long-term development goals (entrepreneurship, workforce development, quality of life).[84] For example, UCD's West Philadelphia Skills Initiative focuses on job training and placement of neighborhood residents in nearby institutions and businesses, and their Just Spaces Initiative is designed to address exclusion in UCD-managed public spaces.

Yet, despite its efforts at community involvement and promotion of inclusion in public space, UCD has been heavily criticized for inequitable development patterns within its jurisdiction. While UCD is celebrated for its success in reducing crime and stimulating investment in commercial and residential real estate, its efforts seem to have done little to address persistent inequalities that existed before its establishment. Neighborhood poverty in the area is high and median incomes have been stagnant, suggesting that while affluent new residents have been attracted to West Philadelphia by UCD's placemaking efforts and improvements to local public schools, low-income residents, overwhelmingly tenants, have yet to see significant personal gains from recent economic development (though improved public safety has likely been to the benefit of all residents). Moreover, there is some suggestion that legacy residents of the area may not be able to stay around to reap the benefits of these improvements. One study notes that, between 1990 and 2010, the percent decline in UCD's Black population outpaced that of West Philadelphia as a whole, all while the city's total Black population grew. The area's white population was stable, despite declining across West Philadelphia.[85] At the same time, between 2000 and 2010, according to this study, the total number of dwelling units in West Philadelphia and UCD fell at a much faster rate than the citywide total as median home values doubled, all typical signposts of gentrification.[86]

The Dudley Street redevelopment, mentioned earlier, offers an interesting comparative look at development outcomes, although the scale of its activities is much smaller than UCD. Like SWP, it is a bottom-up, community-driven, state and local government supported effort that not only transformed but stabilized a blighted neighborhood. The thirty-acre development area included in the development plan and controlled by the community land trust now has a mix of hundreds of affordable housing units along with commercial and green space. The housing includes ninety-seven homeownership units, seventy-seven limited equity cooperative units, fifty-five rental apartments, and ninety-six individually owned homes.

Consistent with its neighborhood plan, the majority of housing units are targeted for families making between 30 and 60 percent of the area median income, approximately $30,000 to $60,000 for a family of four. The sustainability of the Dudley model has been proven in part by the fact that during the economic crisis, from 2008 to 2013, there were no foreclosures of homes even as the surrounding neighborhood had more than 200 foreclosures.[87] Building on its successful model, Dudley Street and ten other neighborhood groups from across that city launched, in 2015, the Greater Boston Community Land Trust Network to expand the CLT model even at a time when acquisition of urban land has been made more difficult because of rising land values. This network has supported and seen the rise of four new CLTs—the Chinatown CLT, Somerville CLT, Boston Neighborhood CLT, and the Urban Farming CLT—across the Boston metropolitan area, and is beginning to push for municipal policies and public resources to support their expansion and growth.[88]

Similarly, the West Side Collaborative, discussed above, was a bottom-up, resident-driven effort that received support from local agencies and the housing court in Buffalo during its operation. In existence for only ten years, between 2000 and 2010, it seems to have been a catalytic force in neighborhood growth and improvement while maintaining the area's ethnic diversity. Examining census and America Community Survey data for the city of Buffalo, and for the West Side in particular, during the collaborative's active years to the present (between 2000 and 2019), is revealing. The West Side has seen a rise in neighborhood homeownership rate, significant growth in home values, and a decline in vacancy rates.[89]

In contrast, in the city of Buffalo as a whole, home values have barely grown, homeownership has fallen, and the vacancy rate has ticked up during the same period. Moreover, though the West Side has been more racially diverse than Buffalo for the last twenty years, since 2000 it has become even more so, with the white population in decline and upticks in Asian and Black population growth in some part due to the increase in the foreign-born population.[90] At the same time, income growth on the West Side has been faster than average and the poverty rate has fallen, while incomes citywide have stagnated and poverty has risen. Since 2000, incomes in the West Side neighborhood have risen faster than rents, such that West Side residents are now no more rent burdened than the citywide average.

While more comprehensive research and analysis is necessary, this cursory examination of available data from top-down and bottom-up partnerships suggests that those who initiate a place governance arrangement are often those who continue holding the most power and, therefore, benefit most. In these complex, multisectoral partnerships—unlike in strictly private place governance structures—resident-led initiatives seem to result in broadly shared benefits.

Conclusion

At a time when the COVID-19 pandemic and the Black Lives Matter movement have accelerated a rethinking of the urban landscape in response to persistent and systemic inequalities and injustices, it matters which actors are driving place governance. Bottom-up place-making's most important feature is that community residents and

Table 3-1. *West Side Neighborhood Change*

	West Side (Zip Code 14213)			Buffalo		
	2000	2008–2012	2015–2019	2000	2008–2012	2015–2019
Population	26,080	23,220	23,113	292,648	261,955	256,480
Population share (%)						
White	47.2	37.7	38.6	51.8	47.1	43.1
Black	17.0	19.5	20.7	36.6	37.2	35.5
Hispanic	27.6	28.1	24.0	7.5	3.3	12.3
AAPI	2.8	9.7	13.4	1.4	9.3	5.9
All other	5.4	5.0	3.3	2.7	3.1	3.2
Share foreign-born (%)	7.6	20.3	25.6	4.4	7.7	10.4
Median HH income ($)	30,683	25,965	36,471	37,767	34,027	37,354
Poverty rate (%)	39.6	45.8	37.9	26.7	30.1	30.1
Median home value ($)	71,608	62,806	111,000	87,537	74,408	89,800
Homeownership rate (%)	32.9	31.7	34.1	43.5	42.3	40.7
Vacancy rate (%)	20.7	20.1	15.8	15.7	17.3	17.0
Median monthly gross rent ($)	712	757	773	703	750	776
Rent-to-income ratio (%)	37.5	45.8	32.0	31.0	35.9	32.0

Source: 2000 Decennial Census and American Community Survey 2008–2012 and 2015–2019 five-year samples, www.census.gov/programs -surveys/decennial-census/data.html; www.census.gov/programs-surveys/acs/data.html

grassroots nonprofits can drive the process and benefit directly from
the social and economic gains that accrue from it. At the same time, resource constraints and limited capacity are real challenges in structur-
ally disadvantaged communities, and residents and community-based
organizations must pool resources with other actors to support transformative placemaking activities. Their success can depend on their
ability to mobilize and sustain those resources over time, a balancing
act of financial dependency on non-public sources of funding and
organizational autonomy.

Public sector leadership and innovation are critical in facilitating
and supporting the pooling of resources to support resident-driven,
bottom-up place governance arrangements. As the examples in this
chapter demonstrate, local public officials and agencies are central to
the identification, facilitation, and transfer of resources to place-based
governance driven or led by residents and grassroots organizations.
For instance, in the previous examples, public authorities facilitated
resident- and community-driven partnerships with different actors by
making available vacant land and structures, utilizing state eminent
domain power, and expending public dollars to subsidize place governance arrangements. Private sector and philanthropic support of
bottom-up efforts is much easier to attract if the public sector is a partner with resident-driven, community-based initiatives.

Importantly, public authorities are facilitating these bottom-up
place governance arrangements as part of their strategy to address the
legacy of systemic racial inequality in their cities. Consider the recent
announcement by the city of Seattle to transfer $1 million and a de-
commissioned fire station to the Africatown Land Trust located in a
historically Black neighborhood, the Central District.[91] The grant
from the city is designed to catalyze inclusive, heritage-rich development in the district, which includes affordable rental housing, homeownership, and community businesses. The fire station will be used
to establish a Center for Cultural Innovation in the neighborhood, a
collaborative effort between the community and the city's Department of Neighborhoods and Office of Planning and Community

Development. This kind of state facilitation and reinforcement of bottom-up place governance presents an opportunity for more robust participation from historically marginalized populations while helping these populations overcome structural and fiscal constraints that are a consequence of systemic racial injustice.

Finally, the public sector's role in facilitating and reinforcing smaller units of resource governance at the hyperlocal level also is critical to realizing the benefits that can flow from a well-constructed polycentric system of place governance at the regional scale—adaptive flexibility, institutional fit, responsiveness to community needs, leveraging local assets, and maintaining fairness and equity.[92] To achieve these ends, polycentric systems must be attentive to the possibility that the preferences of larger and more resourced actors will prevail in collaborative arrangements, leading to outcomes that are unequally distributed and thus reproduce existing power inequalities and injustices.[93] A polycentric system of place governance that facilitates and supports bottom-up initiatives, however, can allow for more robust participation from historically underrepresented groups and bring together actors who are very differently situated in terms of resources. A strong public sector role is thus crucial for a polycentric system that enables historically disinvested communities and those with few resources to co-create goods and services responsive to their needs.

NOTES

1. See Project for Public Spaces, "What is Placemaking," www.pps.org /article/what-is.

2. David Harvey, "From Managerialism to Entrepreneurialism: The Transformation in Urban Governance in Late Capitalism," *Geografiska Annaler*, 71B (1989), pp. 3–17, doi:10.1080/04353684.1989.11879583.

3. See University City District website, www.universitycity.org/.

4. Meagan M. Ehlenz, "Neighborhood Revitalization and the Anchor Institution: Assessing the Impact of the University of Pennsylvania's West Philadelphia Initiatives on University City," *Urban Affairs Review* (2015), pp. 1–37.

5. See University City District website, "Transforming Public Spaces," www.universitycity.org/transforming-public-spaces.

6. Thomas J. Vicino, "New Boundaries of Urban Governance: An Analysis of Philadelphia's University City Improvement District," *Drexel Law Review* 3 (2010), pp. 339–56.

7. See University City District website, "Annual Review," www.ucdannualreview.com/about. In FY2019, 94 percent of UCD's funding came from three sources: board contributions (42 percent), service fees (34 percent), and grant support and tax credits (18 percent). Lenfest Foundation, Penn and Penn Health System, Drexel University, University of the Sciences, and Children's Hospital of Philadelphia all contributed more than $100,000 to UCD.

8. See the Dudley Street Neighborhood Initiative website, www.dsni.org/; Peter Medoff and Holly Sklar, *Streets of Hope: The Fall and Rise of an Urban Neighborhood* (Troy, NY: South End Press, 1994).

9. Harry Smith and Tony Hernandez, "Take a Stand, Own the Land: Dudley Neighbors, Inc., a Community Land Trust in Boston, Massachusetts," in *On Common Ground: International Perspectives on The Community Land Trust*, edited by John Emmeus Davis, Line Algoed, and María E. Hernández-Torrales (Madison, WI: Terra Nostra Press, 2020), p. 288. The majority of housing units are targeted for families making between 30 to 60 percent of the area median income, approximately $30,000 to $60,000 for a family of four. Individuals or families who wish to purchase one of Dudley's affordable homes participate in a lottery system. Once purchased, the homeowner pays a small lease fee for the land the house sits upon, which continues to be owned by the CLT. The homeowner also agrees that if the home is ever sold, which is rare in the Dudley area, the home must be sold at a cost determined by the formula used by DSNI's CLT. The sustainability of the Dudley model has been proven in part by the fact that during the economic crisis, in 2008–2013, there were no foreclosures of DNI homes even as the surrounding neighborhood had more than 200 foreclosures. Ibid, p. 290.

10. Of the twenty community seats, four seats are for Black residents, four are for Latinos, four are for residents with a Cape Verde heritage, four are for white residents, and four are for youth (age 15–18) living in the community.

11. See the NeighborSpace website, http://neighbor-space.org/.

12. The information contained in this paragraph is in large part based on material from its website and a phone interview with NeighborSpace staff on April 18, 2018, by Chrystie Swiney, a research fellow employed by Georgetown University.

13. Sheila Foster, "Collective Action and the Urban Commons," *Notre Dame Law Review* 87 (2006), p. 118.

14. Community Associations Institute, "The Rise and Effects of Home-owners Associations," January 8, 2020, https://communityassociations.net/effects-homeowners-associations/.

15. Robert H. Nelson, *Private Neighborhoods and the Transformation of Local Government* (Washington, DC: Urban Institute Press, 2005), pp. 265–73.

16. Community Associations Institute, "Large-Scale Association Survey Results, Technical Report," Foundation for Community Association Research, 2016.

17. Evan McKenzie "Rethinking Residential Private Government in the US: Recent Trends in Practices and Policy," in *Private Communities and Urban Governance*, edited by Amnon Lehavi (Switzerland: Springer, 2016).

18. Gregory S. Alexander, "Governance Property," *University of Pennsylvania Law Review* 160 (2012), p. 1853. In addition to CICs, he includes marital and domestic partnership property, other forms of joint property ownership (co-tenancies), many types of corporate ownership, and commercial trusts.

19. Alexander, "Governance Property," p. 1862.

20. Robert H. Nelson, "Privatizing the Neighborhood: A Proposal to Replace Zoning with Private Collective Property Rights to Existing Neighborhoods," *George Mason Law Review* 7 (1999), pp. 827, 828

21. Nelson, "Privatizing the Neighborhood," p. 833.

22. Ibid., pp. 833–34.

23. Robert C. Ellickson, "New Institutions for Old Neighborhoods," *Duke Law Journal* 48 (1998), pp. 75, 77 (discussing a similar idea, "Block Level Improvement Districts," which would allow streel level decisions on zoning) and John Myers, "Fixing Urban Planning with Ostrom: Strategies for Existing Cities to Adopt Polycentric, Bottom-Up Regulation of Land Use," Mercatus Research, Mercatus Center at George Mason University, Arlington, VA, February 2020 (proposing legislation laws to allow block or street level land-use decisions, which could address spillover and other concerns and enable win-win bargaining to permit more housing, which is restricted under current land-use rules).

24. Nelson, "Private Neighborhoods," p. 267.

25. Ibid., p. 835.

26. Ibid., p. 836.

27. Nelson, "Private Neighborhoods," pp. 304–5. He also argues that property owners in private communities would net a much larger capital gain when they sold property in their gated neighborhood.

28. Lorlene Hoyt and Devika Gopal-Agge, "The Business Improvement District Model: A Balanced Review of Contemporary Debates," *Geography Compass* 946, no. 2 (2007); Gerald E. Frug, "The Seductions of Form," *Drexel Law Review* 3 (2010), pp. 11, 16–17.

29. See *Kessler v. Grand Cent. Dist. Mgmt. Ass'n*, 158 F.3d 92, 108 (2d Cir. 1998) (rejecting a challenge by non-property-owning individuals residing in a Business Improvement District (BID) arguing that a governing structure that weighed the votes of property owners more heavily than residents violated the constitutional guarantee of "one person, one vote").

30. Ellickson, "New Institutions," p. 92. ("Both theory and evidence indicate that most of the benefits of a localized public good redound to the owners of real estate located within the benefitted territory.")

31. Emily Badger, "How 'Not in My Backyard' Became 'Not in My Neighborhood,'" *New York Times*, January 3, 2018, www.nytimes.com/2018/01/03/upshot/zoning-housing-property-rights-nimby-us.html.

32. Ibid.

33. Ryann Briggs, "The Rise of the 'Overlay': How an Obscure Zoning Tool is Shaping Philly's Future (Again)," WHYY News, January 27, 2021, https://whyy.org/articles/the-rise-of-the-overlay-how-an-obscure-zoning-tool-is-shaping-philly-again/?utm_source=dlvr.it&utm_medium=twitter.

34. Ronald J. Oakerson and Jeremy D. W. Clifton, "The Neighborhood as Commons: Reframing Neighborhood Decline," *Fordham Urban Law Journal* 44 (2017), p. 411.

35. Ibid., pp. 443–44. The authors note, importantly, that the collaborative and the presiding judge on the housing court preferred non-punitive approaches to enforcing the housing code, using the threat of punishment to force property owners to either make needed investments or sell; the ultimate objective was not punishment but reinvestment.

36. Ibid., pp. 444–45. Buffalo's housing court has community liaisons recruited from community organizations and trained to help residents navigate the housing court to get problems resolved and to provide context to judges who can act with lenience in cases where property owners make good faith efforts to correct violations (for example, low income or elderly homeowners).

37. Interview with Harvey Garrett, founder and director of the West Side Community Collaborative from 2000 to 2010 (interview conducted by Jacob Whiton on April 16, 2021, and May 31, 2021).

38. Peter Harnik and Abby Martin, "Public Spaces/Private Money: The Triumphs and Pitfalls of Urban Park Conservancies," *Trust for Public Land*, February, 2015.

39. *Frequently Asked Questions*, Central Park Conservancy Institute for Public Parks, p. 2.

40. Dorceta E. Taylor, *The Environment and the People in American Cities, 1600s–1900s: Disorder, Inequality and Social Change* (Duke University Press, 2009), p. 347.

41. Ibid., p. 356 ("In New York City, for instance, Central Park Conservancy has raised vastly more money than other city parks."); Ibid, p. 352 (noting that Marcus Garvey Park in Harlem, and others, languish in the shadows of fundraising behemoths such as Central Park). See also Murray, "Private Management of Public Spaces," *Harvard Environmental Law Review* 34, no. 179 (2010), supra, pp. 192–93 (reviewing some of the literature exploring the costs of public-private partnerships).

42. Roy Rosenzweig and Elizabeth Blackmar, *The Park and the People* (Cornell University Press, 1992) (discussing the decline of Central Park); Murray, "Private Management of Public Spaces: Nonprofit Organizations and Urban Parks."

43. Kathy Madden and others, *Public Parks, Private Partners* (New York, NY: Project for Public Spaces, 2000), pp. 13–22.

44. Taylor, *The Environment and the People*, p. 352 (noting that Central Park Conservancy agreement with the city allows up to $2 million per year from concession revenues; but for other parks, revenues generated from concessions disappear into a city's general funds).

45. Eugene Kinkead, *Central Park 1857–1995: The Birth, Decline, and Renewal of a National Treasure* (New York: W. W. Norton & Co Inc, 1990), pp. 115–16; See also Murray, "Private Management of Public Spaces," pp. 208–9 (noting that neighbors who live near urban parks, as well as wealthy donors and residents, have long exerted some power over park management—providing donations, labor, advocacy efforts, and planning ideas); Rosenzweig and Blackmar, *The Park and the People*, pp. 509–10.

46. Murray, "Private Management of Public Spaces," pp. 208–9.

47. Rosenzweig and Blackmar, *The Park and the People*, p. 507.

48. Ibid., pp. 510–11.

49. Oliver Cooke, "A Class Approach to Municipal Privatization: The Privatization of New York City's Central Park," *International Labor and Working-Class History* 71 (2007), pp. 112, 121 (citing the 1998 Agreement between the Conservancy and the city of New York Parks and Recreation Department). This agreement seems to have remained quite stable over time, with a few notable changes. "Later versions of the agreement have revised the funding commitments of the Conservancy and the City, and added provisions for catastrophic events, such as cleanup expenses following extreme weather occurrences. The current agreement also defines intellectual property rights for materials relating to the Park and the Conservancy and expands the Conservancy's scope of work to include maintenance in several other New York City parks outside of Central Park." Frequently Asked Questions, Central Park Conservancy Institute for Public Parks, p. 5, https://s3.amazonaws.com/assets

.centralparknyc.org/new_images/report/Institute_PublicPrivatePartnership_FAQ_2019.pdf.

50. Taylor, *The Environment and the People*, p. 350.

51. Forty-three of these are "general" trustees, which are elected by existing trustees, and five are "ex-officio" trustees consisting of the borough president of Manhattan, the NYC park commissioner, the Central Park administrator, the president and CEO of the CPC nonprofit organization, and the president of CPC's Women's Committee, www.centralparknyc.org/board.

52. Central Park Conservancy Bylaws (as amended 6/2017), https://assets.centralparknyc.org/pdfs/bylaws/Central_Park_Conservancy_Bylaws.pdf.

53. Harnik and Martin, "Public Spaces/Private Money," p. 6 (noting that "most conservancies neither own nor hold easements on the parkland; the land remains the city's, and the city retains ultimate authority over everything that happens there"); Frequently Asked Questions, Central Park Conservancy Institute for Public Parks, p. 3, https://s3.amazonaws.com/assets.centralparknyc.org/new_images/report/Institute_PublicPrivatePartnership_FAQ_2019.pdf.

54. Ibid., p. 3 (also noting that capital improvement projects that feature noticeable design changes must receive approval from NYC Parks and go through the city's formal public review and approval process); See also Rosenzweig and Blackmar, *The Park and the People*, p. 521.

55. Jill Simone Gross, "Business Improvement Districts in New York City's Low-Income and High-Income Neighborhoods," *Economic Development Quarterly* 19 (2005), pp. 174, 178.

56. Richard Briffault, "A Government for Our Time? Business Improvement Districts and Urban Governance," *Columbia Law Review* 99 (1999), pp. 365–477, at 441.

57. Gross, "Business Improvement Districts," pp. 179–80.

58. Ibid, p. 184.

59. Taylor, *The Environment and the People*, pp. 302, 356; Cindi Katz, "Power, Space, and Terror: Social Reproduction and the Public Environment," in *The Politics of Public Space*, edited by Setha Low and Neil Smith (New York, NY: Routledge, 2006), pp. 105, 105–21.

60. Research suggests that special districts are formed in large part out of demand for special or additional services by the most affluent citizens. Barbara Coyle McCabe, "Special-District Formation among the States," *State & Local Government Review* 32 (2000), pp. 121, 126 (stating that the probability of special district creation increases with growth in per capital personal income, supporting the notion that more districts are formed as state populations become more affluent).

61. Rosenzweig and Blackmar, *The Park and the People*, p. 519 (citing Central Park Conservancy's attempts to set a policy for what types of events would occur on the Great Lawn, first proposing to continue opera and symphony concert but not mass concerts and political rallies and then finally recommending, after some pushback, that "efforts should be made to limit gatherings to 100,000 people").

62. Briffault, "A Government for Our Time," p. 442

63. David J. Kennedy, "Restraining the Power of Business Improvement Districts: The Case of the Grand Central Partnership," *Yale Law and Policy Review* 15 (1996), pp. 283, 321–23 (pointing to controversies by the Grand Central BID, including being investigated for using its "social services" function to hire low-wage homeless individuals to go out and harass other homeless individuals from sidewalks, doorways, and other public spaces, using violence if necessary).

64. The Urban Institute, *The Impact of Community Development Corporations on Urban Neighborhoods*, June 2005.

65. Alexander von Hoffman, "The Past, Present, and Future of Community Development in the United States" in *Investing in What Works Works for American Communities* (Federal Reserve Bank of San Francisco and Low Income Investment Fund, 2012), pp. 50–51, www.whatworksforamerica.org/the-book/.

66. Amy Laura Cahn and Paula Z. Segal, "You Can't Common What You Can't See: Towards a Restorative Polycentrism in the Governance of Our Cities," *Fordham Urban Law Journal* 43 (2016), pp. 195, 201. ("For decades, municipal and private landowners have left acres of land in neighborhoods . . . abandoned in cities across the Rust Belt and in the Northeast.")

67. Sheila Foster, "The City as an Ecological Space: Social Capital and Urban Land Use," *Notre Dame Law Review* 82 (2013), p. 527.

68. New York City's Green Thumb Program is an example of this kind of support, providing residents with technical support and materials, https://greenthumb.nycgovparks.org/.

69. Elinor Ostrom, *Governing the Commons: The Evolution of Institutions for Collective Action* (Cambridge University Press, 1990).

70. Amnon Lehavi, "Property Rights and Local Public Goods: Toward a Better Future for Urban Communities," *Urban Lawyer* 36, no. 1 (2004), p. 34.

71. Madden and others, *Public Parks, Private Parks*, pp. 51–115.

72. Sheila Foster, "Collective Action and the Urban Commons," *Notre Dame Law Review* 87, no. 57 (2011), pp. 96–98 (describing these kinds of groups and the local government "enabling" efforts that support them).

73. City Parks Foundation, https://cityparksfoundation.org/about-partner ships-for-parks/ (describing New York's Partnership for Parks program); See also Madden and others, *Public Parks, Private Parks*, pp. 107–10.

74. Robert C. Ellickson, *Order without Law* (Harvard University Press 1991), p. 169.

75. Sheila R. Foster, and Christian Iaione, "The City as a Commons," *Yale Law and Policy Review* 34, no. 2 (July 2016), p. 331.

76. Marina Ranga and Henry Etzkowitz, "Triple Helix System: An Analytical Framework for Innovation Policy and Practice in the Knowledge Society," *Industry & Higher Education* 27 (2013), p. 237.

77. Bruce Katz and Julie Wagner, "The Rise of Innovation Districts: A New Geography of Innovation in America," Washington, DC: Brookings Institution, 2009, www.brookings.edu/essay/rise-of-innovation-districts/.

78. See the Cortex Innovation Community website, www.cortexstl.com/.

79. R. Lang, R. D. Roessl, and D. Weismeier-Sammer (2013), "Co-operative Governance of Public–Citizen Partnerships: Two Diametrical Participation Modes," in *Conceptualizing and Researching Governance in Public and Non-Profit Organizations (Studies in Public and Non-Profit Governance*, Vol. 1), edited by L. Gnan, A. Hinna, and F. Monteduro (Bingley: Emerald Group Publishing Limited), pp. 227–46.

80. Thomas J. Vicino, "New Boundaries of Urban Governance: An Analysis of Philadelphia's University City Improvement District," *Drexel Law Review* 3, no. 1 (2010), pp. 339–56; In FY2019, 94 percent of UCD's funding came from three sources: board contributions (42 percent), service fees (34 percent), and grant support and tax credits (18 percent). UCD's total revenue in FY2019 was $11.3 million, www.ucdannualreview.com/fy19financials.

81. See the Southwest Partnership website, https://southwestpartnership baltimore.org/.

82. Vicino, "New Boundaries," p. 354.

83. Meagan M. Ehlenz, "Neighborhood Revitalization and the Anchor Institution: Assessing the Impact of the University of Pennsylvania's West Philadelphia Initiatives on University City," *Urban Affairs Review* (2015), pp. 1–37.

84. Ehlenz, "Neighborhood Revitalization," pp. 8–9.

85. Ibid., pp. 15–16.

86. As documented in UCD's annual reports, the number of area residents with a bachelor's degree or higher climbed by 10 percentage points (from 54 to 64 percent) between 2012 and 2021, providing further indication that neighborhood demographics are shifting. See UCD's State of University City Reports, www.universitycity.org/publications.

87. Smith and Hernandez "Take a Stand," p. 290.

88. Ibid., p. 294.

89. Buffalo Neighborhood change analysis, 2000–2019.

90. Among the foreign-born in the West Side, 71 percent are non-citizens, roughly half from Southern and Southeastern Asia and half from Eastern and Central Africa.

91. Gregory Scruggs, "Plaza Heralds New Era of Afrocentric Development in Seattle Neighborhood," NextCity.org, August 7, 2018, https://nextcity.org/daily/entry/plaza-heralds-new-era-of-afrocentric-development-in-seattle-neighborhood.

92. Elinor Ostrom, "A Frequently Overlooked Precondition of Democracy: Citizens Knowledgeable about and Engaged in Collective Action," in *Elinor Ostrom and the Bloomington School of Political Economy: Polycentricity in Public Administration and Political Science*, edited by Daniel H. Cole and Michael G. McGinnis (Lanham, MD: Lexington Books, 2014), pp. 337–52.

93. Gustavo A García-López and Camille Antinori, "Between Grassroots Collective Action and State Mandates: The Hybridity of Multi-Level Forest Associations in Mexico," *Conservation and Society* 16 (2017), pp. 193–204, www.jstor.org/stable/26393329.

FOUR

Power and Legitimacy in Place Government Ecosystems

A Comparative Analysis

JULIET MUSSO

In Los Angeles, the issue of homelessness has mobilized multiple governance entities. For example, it has entered the agenda of many of the city's ninety-nine neighborhood councils, advisory organizations that meet regularly to deliberate and generate statements of support or opposition to proposed developments within their boundaries. In the Hollywood area, the Central Hollywood Neighborhood Council has focused on data collection, partnering with other local community nonprofits to conduct a volunteer-led count of people experiencing homelessness after the city of Los Angeles cancelled its own 2021 "point in time count," citing the risks of volunteer management during the pandemic. A spokesperson explained: "We will make this year count because it is critical to understand how the homelessness crisis changes every year—especially during a pandemic."[1]

Other councils have lobbied for transitional housing within their vicinities. In March 2021, two neighborhood councils in the port community of San Pedro enacted a resolution requesting that the city make available safe camping facilities, while the Eagle Rock and Highland Park Neighborhood Councils voted in support of a successful city council motion to construct prefabricated "bridge" housing on two sites in northeast Los Angeles.[2] In other communities, the neighborhood councils have served as an arena for stakeholders to air views on the issue. The Echo Park Neighborhood Council has held contentious hearings regarding a communal encampment on the banks of Echo Park Lake, while the Venice Neighborhood Council has been engaged in the review of a proposed supportive housing development.[3]

While neighborhood councils generally have played a mediating role in response to the issue of homelessness, some business improvement districts in Los Angeles have drawn criticism for employing security practices and engaging in advocacy that often is counter to the interests of unsheltered community members.[4] A telling example involves advocacy efforts undertaken by two downtown area BIDs to prevent the creation of an independent neighborhood council in Skid Row, an area of downtown in which many unhoused residents have formed encampments. In 2017, residents of Skid Row successfully petitioned for a vote to secede from the downtown neighborhood council. As reported in the *Los Angeles Weekly*: "Proponents of the Skid Row Neighborhood Council, in their statements and in their petition to the city, made it clear that part of their motivation was to reduce the influence of 'downtown business interests' at a crucial time . . . [when] . . . a $1.2 billion bond issuance . . . is supposed to pay for the construction of 10,000 units of housing for [unsheltered individuals]."[5]

To combat the secession effort, the two area BIDs organized a letter writing campaign asking downtown city council representative

Jose Huizar to permit online voting as an exemption to a citywide ban against it. Two weeks before the election, Council Member Huizar moved to enable online voting; the measure to allow the secession of Skid Row from the downtown council subsequently failed 826 to 766, with online votes disproportionately represented in opposition to the measure.[6] In response to challenges posed by advocates of the Skid Row Neighborhood Council, a panel composed of other neighborhood council members reviewed charges that the late change in voting may have disenfranchised lower income and unsheltered individuals.[7] The panel recommended a new election that did not employ online voting, a recommendation subsequently rejected by the city's Board of Neighborhood Commissioners, which certified the election outcome, leaving Skid Row within the larger Downtown Los Angeles Neighborhood Council.

Lobbying efforts against the formation of a Skid Row Neighborhood Council are illustrative of a broader pattern of advocacy among BIDs that has drawn criticism on grounds that it promotes business development interests at the expense of the interests and rights of individuals experiencing homelessness.[8] To wit, the viewpoint of one influential property owner was expressed in an email that was forwarded to two downtown BIDs and became part of the public record under the California Open Meetings Act: "The implications may not sound politically correct; however, the economic realities are obvious. . . . We have to inform everyone we can that they must actually VOTE. . . . 20,000+ homeless people live downtown and they will be carted up to vote!"[9]

In contrast to BIDs and neighborhood councils, which generally have responded in a reactive fashion to issues around homelessness in Los Angeles, T.R.U.S.T. South LA (*Tenemos que Reclamar y Unidos Salvar la Tierra*), a community land trust in South Los Angeles, has proactively worked since 2005 to counteract residential displacement, steward local housing development, and empower lower income community residents.[10] The CLT manages a 140-unit affordable rental housing development that also includes a medical/dental clinic and commercial space. It is currently developing a limited equity housing cooperative model for preservation of small and medium multifamily housing units adjacent to the University of Southern California (USC) campus. A second CLT in Los Angeles, the Beverly/Vermont Community Land Trust, provides land stewardship for the fifty-unit Eco-Village, which has been operating in Koreatown as an intentional community since 1993.

Until recently, the CLT model has been uncommon in Los Angeles, but it appears to be gaining attention among local policymakers and housing advocates. In September 2020, the Los Angeles County Board of Supervisors enacted a pilot program to provide $14 million in seed money for community land trusts to purchase properties that have gone into tax default and convert them to affordable housing. According to LA County Supervisor and former U.S. Housing Secretary Hilda Solis, who spearheaded the pilot program, the goal is to create fifty-five affordable housing units spread across the five supervisorial districts in Los Angeles County.[11] Community activists also have proposed a nascent CLT, the Liberty Community Land Trust, as a means to community ownership of the Baldwin Hills/Crenshaw Plaza, where commercial redevelopment threatens to displace businesses that serve the area's predominately African American communities.[12] Interestingly, there has not been any movement to create a CLT in downtown Los Angeles, where concerns about city indifference to individuals experiencing homelessness contributed to the attempted formation of the Skid Row Neighborhood Council.

As chapter 6 of this volume discusses, the worsening national housing affordability crisis draws attention to how hyperlocal governance can better serve the needs of residents, including individuals who experience homelessness. This case study highlights institutional responses to this critical issue in Los Angeles, exemplifying how organizations interact in dramatically different ways around a particular (and, in this case, all too common) local challenge based in part on their power and role in the larger place governance ecosystem.

Discussion: Power, Influence, and Impact
in Place Governance Ecosystems

Here we see how place governance entities in Los Angeles have been confronting issues of housing and homelessness in differing ways. BIDs tend to coalesce around protection of commercial interests while neighborhood councils, for the most part, play a mediating role, attempting to find common ground between promoting the values of equity and inclusion and addressing the concerns of residents who object to housing or service development that they perceive—not always with sound evidence—to be detrimental to residential property values or quality of life. While CLTs are less common, they are emerging as a potential means of promoting common good development in the face of high and rapidly increasing land values in the region.

These three types of entities have the common feature of hybridity described in chapter 3 of this volume, each functioning in a public-private or co-productive partnership between city government and other entities, with a focus on developing localized approaches to often challenging issues. Yet the power and influence they yield differs by virtue of their legal authority and governance (why they exist and what they generally are permitted to do); their financing structures and capacity for action (how they are able to do their work); and/or the overall legitimacy they have among the other entities and stakeholders operating in their hyperlocal ecosystem (see table 4-1). The extent of their power in each of these dimensions significantly impacts entities' overall ability to generate their desired—if not always equitable—outcomes in the geographies in which they work.

Even with this understanding, establishing a direct link between the respective power of place governance entities and long-range place-based outcomes is not easy, as these entities tend to shapeshift as political actors within city's decisionmaking processes over time. Robert Chaskin and D. M. Greenberg find in a study of community planning in Chicago that neighborhood organizations and non-profits "often play a kind of interstitial role . . . filling in where

Table 4-1. *Neighborhood Councils, Business Improvement Districts, and Community Land Trusts: Dimensions of Power*

	Neighborhood Councils	Business Improvement Districts	Community Land Trusts
Scope of Authority	Broadest—civic infrastructure; social capital, voice	Generally narrower, with a clean and safe focus; can be broader in practice	Narrowest, preservation of land for public purposes, typically housing or parks
Type of Power	Soft; advisory/lobbying; network politics	Financial but engaged in lobbying and policing	Stewardship of land resources
Typical Governance Structure	Generally elected; often majoritarian but occasionally district or designated stakeholder seats	May be elected or appointed depending on state; typically emphasizes property owners subject to assessment	Elected tripartite; includes residents of property, residents of surrounding area, and public members at large
Community Representation and Voice	Socioeconomic biases raise issues around representational character (descriptive and substantive)	Often property owners' interests dominate, with substantive focus on economic development	While the tripartite board structure attempts to engage broad community, some criticism that there are socioeconomic biases
Capacity and Centrality	Limited resources and advisory character may limit impact	Financing authority increases centrality	Scalability an issue. Reliant on external funding; vulnerable to larger economic forces

governmental action is absent."[13] Their role also is boundary span-
ning in that they often represent "neighborhood interests to both
public- and private-sector concerns."[14] As Jill Gross observes, while
their hybrid structure is not new, we are seeing more complex multi-
actor relationships emerging in response to problems that "demand a
level of collaboration and coordination (horizontally and vertically)
that hierarchical governments within democratic systems are simply not well suited to achieve."[15] The amorphous character of actors
within these networks—both at the jurisdictional level and within
the specific geographies in which they operate—makes roles and responsibilities difficult to assess, especially as they are very context
dependent. A further complexity is that the legal institutions for
localizing and privatizing community voice and service provision
vary across states and municipalities, making it challenging empiri-
cally to generalize regarding their goals, structure, and impact.

Still, a look at three of the entities involved in hyperlocal governance in Los Angeles provides a window into these complicated and
evolving relationships, and how both the source and strength of an
organization's power significantly effects its activities and outcomes.

Federated Civic Voice: Neighborhood Councils

In Los Angeles, ninety-nine elected neighborhood councils, authorized by a 2002 city charter reform, provide a forum for community
stakeholders to speak—usually for two minutes only with speaker
cards submitted in advance—on issues of concern.[16] They produce
community impact statements that become part of the Los Angeles
City Council agenda and permanent record; form alliances to moni-
tor city services, budgeting, and planning; and advocate on an array
of local and regional policy matters. While much of their activity focuses on advisement, they also self-organize to host community
events or make modest investments in neighborhood improvement.

Neighborhood councils are a quasi-federated approach to governance that supports community organizing, deliberation, and spatial
decentralization of political voice within areas that more closely

follow natural community boundaries than do city council districts.[17] In Los Angeles, as in most cities, they function as a system of voluntary neighborhood associations advising the formal organs of city government.[18] In the American urban landscape, the neighborhood council movement was largely a phenomenon of the late twentieth century, through mobilization and, ultimately, city recognition of community action that occurred by means of community-based organizations such as neighborhood block clubs and, in some cities, community action agencies formed during Lyndon B. Johnson's War on Poverty.[19] Typically, neighborhood councils function much like "little city councils," holding regular meetings in which the council will entertain presentations and develop positions that are later communicated to formal city governance institutions.[20] In many cities, neighborhood councils also are vehicles for volunteer mobilization and co-production, mounting local beautification programs and community events such as street festivals.

The typical neighborhood council governance structure involves an elected board composed of residents, business owners, and other community stakeholders, such as representatives from the nonprofit community. In Los Angeles, for example, the ordinance left the structure of neighborhood council boards largely to community discretion, although the authorizing charter specified that no stakeholder group may hold a majority of seats. Board structures vary from simple majoritarian structures to district elections to corporatist structures that identify seats for different groups of stakeholders (for example, homeowners, renters, business owners, and nonprofit representatives).

Cities use an array of approaches to connect neighborhood councils meaningfully to their policy and planning operations, with most neighborhood council systems functioning in a largely advisory fashion. In Los Angeles, neighborhood councils can file formal position statements that become part of the official city council agenda, interact with the mayor's budget process, and provide input to departmental processes.[21]

POWER OF PERSUASION?   While the scope of neighborhood councils is broad, their power is generally "soft," as most council systems have, at most, modest funding and capacity and little or no formal authority. In Los Angeles, the city's neighborhood councils receive annual block grants of $42,000, which may be used to cover operating costs; to provide grants to community schools or nonprofits; or to support community improvement projects.[22]

This limited, diffuse power makes generalizations regarding the actual impact of such systems on policy decisions at the local or the citywide level challenging. Thus, one of the greatest vulnerabilities of the neighborhood council model arguably is irrelevance. Neighborhood associations provide one point of entry among many others for participants to enter into the complex, diffuse networks of civic actors that engage around community action. Chaskin characterizes community action as a "noncentralized democratic system in which responsibilities are shared among levels of formal government and . . . a range of nongovernmental bodies in both the private and nonprofit spheres."[23] Within such a system, even a system anointed with formal city recognition, organizations may lack influence. Based on a study of community action in Chicago, Chaskin and Greenberg argue that neighborhood association activities occur in the interstices between private markets and public agency services. These interstices, they argue, often are unstable and vulnerable to disruption in the event that political leadership or agency priorities change.[24]

The design of neighborhood governance institutions is critical to their effectiveness in empowering local voice. In a study of five well established neighborhood council systems, Jeffery Berry, Kent Portney, and Ken Thomson identify two attributes of governance they deem essential to neighborhood council function and so influence: (1) the scope of jurisdiction that aligns with relatively smaller, "natural" neighborhoods and (2) the establishment of explicit governance mechanisms that connect them to city government. From this standpoint, the relatively small size and boundaries that recognize a sense of place can foster a feeling of belonging and build stronger ties among community stakeholders while providing them an accessible channel through which to reach public officials.[25] This was certainly a motivating factor in the efforts of the Skid Row community to establish their own neighborhood council.

Still, even when a neighborhood council does maintain some level of relevance in terms of its relationship to the city, socioeconomic biases in voluntary participation mean a given council may not always hold such relevance within its own community. Survey research on neighborhood councils in Los Angeles found patterns of identity and interest orientation that suggest they were neither descriptively nor substantively representative of Los Angeles residents. For example, survey respondents were disproportionately white, had higher median incomes, and had higher homeownership rates than the general population of the city.[26] Moreover, when asked to identify the most important interests of the neighborhood, neighborhood council representatives more commonly identified a quality-of-life agenda; this also was evident in content analysis of neighborhood council agendas. In particular, council members reported a keener interest in issues related to development, traffic congestion, and public safety than do likely voters, who tend to place greater emphasis on education.[27]

In short, neighborhood councils in a number of cities have emerged as arenas in which community stakeholders can exercise voice and engage voluntary action to address issues of local concern. These entities often have limited authority and resources, so their impact depends heavily on the ability of hyperlocal leadership to develop networks of influence within and across neighborhoods.

"Clubs" for Local Service Production: Business Improvement Districts

Overlapping with Los Angeles neighborhood councils are forty-two business improvement districts, formed by merchants or property owners for the purpose of self-financing business improvement services. In contrast to neighborhood councils, which have weak fiscal powers and a largely advisory role in governance, BIDs are formalized public or nonprofit entities with specified fiscal authority and, often, professionalized nonprofit management arrangements.[28]

While laws governing BID formation vary from one state to the next, many involve municipal-level authorization of assessments on businesses and properties within a specific area, typically a commercial zone. (See chapter 5 of this volume.) The authorizing municipality collects assessments and allocates revenues to the BID, which then utilizes funds to support business improvement activities and investments that provide a special benefit to property owners and associated businesses within the boundaries of the BID.[29] While neighborhood councils in general present a quasi-federated approach to organizing stakeholder voice, BIDs function in effect as economic "clubs" within which property owners finance local infrastructure investment or enhanced local services within a commercial area.[30] James Buchanan's theory of clubs suggests that excludable public goods can be provided efficiently if those who benefit from a particular public good can self-organize to finance their preferred level, thus avoiding the loss of utility experienced by individuals required by majority rule to pay for a level of services not to their preference.[31] The BID approach to self-funding goods that provide mutual benefit has become increasingly attractive as local governments confront intensifying fiscal constraints due to the joint effects of post-industrial economic restructuring, federal fiscal devolution, and citizen-driven tax limitations.[32]

Unlike neighborhood council boards, where elected members typically engage a broad array of community stakeholders, BID governance boards may be either appointed or elected, and they typically have strong representation by the property owners subject to assessment.[33] The governance and representation of BIDs is conferred to some extent by legal authority, but it also is the result of local decisionmaking. In a 2012 survey by Carol Becker, 40 percent of respondents stated that board members were selected by election, 23 percent by appointment by a mayor, and 21 percent by appointment by the city council, suggesting that, in many jurisdictions, local officials have the power to appoint more representative boards should they deem it important to do so.[34] But in an analysis of state laws regulating BID creation, operation, and termination, Göktug Morçöl and Turgay Karagöz find that while BID laws attempt to ensure accountability, particularly through the establishment of political mechanisms, few state laws ensure "accountability of BID [Downtown Management Organizations] to residents of neighboring areas, shoppers in districts, or the homeless, despite that their actions can affect these groups."[35]

POWER OF THE PURSE   While neighborhood councils were designed primarily for the purpose of organizing neighborhood voice around a range of functions, the legal authority of BIDs allows them to organize the narrower power of the purse, using funds raised through special assessment to pursue the interests of assessed business or property owners.

BIDs are closely related to other localized assessment mechanisms employed by cities to finance a set of public goods. What distinguishes the BID model is that the funds typically are not managed by a city department but through contract with a nonprofit entity. As with governance structure, the laws that affect BID financing vary across states and localities. In California, where local financing is subject to an array of citizen-enacted constitutional restrictions, BIDs face two important financial constraints. First, Proposition 13 restricts *ad valorem* property taxes to 1 percent, so that BIDs typically impose a fixed assessment, such as a per-square-foot fee. Further, such fees and assessments must be used only for "special purposes," meaning that BIDs must take care that there is a clear nexus between the business paying the fee and the purpose for which it is used. In her 2010 survey of BIDs, Carol Becker found that the annual funds raised by BIDs ranged considerably, from a low of $11,000 to about $17 million on the high side, with a mean of about $340,000.

By law, BID powers are intended to be relatively narrow, providing benefits that promote the economic interests of the BID membership. Yet, in operation, as Jill Gross explores further in chapter 5, it can be difficult to determine where "special interests" begin and end, so that many BIDs function much as general purpose quasi-governments within the boundaries of their subscribed places. Most BIDs operate within commercial areas that include spaces that are public in character (streets, sidewalks, parks, and civic spaces). BID activities in those shared spaces frequently extend from those that narrowly benefit the business per se (for example, graffiti removal or advertising) to broader management (for example, security guards patrolling sidewalks or local parks) that affects a wider array of stakeholders, including residents (housed or un-housed). Considering that BID governance generally is not representative of all these stakeholders—and, therefore, does not include their voice in decisionmaking—such "mission creep" may not always be supported by the broader community and can in fact undermine the perceived legitimacy of the BID to engage in certain activities at all.

Perhaps most controversially, many BIDs use their financial capacity to engage in lobbying and political advocacy on commercial issues of interest to local businesses and property owners. In Los Angeles, the Business Improvement District Division, which supports BIDs, dedicates a section of its website to a discussion of the circumstances under which BID employees (and board members) must register with the city as lobbyists.[36] The downtown BIDs clearly exercised this power in the Skid Row case, but it is not unique. Based on an analysis of California BID financial reports and activities, Jeffery Selbin and others argue that BIDs maintain a hostile stance toward the rights of unsheltered individuals, both policing them aggressively in public places and actively lobbying for an agenda that disempowers them.[37]

Indeed, as the Skid Row example illustrates, the BIDs, ironically, had greater influence in this particular policy arena than the neighborhood councils—which ostensibly hold the power of persuasion. In this instance, the BIDs also wielded their power in a manner that failed to promote equity and reduced local participatory agency. Such lobbying activities call into question the notion that BID activities only narrowly impact members of their dues paying "club."

"Nonprofitization" of Land Management: The Community Land Trust

The third approach to place governance identified in the example is the Community Land Trust, in which a nonprofit holds land in perpetuity for common public purposes, such as affordable housing or park construction.

The CLT model, like the BID, has some character of hybridity, although it is "more private" than BIDs or neighborhood councils inasmuch as it does not invoke powers of taxation (as do BIDs) or engage with a broad array of public issues (as do neighborhood councils). The historical antecedents of the CLT model often have made it attractive to organizers seeking to challenge traditional economic development. James DeFillippis and others observe: "CLTs were borne out of the civil rights and Black Power movements and were based on the . . . recognition that control over land, and the meanings of land as either something to be valued for its uses or something to be valued for its price, were vital political economic questions."[38] While the detachment of land from markets has been recognized as a useful means of providing affordable housing, the CLT model also has historically sought to engage community members in decisionmaking around the transformation of local places.[39]

Land trusts have become active advocates of preventing displacement, promoting affordable housing, and supporting more equitable access to parks within urban areas during a time in which fiscal austerity and neoliberal reforms make it increasingly difficult for municipalities to support and maintain them. The model of a housing-focused CLT is to acquire land within a defined spatial area, and either to lease the land to entities that develop a public-interest amenity (for example, a park or affordable housing), or issue long-term leases to individuals who then own housing built on the land. John Emmeus Davis describes three key characteristics that distinguish a community land trust from other types of land trusts. First, the CLT is a nonprofit landholder that makes corporate membership available to all residents within the place in which it operates. This feature is similar to the broad stakeholder focus of a neighborhood council, and is much broader and more inclusionary by design than are many BIDs. Second, the CLT is governed by a board elected by a majority of the CLT membership. Again, this is not dissimilar to neighborhood council board selection, where members of the stakeholder community elect governing boards, and it is likely to be more inclusionary than are many BID boards. Third, the classic design of the CLT board is a corporatist governing board structure in which there are equal numbers of seats for leaseholders (individuals living on or utilizing CLT land); residents of the place in which the CLT operates; and representatives of the public at large, typically members of public or nonprofit entities or those who advocate for lower income individuals.[40] The intent of this tripartite board structure is to create a participatory structure that engages all members of the community in which the CLT operates in its governance.[41]

In contrast to the BID, which seeks to promote economic development and, by extension, property and land values, the goal of the CLT is to detach land use from exogenous market forces that tend to drive escalation of exchange value. This is accomplished through the use of a long-term lease, typically for ninety-nine years, which removes land from the market for a longer tenure than most affordable housing programs. And, as the historical roots of the CLT are in the civil rights movement, most land trusts explicitly embrace goals related to equity and inclusion.[42]

POWER OF LEGITIMACY   Of the governance models reviewed in this chapter, the CLT has the narrowest scope of power, and typically is the most "hyperlocal" in that CLTs usually focus on one or more specific parcels of land within a community. The mission of most CLTs also is narrow, focusing explicitly on the acquisition and management of land within a designated place.

CLTs function as nonprofits without the dedicated fee structure of the BID and, as such, are dependent on resources for land acquisition from either local governments or private funders. The CLT model can face challenges in accessing financing for land acquisition, particularly within urban areas that experience high and rapidly increasing land values. Because CLTs function as land stewards, they need either to be gifted land, allocated land resources to manage by a local government, or have the resources to acquire the land, which, in some housing markets, may require a substantial financial investment. As Davis explains: "Very few of the first CLTs got started without an occasional dose of 'miracle financing' from a wealthy individual, a local church, a national religious order, or a faith-based charity like the Campaign for Human Development."[43] Since 1992, many CLTs can qualify as a Community Housing Development Organization under the National Affordable Housing Act, which means they are able to receive federal funding for both projects and technical assistance.[44] Nevertheless, the CLT model will likely be most effective when implemented within communities that have sources of wealth that are politically sympathetic to the cause of affordable housing or other public interest land uses.

Although most CLTs are developed from the grassroots, state and local governments facing an acute affordable housing shortage are beginning to look toward CLTs as a means of approaching the construction and long-term preservation of affordable housing.[45] In California, for example, policymakers increasingly view CLTs as one tool that can be used to produce such housing within a highly fiscally constrained environment, and have recently enacted legislation to provide advantageous property tax treatment to homes owned by CLTs. There also are examples of city-initiated land trusts for construction of affordable housing. For example, in 2006, the city of Irvine, California, established a city-sponsored CLT to manage the development of affordable housing on land acquired when the Marine Corps closed the El Toro Air Station.[46] While recent interest is encouraging, the need to establish a sustainable funding source (analogous to the BID assessments) makes the CLT model vulnerable to the pressures of real estate markets. The model is sustainable once land is acquired because holding it in trust preserves housing services from the increasing costs associated with rising land values.[47]

With the narrowness of CLT's political influence and their limited financial toolbox (so far), perhaps their greatest power is legitimacy. While legitimacy is a slippery concept, it arguably emerges from a good fit between a place governance organization's scope and its stakeholders. In the case of CLTs, this fit is almost the inverse of BIDs. Whereas the scope, costs, and benefits of a BID are broad and ever growing, a CLT's scope, costs, and benefits are clear and small; whereas a BID's board is far narrower than the full range of parties affected, a CLT's board is far broader. The tripartite structure of the CLT most clearly distinguishes the CLT model from a neighborhood council or BID, as seats are designated for key stakeholders within the community served by the land trust. While this structure was endorsed by the federal government in 1992 and recognized in 2006 by the national CLT network, governing board structures vary, and CLT board structures may not be descriptively representative of an area's residents.[48] However, this attempt at accounting for the full costs and benefits of place governance through representation gives CLTs the strongest claim to legitimacy of the three examples provided.

Conclusion

While the complexity of local government policy ecosystems makes it difficult to discern how specific institutions affect urban outcomes, a comparison of different institutional approaches to local placemaking highlights variations in their scope, governance structure, and financing, as well as implications for sources of power and legitimacy. For example, neighborhood councils frequently have a broad scope, focusing on an array of community-level issues, but soft power, which requires the exercise of voice rather than financial or regulatory power.

In contrast, BIDs are able to leverage financial resources for purposes of community improvement, but too often they are (or are perceived to be) acting in narrower business or property interests, which, in turn, may raise questions about representative legitimacy.

While BIDs arguably act to increase land values, CLTs seek to preserve the use value of land in the public interest. While their board structure seeks to engage a broader public in governance, these entities often operate at a micro-level and with resource constraints that may limit scalability. Local officials or other community advocates might keep in mind these design trade-offs when seeking to foster institutional approaches to local placemaking.

In developing place governance institutions, leaders need to think about their institutional vulnerabilities and consider building in institutional safeguards that can improve their function. For example, to increase the centrality of neighborhood councils, local officials can design formal spaces for engagement with the city, such as participatory budget deliberations or planning procedures. Provision of resources to support outreach and co-productive activities with a particular focus on inclusionary practices can help overcome the socioeconomic biases in participation that make such organizations less broadly representative. In the case of BIDs, the dominance of business interests can be addressed through the appointment of other community stakeholders to boards and the appointment of leadership that takes an inclusionary approach to place governance. And while CLTs are gaining attention as a means of investing in and managing public resources, such as affordable housing, there is a need for upfront public investment for purposes of land acquisition. Also, while their board structure, in theory, helps to build a broader community focus, it too may suffer from the typical socioeconomic bias in participation and warrant attention to inclusionary practices.

In sum, as local agents have sought to address local concerns and challenges, there has been an emergence of varied approaches to place-based governance. Each of these forms has hybrid characteristics, combining elements of public and private action to fill gaps in power and policy attention. While each can contribute in important ways to placemaking, all are circumscribed in some way with respect to resources, authority, and legitimacy. As such, attention to design can improve the impact of local governance institutions and make them more responsive to a broad array of community needs.

NOTES

1. CBS Los Angeles, "Hollywood Groups to Hold their Own Homeless Count," February 25, 2021, https://losangeles.cbslocal.com/2021/02/25/hollywood-groups-to-hold-their-own-homeless-count/.

2. T.A. Hendrickson, "City Council Approves Motion to Build Prefab Shelters for the Homeless in Need," *Boulevard Sentinel*, March 17, 2021, www.boulevardsentinel.com/city-council-approves-motion-to-build-prefab-shelters-for-the-homeless-in-nela/; Donna Littlejohn, " San Pedro Neighborhood Councils Back Proposal to Allow Safe Homeless Campsite on Two Port of Los Angeles Parking Lots," *Daily Breeze*, March 11, 2021, www.dailybreeze.com/2021/03/11/san-pedro-neighborhood-councils-back-proposal-to-allow-safe-homeless-campsite-on-2-port-of-la-parking-lots/.

3. Benjamin Oreskes and Doug Smith, "How a Commune-Like Encampment in Echo Park Became a Flash Point in LA's Homelessness Crisis," *Los Angeles Times*, March 13, 2021, www.latimes.com/homeless-housing/story/2021-03-13/echo-park-encampment-exposes-bigger-la-homeless-issues.

4. Jeffrey Selbin, Stephanie Campos-Bui, Joshua Epstein, Laura Lim, Shelby Nacino, Paula Wilhelm, and Hanna Stommel, "Homeless Exclusion Districts: How Business Improvement Districts Use Policy Advocacy and Policing Practices to Exclude Homeless People from Public Space," UC Berkeley Public Law Research Paper, Policy Advocacy Center, University of California Berkeley (2018); and Wonhyung Lee, "Downtown Management and Homelessness: The Versatile Roles of Business Improvement Districts," *Journal of Place Management and Development* 11, no. 4 (2018), pp. 411–27.

5. Jason McGahon, "Who Killed the Skid Row Neighborhood Council?," *Los Angeles Weekly*, June 21, 2017, www.laweekly.com/who-killed-the-skid-row-neighborhood-council/.

6. According to the *Los Angeles Weekly*, "Who Killed the Skid Row Neighborhood Council," of the total votes, 807 no votes and 581 yes votes came via online voting.

7. Matt Bloom, "Panel Recommends Investigation into Skid Row Neighborhood Council Election," KPCC, 2017, https://archive.kpcc.org/news/2017/05/04/71497/panel-recommends-investigation-into-skid-row-neigh/.

8. Selbin and others, "Homeless Exclusion Districts."

9. Email from Scott Gray, director of operations at Capital Foresight, quoted in McGahon, "Who Killed the Skid Row Neighborhood Council."

10. Ashley Camille Hernandez, Sandra McNeill, and Yasmin Tong, "Increasing Community Power and Health through Community Land Trusts," T.R.U.S.T. South LA, December 2020, https://trustsouthla.org/wp-content /uploads/2021/02/Increasing-Community-Power-Thru-CLTs-REPORT -TCE-BHC-Dec2020.pdf.

11. Zole Matthew, "How Community Land Trusts Could Make Los Angeles More Affordable, *LAist*, February 2021.

12. Lisa Olivia Fitch, "Delay in the Sale of the Baldwin Hills Crenshaw Plaza, *Our Weekly Los Angeles*, February 18, 2021, http://ourweekly.com/news /2021/feb/18/delay-sale-baldwin-hills-crenshaw-plaza/.

13. Robert J. Chaskin and D. M. Greenberg, "Between Public and Private Action: Neighborhood Organizations and Local Governance," *Nonprofit and Voluntary Sector Quarterly* 44, no. 363 (2015), pp. 248–67.

14. Ibid.

15. Jill Gross, "Hybridization and Urban Governance: Malleability, Modality, or Mind-Set?," *Urban Affairs Review* 53, no. 13 (2017), pp. 559–77.

16. Juliet Musso, Christopher Weare, Tom Bryer, and Terry L. Cooper, "Toward 'Strong Democracy' in Global Cities? Social Capital Building, Action Research, and the Los Angeles Neighborhood Council Experience," *Public Administration Review* (January/February 2011), reprinted in *Debating Public Administration: Management Challenges, Choices, and Opportunities*, edited by Robert F. Durant and Jennifer R.S. Durant (New York: Routledge, 2013).

17. Richard Box and Juliet Musso, "Experiments with Local Federalism: Secession and the Neighborhood Council Movement in Los Angeles," *American Review of Public Administration* 34, no. 3 (2004); Erwin Chemerinsky and S. Kleiner, "Federalism from the Neighborhood Up: Los Angeles's Neighborhood Councils, Minority Representation, and Democratic Legitimacy," *Yale Law and Policy Review* 32 (2014), pp. 569–81; and Jun Kyu-Nahm and Juliet Musso, "Participatory Governance and the Spatial Representation of Neighborhood Issues," *Urban Affairs Review* 49 (January, 2013), pp. 71–110.

18. Jeffrey Berry, Kent Portney, and Ken Thomson, *The Rebirth of Urban Democracy* (Brookings Institution, 1993); Archon Fung, *Empowered Participation: Reinventing Urban Democracy* (Princeton University Press, 2009); Musso and others, "Toward Strong Democracy in Global Cities?"

19. Berry, Portney, and Thomson, *The Rebirth of Urban Democracy*.

20. Neighborhood councils are distinguished from homeowners' associations or common interest developments, which are typically smaller-scale legal

associations of homeowners organized for the purposes of self-financing local conveniences such as recreational amenities or funding common space maintenance (see chapter 3 of this volume).

21. Musso and others, "Toward 'Strong Democracy in Global Cities'"; Pradeep Chandra Kathi and Terry L. Cooper, "Democratizing the Administrative State: Connecting Neighborhood Councils and City Agencies," *Public Administrative Review* 65, no. 5 (2005), pp. 559–67.

22. In addition, two departments—the Office of the City Clerk and the Department of Neighborhood Empowerment—provide substantial operating and technical assistance.

23. Robert Chaskin, "Fostering Neighborhood Democracy: Legitimacy and Accountability within Loosely Coupled Systems," *Nonprofit and Voluntary Sector Quarterly* 32, no. 179 (2003), pp. 161–89.

24. Chaskin and Greenberg, "Between Public and Private Action."

25. Berry, Portney, and Thomson, *The Rebirth of Urban Democracy.*

26. Juliet Musso, Christopher Weare, Mark Elliot, Alicia Kitsuse, and Ellen Shiau, "Toward Community Engagement in City Governance: Evaluating Neighborhood Council Reform in Los Angeles," Project Report, Civic Engagement Initiative, University of Southern California. (2007), www .researchgate.net/publication/265032511_Toward_Community_Engagement _In_City_Governance_Evaluating_Neighborhood_Council_Reform_in _Los_Angeles.

27. Ibid.

28. Richard Briffault, "A Government for Our Time? Business Improvement Districts and Urban Governance," *Columbia Law Review* 99, no. 2 (1999), pp. 365–477; Seth Grossman and Marc Holzer, *Partnership Governance in Public Management: A Public Solutions Handbook* (New York: Routledge, 2015); Göktug Morçöl and Ulf Zimmermann, "Metropolitan Governance and Business Improvement Districts," *International Journal of Public Administration* 29, no. 1–3 (2006), pp. 5–29; Göktug Morçöl and D. Gautsch, "Institutionalization of Business Improvement Districts: A Longitudinal Study of the State Laws in the United States," *Public Administration Quarterly* 37, no. 2 (2013), pp. 238–77; and Suzanna Schaller, *Business Improvement Districts and the Contradictions of Placemaking: BID Urbanism in Washington, DC* (University of Georgia Press, 2019).

29. While property owners are responsible for paying the assessment, the costs of the assessment would to some extent be passed on to any tenant businesses. And because, presumably, property owners are renting a basket of services that include real estate as well as area amenities, benefits also would accrue to businesses.

30. Schaller, *Business Improvement Districts and the Contradictions of Placemaking*; James Buchanan, "An Economic Theory of Clubs," *Economica* 32, no. 125 (1965), pp. 1–14.

31. Buchanan, "An Economic Theory of Clubs."

32. Roderick Kiewet and Mathew McCubbins, "State and Local Finance: The New Fiscal Ice Age," *Annual Review of Political Science* 17 (2014), pp. 105–22.

33. Göktug Morçöl and Turgay Karagöz, "Accountability of Business Improvement Districts in Urban Governance Networks: An Investigation of State Enabling Laws, *Urban Affairs Review* 56, no. 3 (2020), pp. 888–918.

34. Carol Becker, "Democratic Accountability and Business Improvement Districts," *Public Performance & Management Review* 36, no. 2 (2012), pp. 187–202.

35. Morçöl and Karagöz, "Accountability of Business Improvement Districts in Urban Governance Networks."

36. City of Los Angeles, Office of the City Clerk, Business Improvement District Division, https://clerk.lacity.org/clerk-services/bids/administrators/policies-and-guidelines/bids-and-lobbying.

37. Selbin and others, "Homeless Exclusion Districts."

38. James DeFillippis, Olivia Williams, Joseph Piece, Deborah Martin, Rich Kruger, and Azadeh Hadizadeh Esfahani, "On the Transformative Potential of Community Land Trusts in the United States," *Antipode* 51, no. 3 (2019), pp. 795–817.

39. Ibid.

40. John Emmeus Davis, "Origins and Evolution of the Community Land Trust in the United States," 2014, https://community-wealth.org/sites/clone.community-wealth.org/files/downloads/report-davis14.pdf.

41. Emily Thaden and Jeffrey S. Lowe, "Resident and Community Engagement in Community Land Trusts," Lincoln Institute of Land Policy Working Paper, 2014, www.lincolninst.edu/publications/working-papers/resident-community-engagement-community-land-trusts.

42. Davis, "Origins and Evolution of the Community Land Trust in the United States."

43. Ibid., p. 46.

44. Ibid.

45. Rick Jacobus and Michael Brown. "City Hall Steps In: Local Governments Embrace Community Land Trusts, *Shelterforce* (2007), pp. 12–15, reprinted in *The Community Land Trust Reader*, Lincoln Institute of Land Policy (2010).

46. Ibid.

47. Julie Curtain and Lance Bocarsly, "CLTs: A Growing Trend in Afford-able Home Ownership," *Journal of Affordable Housing* 17, no. 4 (2008), pp. 367–94; Davis, "Origins and Evolution of the Community Land Trust in The United States."

48. John Emmeus Davis and Rick Jacobus, "The City-CLT Partner-ship: Municipal Support for Community Land Trusts," edited by John Em-meus Davis, Lincoln Institute of Land Policy (2008), www.lincolninst.edu /publications/policy-focus-reports/city-clt-partnership.

FIVE

Who Benefits from Place Governance and Who Is Accountable for Its Oversight? The Case of Business Improvement Districts

JILL SIMONE GROSS

Placed-based investment has long been viewed as a core tool through which municipalities endeavor to retain, attract, and anchor local assets (economic, social, physical, and cultural). In this context, placemaking is the strategic application of such investment, designed to build or capitalize upon the unique socio-spatial characteristics of an area and its population. When placemaking is conducted through channels inclusive of owners, tenants, residents, and other users of these places through processes that generate trust and a shared sense of ownership, then placemaking is more likely to be truly impactful and transformative—with a more equitable distribution of benefits and costs.

As Sheila Foster and Juliet Musso explore in chapters 3 and 4, a wide spectrum of place governance entities and structures comprised of varying actors are involved in an expansive range of placemaking activities, often within overlapping geographies. But who is positively or negatively affected by that work—and who is accountable in the process—depends upon both the institutional structure and makeup of organizations themselves, as well as the choices made by those groups around where, how, and in what efforts they engage.

This chapter focuses specifically on business improvement districts (BIDs) in this context. BIDs are public-private partnerships financed by supplemental taxes paid by BID property and business owners within a defined area and returned to that area (the district) for locally determined services. BIDs have become common, but they are not all alike. BIDs vary in legal form (that is, structure and powers), stakeholder representation (that is, who is included and excluded from the decisionmaking process, and the balance of power among stakeholders), function (that is, the developmental approach taken), and impacts (that is, beneficiaries and victims).

BIDs were first created as special purpose authorities to attract, retain, and manage commercial corridors in cities. They were the urban answer to suburban shopping malls. However, over time, they have taken on a much broader scope of development activities aimed at serving a wider range of goals. Today, one can find BIDs engaged not only in investments in the economic development of a place but also in areas such as transportation planning, housing development, social service provision, and capacity building—with activities ranging from public space management and programming to job training to homeless service provision. They can serve as planners, advocates, and even policymakers.

For the BID, each expansion of function, and each successful outcome, brings with it a new set of challenges. As a BID's portfolio expands or shrinks, and as the owners, renters, shoppers, and residents of an area change, the BID is confronted with the demands of adaptation: Whose interests are served? What agendas are pursued? Who benefits? Who is accountable? Can the BID adapt or will the changes tear it apart?

The reality is that BIDs are hyperlocal institutions built upon shifting sands. While initially created to anchor and attract economic growth, growth itself generates change. Change may induce added competition among local stakeholders or cause displacement when land values increase. And it may generate conflict not only within the BID itself but also between the BID and the surrounding communities who may lack a voice within the BID decisionmaking structure. Though held up as tools of community development—and, by extension, community *building*—a BID can just as easily become an agent of community *breaking*, or even *erasing*.

This chapter explores how and under what circumstances this can occur. If, as Jennifer Vey and Hanna Love at the Brookings Institution assert, transformative placemaking is about remaking "the relationship between place and economy in ways that generate broad-based and locally led prosperity . . . not only in high amenity areas but in those areas that have long been overlooked and undervalued by the public and private sector," the BID model may well build organizations that can fulfill that ambition. However, as the case studies explored here illustrate, aspects of stakeholder representation, decisionmaking, and accountability may need to be rethought to do so.[1]

Business Improvement: Why, What, and in Whose Interest?

BIDs were introduced in North America in the early 1970s when many cities in the northeast were losing white middle-class populations and their tax dollars to the suburbs. Cities were faced with increased service demands, less money, and less support from state and federal governments. BIDs were conceived of as decentralized mechanisms to support the development and maintenance of commercial areas and provide for the upkeep of capital improvements. Policymakers saw

Table 5-1. *General BID Types*

Community BIDs	Main Street BIDs	Corporate BIDs
Operate on small commercial strips that are primarily composed of retail and service-based businesses. With smaller total budgets (assessment revenue less than $300,000), they tend to focus on place keeping and business retention. Small staff, often part-time. Small governing boards.	Operate in medium-size, mixed-use areas, with small and medium retail, commercial, and governmental businesses. With medium-size budgets (assessment revenue $300,000 to $1.5 million), they focus largely on placemaking via marketing and area promotion. Medium-size staffs, mix of full-time and part-time. Medium-size governing boards.	Operate in large retail areas, and include commercial, corporate, and government businesses. Large budgets (assessment revenue from $1.5 to $15 million or more). These BIDs engage in placemaking, marketing, area promotion, and capital improvements. Large staffs, full-time and part-time. Large governing boards.

Note: The data on assessment revenue by BID type was derived from an analysis of BIDs in New York City.

BIDs as a means of harnessing the power of the private sector for public purposes.

While there are many types of place governance institutions, the BID has been promoted by local governments in virtually every state in the United States, such that it has become almost ubiquitous.[2] BIDs range in size from large corporate entities covering geographic areas with substantial commercial and office space to small organizations managing main street districts or community retail strips.[3] Table 5-1 illustrates the broad types of BID by structure and function. There are always exceptions; for example, a main street BID might, in special cases, take on capital improvement projects, and community BIDs might get involved in area promotion. The model, therefore, is an extrapolation derived from the common activities of BIDs of different sizes and scales.

Today, an estimated 1,500 BIDs operate in the United States alone.[4] Consider, for example, that in New York City today there are seventy-six BIDs, serving 93,000 businesses, over an area of 292 linear miles of streetscape, containing almost 45,000 properties, financed through assessments revenues totaling $137.4. million.[5] In Washington, DC, there are currently eleven BIDs, jointly controlling $55 million in assessment revenue.[6] While in the cases of New York City and Washington, DC, BIDs have become tools of urban placemaking, they are not exclusive to the urban core, there or elsewhere. In the case of the Atlanta metro area, for example, there are currently thirty-four BIDs, with the vast majority serving the suburban parts of the region.[7] Atlanta metro area BIDs collectively include properties with an assessed value of $16.9 billion.[8]

BIDs are "self-taxing, self-help, public private partnership organizations," that control, manage, and develop commercial areas. BIDs operate within boundaries defined by local property and business owners, in concert with local governments, and they are formally codified through state enabling laws, local ordinances, charters, and contracts.[9] In combination, these define formation and dissolution processes, membership, how BIDs are governed, voting and decisionmaking procedures, processes for setting up assessment formulas, budgeting, boundaries, and lines of accountability.[10] BIDs are sometimes instigated by municipalities and, in other instances, by a local group of property and business owners.[11] Most will require either that the majority of property and/or business owners within the proposed district boundaries approve formation, or that a majority do not oppose formation. Public hearings are usually a requisite part of the process as well, though once formed no such requirements exist.[12]

Once established, BIDs are financed through assessments on commercial property. Though there is some variation, three broad formulas are used (or some combination of the three). In some localities, assessments are calculated according to property value. In others, spatial elements such as overall square footage or the amount of frontage taken up on the commercial street are the basis. The BID is normally administered either by a nonprofit management association or by a quasi-governmental public authority, with decisions within the BID generally placed in the hands of a board of directors.[13] The voting structures within BIDs vary, but most are governed by a set of property and business owners who pay the assessed fees, with voting weighted to favor property owners according to the amount of property they control. In most BIDs, local government officials (or their representatives) are appointed by the municipality to serve as either ex-officio or voting members of the governing board.

The formal power holders in most BIDs, then, are property owners. This group is perceived to have a greater stake in an area by virtue of their ownership, and are, as those who pay, in principle meant to be the most direct beneficiaries of BID activities. However, this perception fails to recognize the incredible diversity of the wider group of area stakeholders and their own levels of commitment to local place governance. Within BID boundaries, there are landowners, merchant owners who are renting space, nonprofits, religious institutions, street vendors, shoppers, residents, and homeless populations—all of whom may live or work within BID boundaries and are thus often affected by BID decisions. There also are stakeholders who are affected by the BID but may be based in surrounding areas. These groups typically are not formally incorporated as voting members of BID governing boards and, thus, the degree of commitment to them will vary.[14] While there are progressive groups of owners who may well be concerned with the broader public in an area, there is generally no legal mandate requiring it.

There also are diverse needs and interests among the property owners themselves within a district. Some owners are deeply involved in their community. This includes resident owners, some heavily invested in transformative placemaking while others may prefer things as they are. But often, particularly in areas that have experienced extensive disinvestment, owners are absentee and their interests may be narrowly defined in terms of profit potential alone. Meanwhile, some owners simply may not be interested in or able to be actively involved in BID activities at all. Such interests are constantly in flux as growth and decline generate changes in the composition and interests of stakeholders over time.

In the ideal situation, BIDs organize local stakeholders, advocate on their behalf, provide services not offered by the municipality, and endeavor to be tools that support places—culturally, economically, socially, environmentally, and politically. But in reality, BIDs serve many different people and groups across their life cycle. Some BIDs seek to maintain the status quo through preservation of existing interests. Some evolve along with their communities, actively working with stakeholders to address changing local needs. And some pursue growth at all costs, even if this leads to displacement of existing businesses and residents and, with them, the culture and history of the place itself.

The Bid as Builder, Breaker, or Eraser

The Fulton Mall Improvement Association (FMIA) was incorporated in 1976 as a special assessment district (the precursor to BIDs in New York), with the primary goal of helping to bring "the middle-class shopper back to Brooklyn."[15] The FMIA BID was formed by a group of business leaders between 1967 and 1973 to explore ways to respond to economic decline in the area. At the suggestion of the Economic Development Corporation of the City of New York, FMIA was seen as something of a "quid pro quo."[16] The city would agree to allocate funds to "improve" this commercial thoroughfare by widening sidewalks and providing wayfinding signage, street furniture, trees, and lighting. In exchange, it was expected that the property owners and merchants would form a BID, pay a small supplemental tax, and use these funds to maintain area capital improvements through investments in sanitation, security, and marketing.[17]

In the ensuing decade, FMIA saw Fulton Street transition from a white middle-class shopping center to a largely African American, Caribbean, and Puerto Rican commercial and cultural district. The Albee Square mall was built in 1977 in the core of the district and was occupied largely by merchants serving Brooklyn's thriving hip-hop culture.[18] At the time, the BID provided sanitation and security services, engaged in marketing activities in support of local businesses, helped local merchants negotiate affordable rents with the property owners, worked with local street vendors, and helped retain the district's last remaining anchor, a Macy's department store. While FMIA was at this time engaged in processes of community building, it did so in ways many of its original property owners did not anticipate. FMIA investments did not initially lure back the white middle class or the shops they patronized. Instead, it served to solidify the area as a center of commerce for Brooklyn's burgeoning working and middle-class communities of color.

Over time, however, the BID would ultimately struggle to build unity among old and new stakeholders.[19] The small merchant tenants (a minority voice), many of whom were immigrants subletting spaces and independent business owners, sought to hold onto their existing clientele and support the vibrant hip-hop scene. The BID, due to its institutional structure, cleaved more directly to the interests of the property-owning majority on the governing board, who sought to increase land values through the attraction of a more affluent set of businesses and, by extension, shoppers.[20]

In 2004, with the support of the FMIA, developers, real estate interests, and area boosters, the city of New York approved the Downtown Development Plan, which rezoned the entire area to allow for mixed-use high-rise development. The plan was based on the implicit assumption that downtown Brooklyn was an underutilized asset.[21] In the FMIA district, long-term property owners—many of whom were absentee—saw immediate benefits as the value of their properties increased. Small merchant renters, on the other hand, faced eviction as owners sought to capitalize on the development frenzy unleashed by the rezoning. While the BID engaged stakeholders in dialogue, few were empowered to influence the outcomes, and only a narrow set of community interests reaped direct benefits. While the BID may have helped small merchants in the early years to remain, it did little to help them now from being displaced.[22]

The BID had entered a period in which it no longer served as a community builder but had, instead, become a community breaker. The immigrant merchants, independent business owners selling to the hip-hop cultural community, and the working-class communities of color were treated more as placeholders while the regional economy was revived. In fact, what some local residents saw as a thriving community was seen by non-users as a blighted community.[23] It was the latter view that prevailed, a reflection of the power holders in the BID and their views of what constituted successful economic development. In addition, it revealed the less-than-transparent process through which revitalization and management of the area occurred.[24]

The BID, which supported the rezoning efforts, became a part of the process that broke the bonds between the diverse set of community stakeholders present in the district at this time. The corridor entered a period of conflict and division, which then led to what can only be described as a period of community erasing. The Albee Square Mall was demolished in 2004 and replaced by a 1.5 million-square-foot high-rise, mixed-use development that has become home to big box retail stores, restaurants, and the like.[25] While a shiny new center of economic activity has found its way into this dynamic economic hub, it is no longer a center for small independent merchants, immigrant entrepreneurs, or communities of color.[26] Most of these groups have either been erased or their narrative has been appropriated to appeal to the newest arrivals. By 2017, the Real Estate Board of New York reported that this stretch of Fulton Street had become "the most expensive . . . commercial space in Brooklyn."[27]

This vignette illustrates the complex and challenging terrain upon which BIDs operate, and the many roles they can play in communities as *builders*, *breakers*, and, at times, *erasers*. The story reminds us that BIDs face a fundamental challenge as place builders; they are formed to "improve" commercial areas, but what counts as improvement is likely to be interpreted differently by different stakeholders in and around the district area. It also matters a great deal who is invited to the decisionmaking table and who has power over these decisions.

When BIDs take on the role of builder, they are actively engaged in building cohesion among the diverse set of stakeholders in an area. Builders endeavor to work with these groups to build a shared vision of place, and to use BID resources and revenues to serve this vision. When BIDs are taking on the role of builders, they are more likely to adopt public-facing decisionmaking processes that are inclusive. They do this through the use of fair voting processes that incorporate non-owners, and through public hearings, community-visioning processes, and the like. Builders engage in activities in the interests of the broadest stakeholder base, pursuing strategies in which most stakeholders achieve some modicum of gain, while also sharing the losses as broadly as possible as well (that is, win a little lose a little). As an ideal, the builder BID is likely to support transformative forms of hyperlocal placemaking. It may create something new or tinker with existing places through capitalizing on existing assets, but centers the needs and interests of the broadest base of both owners and users of an area.

But BIDs can just as easily serve to represent narrow subsections of an area's stakeholder base. In these instances, the BID may divide the community rather than unify it. Here, the beneficiaries are likely to be a select group—typically the largest property owners, as the BID model is designed specifically to support their interests. The programs they adopt are more likely aimed at advantaging this subsector to the direct (or indirect) disadvantage of other stakeholders. This is what is meant when the BID is referred to as a community breaker. This, in turn, leads to greater competition among stakeholders with divergent interests, with obvious winners and losers in the process. Often, the breaker becomes an agent of displacement in that it may seek to lure and anchor some stakeholders while pushing others out.

Finally, sometimes BIDs play the role of erasers. In this situation, the BID engages in activities designed to completely remove the existing commercial, industrial, or social identity of an area, and those businesses associated with that past. The eraser pursues strategies designed to replace an area's assets, culture, and heritage with something new, removing existing businesses and purging areas of users such as street venders and people experiencing homelessness. They may even seek to replace existing shoppers by building a more lucrative commercial area to entice higher-income visitors. In short, erasers are BIDs that see the existing conditions in an area as something to be eliminated, pushing to rub out the past to create a blank slate on which to build new types of development. Thus, on the continuum of stakeholder representation, the eraser tends to represent the narrowest of stakeholder groups and to adopt decisionmaking processes that are likely to be opaque and heavily weighted toward landowners exclusively.

Three Bid Case Studies in Community Building, Breaking, and Erasing

As the FMIA story tells us, BIDs are likely to take on different roles over time as contexts change, structural forces shift, and populations move. As the fortunes of communities change, so, too, do BIDs. A look at the evolution of three other BIDs—in New York City, Washington, DC, and Atlanta—shows how those changing fortunes build, break, or erase over the course of time. States (and some municipalities) have slight variations in their BID enabling laws, which define their formation, approval, administration, financing, and the general services they provide. These institutional nuances affect BID decisionmaking and representation and, by extension, the dynamic roles BIDs play in communities as builders, breakers, or erasers (see table 5-2).

The Challenges of Balancing Growth and Community Cohesion in an NYC Immigrant Community: The 82nd Street Partnership

The 82nd Street Partnership BID is located in the Queens neighborhood of Jackson Heights, one of the most ethnically diverse communities in New York City. Day-to-day operations are managed by a nonprofit district management organization with an executive director and seven staff members responsible for outreach, events, and cleanliness. The partnership is governed by a board made of twenty-one voting members: ten property owners, four commercial tenants, and four public officials (a council member, the borough president, the New York City comptroller, and the commissioner of small business services). There are an additional three non-voting public officials from the two community boards and one member of the New York City council. The board is weighted in favor of property owners (in keeping with the New York City administrative code, subsection 4), and all but two of these property owners are in real estate and development or finance. There are forty-four properties in the district, 194 commercial spaces, and one small plaza. In 2018, this BID received $254,450 in assessments from BID properties, $60,000 in grant funding, and $9,350 in fees for services. In combination, this generated a total revenue for this BID of $323,800. Some 57 percent of the BID's revenue is spent on administration, and the remainder is applied—in alignment with its stated mission of enhancing quality of life and economic growth—to locally determined services such as marketing, business services, community events, sanitation and maintenance, graffiti removal, street plantings, and community art installations.[28]

Table 5-2. *Who Governs?*

	Formation	Approval	Administration	Financing	General Services
New York[1]	BIDs are initiated by a place-based community of interest. The composition of interests is not mandated. The group could include owners, residents, or a broader base of users. BID formation requires an assessment of community needs be conducted to justify BID formation. The BID collects letters of support. This group also identifies preliminary boundaries, proposes an annual budget, creates the assessment formula, and identifies programs and services to be provided.	The BID plan is then presented to the local community board, the borough board, the department of city planning, the city council, the mayor, and the comptroller for public approval and input. Public hearings are held to gather information and support. The BID can be approved provided 51% of property owners do not oppose its formation.	BIDs are administered by a nonprofit district management association (DMA). Members select a board of directors composed of commercial property owners, business owners, and, occasionally, a residential tenant within the BID boundaries. A majority must be property owners, some commercial tenants, and residents (though there are no requirements for how many. Thus these groups are always the weak partners in the BID board). Four appointed representatives from local and municipal government also are required.	BIDs are financed through a special assessment collected by the city and paid for by property owners. Formulas vary and may be based on square feet, street frontage, assessed value, or some combination. The assessment can be passed on to tenants. BIDs also can charge fees for services and sponsoring events and can receive grants.	BIDs are primarily empowered to provide supplemental services deemed to be for the benefit of the long-term economic health and development of the district. Services might include maintenance, marketing, safety, capital improvements, landscaping, commercial development, or community services.

(continued)

Table 5-2. *Who Governs?* (continued)

	Formation	Approval	Administration	Financing	General Services
Wash-ington, DC[2]	BID formation requires council member support and must be officially registered by the mayor. Here, a more specific distribution of stakeholder support is required for forma-tion: property owners representing 51% of the assessed property value in the area, 25% of the individual taxable properties, and 51% of commercial tenants must sign onto the statement seeking approval for formation.	BID powers are vested in a board of directors, the majority of whom must be owners but also may include residents, commu-nity members, and government officials. Amendment to the bylaws of the BID requires approval by 2/3 of board and ratification by a majority of members present or proxy. Property owners in adjacent areas can become members through payment to the BID.	The BID is administered by a nonprofit and governed by an unpaid board of directors that includes owners (or their agents) and commer-cial tenants. They can also include residents, commu-nity members, and govern-ment officials. The majority must be owners. Each BID establishes its own bylaws regarding elections.	Assessments vary by BID but can include square footage of land in the BID, space occupied in commer-cial buildings, and number of hotel rooms and residential units. BIDs can supplement their assessment through gifts and grants. BIDs can borrow money and issue bonds. The BID can hire people to carry out BID services and functions.	BIDs provide services to promote the economic health of the area as a center of business and community. BIDs operate in the general interest of residents, employers, workers, property owners, commercial tenants, consumers, and the general public.

Atlanta[3]	Each affected jurisdiction must agree to CID/BID formation. Commercial or industrial property owners must gather support from all affected property owners. Certification also is required from tax commissioner. Boundaries are designated by city council.	The BID plan is enacted by municipal resolution; a majority of owners of real property that will be subject to assessment; and owners controlling at least 75% of the value of property in the district.	The BID is administered by an uncompensated governing board: one member appointed by the mayor, two by the president of the city council; the remainder are elected by the property owners, some elected by majority of members (one member one vote), some by equity votes (votes weighted to account for assessed value of property owned). Board members serve four-year terms, staggered.	Funding consists of assessments, fees, and taxes on real property (normally not residential), no more than 2.5% of aggregate assessed value of property. Assessment should be based on services provided. BIDs may incur debt; borrow; execute bonds; and acquire, lease, or dispose of property.	Services include road construction and maintenance; parks and recreational spaces; stormwater, sewers, water, and disposal systems; public transportation; parking; and other services needed in high growth non-residential areas.

[1] See New York City Administrative Code, Chapter 4: City Business Improvement Districts and New York City Department of Small Business Services, "Starting a Business Improvement District: A Step-by-Step Guide," 2003, swww.nyc.gov/html/sbs/downloads/pdf/bid_guide_complete.pdf.

[2] See The Code of the District of Columbia, Chapter 12 Subsection VIII, Business Improvement Districts.

[3] See Atlanta Code of Ordinances, Part 1—Charter and Related Law, Chapter 3 Community Development, Article 2, Community Improvement Districts.

Thus, in terms of scale, this BID would be considered a "community" BID that is on the cusp of becoming a "main street" BID (see table 5-1).

This commercial strip on 82nd Street was developed between 1910 and 1939 to support the surrounding white, middle-class, garden-apartment community, one of the first in the United States.[29] As geography professor Ines Miyares highlights, along 82nd Street, a shopping center was built, "with English Gables designed to give the street a European Village atmosphere."[30] The area, like many in the urban core, experienced significant population loss in the 1960s and 1970s before seeing a rise in Latinx and Asian immigrants. The 82nd Street Partnership was formed in 1983 by local property owners, with the espoused goal of enhancing "quality of life," though in the minds of some this was simply code for erasing the newer, more densely packed small immigrant businesses—mostly tenant-based—that were seeking a foothold in the area. The Partnership was a business association with no designated resource stream and an agenda that leaned toward the preservation of the European village design, with the expectation that new businesses would work within existing design parameters along the commercial strip. The area was incorporated as an improvement district in 1990, providing it with a designated resource stream to advance its mission of "marketing" and "preserving" its historic character.[31] This vision was reinforced in 1993 when, with BID support, the neighborhood was officially designated as a historic district, illustrating the expansion of the BID's role into neighborhood planning processes.

Though the physical contours of the area remained unchanged during this period, the demographic character continued to evolve. By 1998, researchers identified the area as "one of the nation's most ethnically mixed neighborhoods [composed of] White, Latino and Asian, as well as middle- and working-class residents."[32] However, at the time, the BID did little to incorporate the interests of these new populations; the executive director, in place for almost a decade, served as a force for the maintenance of the status quo. For example, the BID ostensibly existed in large part to support the needs of local businesses by providing assistance in navigating the city's permitting systems and otherwise helping them to successfully operate in the area. Yet by 2010, more than half of the businesses around the 82nd Street corridor had violations with the city due to lack of conformance with the landmark status. Violations led to fines, which can be devastating to small businesses operating on shoestring budgets; by failing to work with the large and growing number of small immigrant businesses around these landmarking issues, then, the BID may have been indirectly pushing these businesses out. By narrowly representing the desires of a narrow group of existing property owners—while making few efforts to support this commercial strip as a new immigrant commercial district—the BID essentially became a community breaker. In response, the public sector actors on the BID governing board began to push for a change in administration. The executive director was forced to resign and was replaced with an appointee recommended by the New York City Department of Small Business Services.

The dynamic that subsequently unfolded reveals that accountability in BIDs is not always a straightforward issue. On top of the action, or inaction, of the prior executive director, the engagement of local government officials served to further break down trust between public and private sector partners, as some felt that the public sector had usurped the authority of the BID itself. The new executive director remained for two years, and while he brought important capital improvements to the area's public spaces and helped work with local business to prevent and resolve violations and costly fees, the local property owners continued to view him with suspicion due to the way in which he was brought into the BID.

Not surprisingly, this BID has continued to be at the center of many of the battles over the branding of this area; it remains caught between those who look back to the historic white, European, middle-class population and those who look forward to the new immigrant community—each seeking to shape this unique, evolving place in their preferred image. This case illustrates that efforts to build places can generate unique challenges, especially when the stakeholder base changes. Indeed, while BIDs may be effective tools of economic growth, they are not necessary equally equipped with the skills required to create social capital. Thus, while they are certainly place builders, they are not inherently transformative place builders. There also are few incentives in the property-led BID model to pursue this path when the new immigrant community tends to be renters and, therefore, marginalized voices in the BID's legally designated decision-making structure.

BID funding formulas tend to promote zero-sum thinking because, unless the boundaries can be expanded, replacing older businesses with new, higher-rent businesses is one of the few mechanisms (beyond grant writing, fees for services, and donations) to increase BID revenue streams. But expansion, which typically requires public approval, brings its own challenges. In 2014, the local city councilmember announced plans to extend the geography of the 82nd Street Partnership BID, from a territory on two blocks of 82nd Street to one covering some fourteen blocks along Roosevelt Avenue. This move served to break stakeholder communities even further. The expansion would have increased the number of businesses from 200 to 800, and the number of property lots from forty-four to 440. The effort was rebuffed by many commercial tenants, informal street vendors, some residents, and homeless advocates. Of course, this coalition lacked any real formal power within the BID structure, and thus their ability to influence decisions tended to be through more informal mechanisms of protest. Though supportive of the services the BID would provide, this group of BID users felt the governance structure of the BID was problematic, and that expanding the district would advantage only the owners rather than the other district users.[33]

In reaction to the growing divisions that emerged in response to the proposed boundary changes, the BID began to promote strategies designed to build collaboration through increased representation of voices that had been absent in the past. Thus began a phase in which the BID could be viewed as pursuing an approach more akin to being a builder, through efforts to enhance accountability and responsiveness, and to give voice to a much broader range of stakeholders. In 2015, following the decision by a local civic group (Make the Road New York) to withdraw support for the expansion, the local council member suggested that a new BID board be created. He proposed increasing its size from twenty-one to twenty-five members, that at least eight seats (an increase of four) be designated for commercial and residential tenants of the district, and that one seat each be held for representatives of the street vendors, youth, and the LGBTQ community.[34]

Given that the existing BID governing board was entirely controlled by property owners, this represented a potentially important rethinking of BID governance and an acknowledgement that places are shaped by the users of these spaces as well as the owners. In the end, though, the expansion effort failed, the voting structure on the BID board remained unchanged, and the stakeholders continue to be divided. The BID seems to have reverted back to its role as a breaker, supporting the select interests of property owners over the broader base of stakeholders in the area. The proposed voting structure, while more representative, did not gain broad support, as it was clearly a more tokenistic effort to pacify opposition without providing any real power to the broader range of BID area users. Still, given the legal structure of BIDs in New York, anything more radical would have required a legislative change, as BID law does now allow renters or the broader set of non-owning users of the district to occupy a controlling majority in BID decisionmaking. In the case of New York, it appears that BIDs simply are not designed to be strong agents of transformative placemaking.

Building a Mixed-Use Community while Erasing Another: The Mount Vernon Triangle CID, Washington, DC

The Mount Vernon Triangle Community Improvement District (referred to here as MVT CID or the BID) located in Washington, DC, is somewhat unique by virtue of its effort to earmark itself as a mixed-use business improvement district. Created in 2004 in an area with both commercial and residential property, this BID stretches across some seventeen blocks of downtown DC and includes 4.8 million square feet of real estate. It collects assessments of $861,096, making it a "main street" BID on the path toward becoming a "corporate" BID (see table 5-1). The BID has an eighteen-member governing board that incorporates an interesting mix of members, reflecting not only property owners and commercial interests but also local community leaders. This is an important feature of the BID model in this case—as specified in the DC code—and is one of the only examples in this analysis of a BID structure that mentions an interest in incorporating a broader range of stakeholders (see table 5-2). As such, one would expect that DC BIDs have the formal capacity to be community builders, with an ability to take on a more transformative place-making role. However, even with the inclusion of this language, they, like the other cases discussed here, still demand that property owners hold the majority voice on the governing board. Thus, the rhetoric overstates the reality.

Like most BIDs, the Mount Vernon Triangle organization has focused its efforts on the goal of enhancing the quality of life in the area. But a look at the BID's bylaws illustrates that, from the start, the BID saw its role in a very specific way: to "lessen the economic blight of the area," "promote development," and "combat community deterioration by eliminating the physical and economic causes of such deterioration."[35] Such language opened the door for the BID to take on the role of eraser by promoting activities that would serve to remove those aspects of the area deemed to be the cause of blight. The reasoning for this is clear. This BID is located within the historic Northern Liberty Market area, a center of commerce from 1875 to the mid-1960s, but one that lost much of its residential and economic base in the ensuing decades. Over time, it became a conduit for bringing workers into and out of the district, but not for retaining these groups as owners or users of the commercial area. The area was labeled a "blighted community" by city planners in 1961. Subsequently, federal funds were used to clear the area for the development of a convention center. Renewal led to property speculation and rents skyrocketed. Researchers estimated that some 90 percent of area businesses and organizations were displaced by 2015. Property owners have been the beneficiaries while renters have been the victims.[36]

In comparison with our other case studies, this BID does appear to engage a slightly broader base of non-owning stakeholders, including residential property owners, nonprofit service providers, and religious institutions. However, these groups are a minority on the governing board and thus lack the capacity to truly shape the decisions of the BID in any meaningful way. Though residential property is an important part of the district's makeup (by 2018 there were 4,545 residential units in the MVT CID), there is only one resident sitting on the eighteen-member governing board.[37] The remaining members include property developers and managers, commercial businesses, and several local religious leaders.

The MVT CID is one of the few improvement districts in Washington, DC, to include residential property as a core element of its identity. In 2004, when the BID began operation, the area was in the nascent stages of redevelopment. The BID envisioned itself as a force of "transformative placemaking," converting what it saw as an area of abandonment into a "new" neighborhood, as a community builder. At the time, they described the area as "30 acres of parking lots and fields, bleakly interrupted by an office building, a subsidized high-rise and the gash left where Interstate 395 sliced through."[38] Thus, unlike the FMIA case, which cycled through processes of making, breaking, and then erasing, the MVT BID believed itself to be working within a place that had already been erased by structural forces well before it arrived on the scene.

The BID saw the area as poised for massive change. In 2000, planners estimated that it could accommodate 3,200 new housing units and three million square feet of hotels, offices, and stores.[39] By 2004, developers were pushing for more residential development, with proposals to add 5,000 square feet of housing, two million square feet of office space, 800 hotel rooms, and 200,000 square feet of retail space by 2011.[40] Though the MVT CID speaks of itself through the lens of equity and justice, not all stakeholders would agree. For example, the BID has endeavored to creatively link its past and present through initiatives like the "Real History, Real Life" project in which coasters were created for use by local area bars and restaurants—on one side, a story from the area's history, and on the other, a story of its new developments. According to the District's President:

> Mount Vernon Triangle today reflects not only one of the fastest growing downtown neighborhoods but also its years as one of the original downtown business and residential communities in Washington, DC. As a Mount Vernon Triangle resident, I am both proud and thrilled that we have found such a creative, fun and inclusive way to weave together the rich historical fabric and history of the community to the new and exciting developments to come.[41]

The history is being used to brand the area for new users, while the physical remnants have largely been removed.

Indeed, BID property owners, alongside public partners, viewed the locality as something of a blank slate that could build upon select remnants of its past while envisioning a new future. The district's 2019 annual report notes how MVT "has proven the benefits inherent in . . . changing perceptions of an area once thought to be blighted and unworthy of investment."[42] However, the success of placemaking efforts toward this end can pit old and new against one another, and risks displacement of lower-income residents and businesses due to the inevitable pressures of gentrification. As this or any BID grows, and the stakeholders change, to what degree can they harness these new visions and operationalize them in the physical spaces of the community, given their legal structures and the limitations they pose?

This challenge seems especially significant for BIDs located in areas zoned for mixed use. Here, the MVT CID endeavored to attract an affluent residential base to the area. In this environment, success in luring new residents could disenfranchise those already there; residential demands also may conflict with commercial property interests. As an example, one business in the area, a strip club that long preceded the BID's arrival, spent two years renovating their space only to find that, by the time they opened their doors, the neighborhood had changed. Few of the residential tenants desired this type of business in the locality.[43] This simply illustrates that, for some stakeholders, BID success may well result in the failure of their own business, or even its displacement.

In the case of BIDs in Washington, DC, there exists a critical structural difference shaping governance, which, by extension, impacts beneficiaries and lines of accountability. Because DC is not a state, each BID must go through its own approval process, and the mayor has regularly allowed exceptions to the DC code for BIDs. For example, though formation technically demands that a majority of both property owners and commercial tenants in the area approve, the municipal government has exempted most DC BIDs from this requirement, based on the argument that, as former director of the Adams Morgan Partnership BID put it: "Since tenants may be more short-sighted and focused on the cost to them, if we 'did the right thing' and went for approval we would not get the BID."[44] Thus, tenants' rights have occasionally been obviated by the municipality when they are viewed as obstructing BID actions. As a result, the voices of the owners of real property are empowered while tenants tend to be viewed more as a burden.

In the case of the MVT CID, though both residents and commercial tenants pay assessment fees, they remain weak partners when it comes to governance. The governing board members are elected by "tax paying property owners."[45] Those tenants who are contributing to the owner's assessment fees get one half of one vote for each dollar paid. The owners, by contrast, are allocated one vote per dollar spent on assessment. And there is only one seat for residents on the governing board. As geographer Nathaniel Lewis, who has studied BIDs in Washington, DC, comments: "The fragmented nature of BID oversight has also frequently left the public interest subject to the preferences and relationships of the few private actors who run a BID."[46]

Meanwhile, the BID's efforts to promote residential development has been labeled by some to be an agent of gentrification, serving as an eraser and a breaker at times. According to their 2018 annual report:

Despite comprising just 0.50% of all taxable DC land area, properties in Mount Vernon Triangle in FY 2018 were responsible for 1.0%—or $3.4 billion—of the city's total appraised property value, and 1.4% of city real property tax collected—rising from 0.97% in FY 2009. Real property taxes generated in the MVT CID rose at a compound annual growth rate of 8.3% between FY 2009 and FY 2018. That is more than twice as fast as the D.C.-wide average of 3.9% over the same period."[47]

Thus, though the BID proports to attract housing for low-income residents and seniors, its affordable housing is pegged to the area median income, which rises along with area property values. The result is that, even with the construction of "affordable housing" in the BID area, for the few low-income residents that remained over the long term, the area is becoming increasingly unaffordable. According to one community activist, the MVT CID has raised the median income of the area by 37 percent.[48] Not surprisingly, in the minds of some, the MVT CID appears to move between two roles as eraser and builder.

From Builder to Breaker: The Evermore CID, Gwinnet County, Georgia

The Georgia Community Improvement District model represents a slightly different type of BID, in that it emerged to support suburban commercial property owners—with a specific focus on the planning and maintenance of roads, traffic flows, recreational areas, sewers, transportation, and parking.[49] In this spirit, the Evermore CID was specifically designed to support economic development through investments in transportation, land-use planning and management, and small business supports. While in the other examples, these additional land-use and planning roles came about in a more organic and even ad hoc manner, in Atlanta, these roles were baked into the design.

Atlanta's CIDs were initially promoted in the 1980s by a prominent developer/property owner, a state legislator, and a group of local business owners to benefit owners (property and business) and residents. However, as is true in the other cases, the commercial property owners rule. Political scientists Andrew Ewoh and Ulf Zimmerman found that the executive directors of many of Atlanta's CIDs tended to believe that tenants and residents would be represented indirectly by the public officials serving as appointed members of the CID governing board.[50] In addition, because CIDs were created to construct, manage, and oversee capital improvement projects, they do not serve simply as agents of placemaking via economic development, but they also are acting as planners and project managers overseeing road and transport projects in partnership with Atlanta's county and municipal governments.

The Evermore CID was created in 2003 by a small group of suburban commercial property owners located along a 7.5-mile section of Highway 78. The area is relatively large, and includes some 785 businesses and property owners. With assessment revenue of roughly $950,000, it falls into the "main street" category of BIDs, on the cusp of becoming a "corporate" BID.[51] In addition to its assessment revenue in 2019, the CID received funds from intergovernmental grants and from interest on its revenues. Its revenue totals $1.4 million, which it uses for some traditional BID services such as security and maintenance while primarily supporting transportation and beautification projects.[52]

Evermore CID is administered by a nonprofit and controlled by an eight-member governing board comprising six elected property owners and two appointed officials from the county. This group sets the agenda for the organization's activities and investments in the area. Assessments are drawn from commercial property and business owners. Not only is voting controlled by property owners, but the voting structure also provides greater voice for those who control a larger proportion of the property in the district. Thus, of the six elected board members, three are chosen based on the single vote of each property owner, and three are selected following what they term an "equity-vote," in which the vote is weighted to the amount of assessed value of the respective member. Neither tenants, residents, nor other users of the district have any direct influence over CID operations.

This CID was formed in response to a very specific problem: the planned construction of a highway median by the Department of Transportation to enhance auto traffic flow. Stakeholders feared this would have catastrophic impacts on local business, believing the new median would make it far more difficult for shoppers to access businesses located on each side of the roadway. Thus, this CID formed for the purposes of organizing local businesses, lobbying, and investing in the economic future of the area. In essence, they sought to ensure that they would remain a place for the community to conduct business rather than become a transit corridor where they would be bypassed. They hoped to "turn Highway 78 into a pleasant upscale destination rather than a road to somewhere else."[53] This CID began as a community builder, working to unify its stakeholders in support of ongoing placemaking initiatives designed to build an identity while also protecting their investments in the local economy.

The CID was originally known as the Highway 78 CID, but the governing board realized early on that if they sought to attract more economic activity to the area, they needed to promote a more positive image of the area as a destination rather than as a conduit. In 2007, they changed the name to "Evermore" based on a survey conducted with some 250 residents in and around the area. This survey engaged the users of the area and found that most associated the area with the highway. Further, the survey revealed that this particular stretch of roadway was viewed as a dangerous place that generated road rage due to traffic congestion rather than a nice place to shop and do business.[54] The new name was adopted in an effort to rebrand the area as a destination, and by 2008, the CID was in full swing, working to achieve the stated goals of investing in the area's physical environment with landscaping, capital improvements, and engagement with the transit authority.

While this approach worked well for a while, in 2009, the governing board became divided about the role of the executive director (ED) and who to hire for the position. The result was almost two years of conflict, stagnation, and court battles.[55] Initially, there was something of a power struggle over decisionmaking, with some board members feeling the ED was usurping the board itself as the decisionmaker for the CID.[56] The split was even, leaving the CID deadlocked and preventing it from carrying out many of its duties in the area. Two board members were then recalled, and divisions occurred between original CID members and newcomers. Four members actually shut the board down for three months by boycotting the meetings and preventing a quorum. Things got so bad that the CID chair proposed that the entire governing board resign, and six of the eight did so.[57] Two consecutive executive directors were removed, leading ultimately to the decision to appoint the county district commissioner (a public official elected by residents of the county) as chair and interim leader of the CID. The hope was that this would unify the board and allow the CID to continue operations and service provision.[58]

These events illustrate the profound ways in which a lack of trust and an inability to generate cohesion within a BID's governing board can cause a district to stagnate—shifting its role from a community builder to a community breaker. As one member commented, "I wish they would find a way to work harmoniously rather than maintaining factions against each other."[59] The story shows that property ownership in and of itself does not inherently lead to shared vision, particularly in the face of divergent views regarding leadership and management. Moreover, it highlights the importance of recognizing the human dimension of place governance, suggesting that BIDs may well need to think about the importance of building social capital alongside economic capital. Unable to unify a changing group of stakeholders behind a shared vision, a BID can easily come to a standstill.

Eventually, the Evermore CID reached an agreement, a new executive director was hired, and the CID was back in business. The prior conflicts did not prevent the CID from growing its membership and expanding its portfolio of activities. Still, while the benefits of a BID are primarily increased property values, here the outcomes are less clear. Researchers found that, as highway improvements were made, the result was a rise in the number of vehicles passing through the district each day—which, as of 2015, had not led to the anticipated growth in property values. On the contrary, values came down due to a lack of new commercial development—perhaps, in fact, because the area prioritized auto travel—and the long-term impacts of the recession.[60] However, in other regards, the stakeholders benefited from capital improvements that provide enhanced access to the area from the highway, the creation of networks of communication with transportation authorities and local government, as well as a range of smaller beautification projects.

Conclusions and Takeaways

Over the past several decades, BIDs have become central tools for placemaking. They arrived at a time when governments were contracting due to resource constraints, and became publicly sanctioned, privatized forms of distributive local governance. Local taxes could be spent on locally defined commercial needs with an underlying assumption that these investments would have a trickle-down effect—with broad benefits—on surrounding communities.

However, as each of these cases reveals, the governance structure of BIDs—even after accounting for variations—contains within it a fundamental and potentially problematic feature. In most of these entities, decisionmaking power is weighted toward one group: property owners. Furthermore, the more property an owner controls, the more likely it is that they also will be able to control BID activities to the exclusion of the many other stakeholders that use and occupy commercial districts. Thus, for all the positive impacts they can have and in fact have had on communities, BIDs also have disproportionately served the interests of select stakeholders, abetting processes of gentrification, displacement, fragmentation, and polarization.[61]

As the cases presented here reveal, BIDs are not static. BID governing boards make choices about how to allocate resources, how to capitalize on local assets, and which assets to promote. In some locales, and at some moments, the BID itself works to support and build cohesion and a shared vision among both owners and users of BID spaces. In other cases and times, they work to preserve the area and the select vision of a narrow subset of area stakeholders. At some moments and under some conditions, they will act as agents of transformation and at others, as maintainers of the status quo.

Despite this constant flux, however, three clear patterns have emerged from these case studies that offer insight into how BIDs become builders, breakers, or erasers at different moments in their life cycle.

BIDs are more likely to take on the role of community builder when they are required by law or by conditions (economic decline or crisis) to engage the broadest base of community interests in decisionmaking processes. The structure of governance and participation is an important institutional feature of BIDs that significantly impacts their role in the community.[62] When a BID is dominated by the interests of property owners—as it often is—its agenda is more likely to be premised on growth at any cost, and on removing or excluding voices and activities perceived to prevent this goal. But with the exception of initial formation, which may require a public hearing, rarely are BIDs actually required or otherwise

motivated to be inclusive of a broader agenda set by a broader constituency of stakeholders. Indeed, this was clearly illustrated in the
Atlanta case when the BID began as a builder but later became a
breaker. The reality is that, because people and capital are mobile, the
only way to ensure that both remain at the heart of BID activities is
to require their inclusion in these organizations by law. This could
mean adding and/or reserving seats on the BID governing board
specifically for other users of the BID area and providing tenants with
equitable voting power within BID boards. BIDs also could be legally
required to hold regular community forums to share information
on BID activities and community dialogues to ensure that information flows in both directions. In this way, trust and responsiveness
will be enhanced. BIDs also could be subject to regular public and
community-based review throughout their life cycles to ensure accountability to a broader range of changing BID users over time.

**BID efforts to "build" by meaningfully engaging all parts of its
constituency require skill and capacity.**   Even absent legal requirements to include a broad range of community stakeholders in
governance and decisionmaking, BIDs can choose to give voice to
these groups through informal mechanisms. Using the methods of
participatory policy and planning—from charrettes to focus groups
to community mapping or visioning sessions—can lead to better
understanding of the needs of distinctly different sets of interests.
These community engagement methods also can serve to empower
and educate participants and build the trust needed to effectively
plan and implement initiatives that yield widespread benefits for the
area.[63] That said, not all BID leaders possess the time and resources
needed to organize and engage the community effectively, if at all.
We saw this in the case of the 82nd Street Partnership, in its inability to unify stakeholders around efforts to expand the BID
boundaries, and in the Mount Vernon Triangle, which has struggled
to engage a changing set of stakeholders—old and new, residential
and commercial. BID capacity to promote more inclusive dialogue

requires practitioners trained to use conflict as an impetus to build a more expansive vision rather than becoming hamstrung by it. This would suggest that when BIDs provide space for the expression of different opinions, they may be in a stronger position to understand community needs and be more responsive to them. Similarly, such awareness also can aid a BID in helping community members better understand what is at stake and create shared visions for the future. These processes are critical if the goal is transformative placemaking.[64]

BIDs cannot survive without adapting to the changes in both the economy and in the base of stakeholders within and around the BID area. BIDs are in many ways at the front lines of the growing polarization in our communities today—including rising inequality, increasing segregation, gentrification, and fragmentation of our political, economic, social, and environmental systems. Their ability to navigate change—and, especially, to mitigate its most negative impacts—is challenged by the fact that their very mission is centered upon what are often conflicting goals. Indeed, many of their investments and activities are focused on both maintaining and marketing their areas—supporting existing local business while promoting the area to encourage new development. What each of the cases in this chapter illustrate is that BIDs cycle between these dynamics at different times, variably aligning their decisions and efforts with the needs and preferences of new or existing stakeholders, new or old leadership, and the local economy as it once was or as it is evolving.

The shift between builder, breaker, and eraser often depends upon the ability of the BID to be adaptable and responsive under this constantly changing set of conditions. Organizational theorists Mary Uhl-Bien and Michael Arena suggest that when conflicting ideas are given the space to be aired, they can "create new views of problems and generate new insights for solutions."[65] The 82nd Street Partnership promoted a more inclusive governing board when it was faced with stakeholder conflict around boundary expansion. And though the expansion did not happen, the dialogue and conflict among local stakeholders allowed new ideas to emerge that might be the basis for future institutional adaptations in BID decisionmaking.

BIDs can be important tools for hyperlocal placemaking. What each of these cases has revealed is that while most BIDs were created to generate and manage economic and physical assets, social assets may well be just as important. By engaging in dialogue with a broader base of owners and users, BIDs increase the likelihood that they also can act as agents of transformation. By creating governance structures that incorporate and empower these stakeholders, BIDs increase their capacity to adapt to changing contexts and to be reliable community builders rather than community breakers or erasers.[66]

NOTES

1. Jennifer S. Vey and Hanna Love, "Transformative Placemaking: A Framework to Create Connected, Vibrant, and Inclusive Communities," Brookings Institution, November 19, 2019, www.brookings.edu/research /transformative-placemaking-a-framework-to-create-connected-vibrant-and -inclusive-communities/.

2. Richard Briffault, "A Government for Our Time—Business Improvement Districts and Urban Governance," *Columbia Law Review* (1999), pp. 365–477; Jerry Mitchell, *Business Improvement Districts and the Shape of American* Cities (SUNY Press, 2009); Gökug Morcol and Douglas Gautsch, "Institutionaliza-tion of Business Improvement Districts: A Longitudinal Study of the State Laws in the United States, *Public Administration Quarterly* (Summer 2013), pp. 240–79; and Elisabeth Peyroux, Robert Pütz, and Georg Glasze, "Business Improvement Districts (BIDs): The Internationalization and Contextualization of a 'Travel-ling Concept,'" *European Urban and Regional Studies* (April 2012), pp. 111–20.

3. Edward T. Rogowsky and Jill Simone Gross, "Managing Development in New York City: The Case of Business Improvement Districts," in *Manag-ing Capital Resources for Central City Revitalization*, edited by Fritz Wagner, Tim Joder, and Anthony Mumphrey Jr. (New York: Garland Press, 2000), pp. 81–115; Jill Simone Gross, "Business Improvement Districts in New York City's Low-Income and High-Income Neighborhoods, *Economic Development Quar-terly* (2005), pp. 174–89; and "Business Improvement Districts in New York: The Private Sector in Public Service or the Public Sector Privatized?," *Urban Research & Practice* (2013), pp. 346–64.

4. Robert Stokes and Julia Martinez, "Business Improvement Districts," in *Oxford Bibliographies in Urban Studies* (Oxford University Press, 2020).

5. New York City Small Business Services, "FY20 NYC Business Improvement District Trends Report," 2021, p. 12.

6. Office of the Chief Financial Officer, "2020 IDO Business Improvement Districts Transfer," DC Gov, 2020, https://cfo.dc.gov/sites/default/files/dc/sites/ocfo/publication/attachments/id_bidt_chapter_2020j.pdf.

7. Note that in Georgia there are two BID models in use. Community Improvement Districts operate in suburban areas with a strong focus on transportation, and Business Improvement Districts operate in urban areas with a focus on economic revitalization. I am using the term *BID* generically, though the cases discussed here are derived from the suburban group known as "community improvement districts."

8. Georgia Tech, "Ready for the Smart(er) City: How Community Improvement Districts (CIDs) are Building the Future," February 2021, www.cidreport.com/read-the-full-report.

9. Gross, "Business Improvement Districts," p. 174.

10. Most BIDs in the United States require local government approval of their budgets annually, though a handful leave this decision to the BID governing board (for example, Washington, DC, BIDs).

11. While there have been some efforts to create districts in residential areas, these have yet to take root. See Robert Nelson, Erika Christensen, and Eileen Norcross, "From BIDs to RIDs: Creating Residential Improvement Districts," *Mercatus Policy Series, Policy*, Comment 20 (2008).

12. There are exceptions, for example in New York, when a BID partners with a developer on projects that require a change in zoning for an area—for example, building taller or at a higher density—this will trigger a planning process known as the Uniform Land Use Review Process (ULURP). ULURP legally requires public hearings be held.

13. Göktuğ Morçol and Turgay Karagoz, "Accountability of Business Improvement District in Urban Governance Networks: An Investigation of State Enabling Laws," *Urban Affairs Review* (May 2020), p. 906.

14. Morçol and Karagoz, "Accountability," p. 896.

15. Special Assessment Districts were the first form of BID created in New York. At the time, because there was not yet any state enabling legislation for these entities, each required state approval for its creation. In the early 1980s, the laws changed. BIDs no longer required state approval; instead, the city assumed control over formation, approval, and oversight processes. Quoted in Frank J. Prial, "Mall Stands Alone in Brooklyn 'Renaissance,'" *New York Times*, April 9, 1982, p. B1.

16. Rogowsky and Gross, "Managing Development in New York," p. 95.

17. Quoted in Marcia Chambers, "Federal Government Grants $2.9 Million to Build Fulton Street Mall," *New York Times*, January 20, 1977, p. 41.

18. Rosten Woo, Meredith TenHoor, and Damon Rich. *Street Value: Shopping, Planning, and Politics at Fulton Mall* (Princeton Architectural Press, 2010), p. 191.

19. Vicki Weiner and Randall Mason, *Fulton Street Mall: New Strategies for Preservation and Planning* (New York: Pratt Center for Community Development and Minerva Partners, March 2006).

20. New York City Administrative Code, Title 25 Land Use, Chapter 4: City Business Improvement Districts Subsection 25-414 District Management Association.

21. Mitchel Moss, "Downtown Rising: How Brooklyn Became a Model for Urban Development," in *The Brooklyn Way: Putting Together the Pieces of a 21st Century*, edited by Mitchell Moss Tucker Reed, and Karen Brooks Hopkins (New York: Downtown Brooklyn Partnership, 2016).

22. See *My Brooklyn*, directed by Allison Lirish Dean and Kelly Anderson, New Day Films, 2012.

23. Prial, "Mall Stands Alone."

24. Adding to the lack of transparency, in 2008, FMIA entered into an arrangement with the Downtown Brooklyn Partnership, a local development corporation, to provide agreed upon services. The DBP also oversees the management of two nearby BIDs (MetroTech and the Court-Street Schermerhorn). With this, another layer of bureaucracy is added to decision-making. Together, they continue to erase and replace the grittier history of the area with investments that might attract residents from Brooklyn's luxury high-rise community. The area has continued to thrive, albeit in different ways, and the BID continues to operate on shifting sands.

25. Fulton Street Mall Improvement Association, Annual Report, 2009.

26. Allison Lirish Dean, "Albee Square: When the Mall's No Longer Home," *Gotham Gazette*, July 20, 2007, www.gothamgazette.com/index.php /development/3612-albee-square-when-the-malls-no-longer-home.

27. Quoted in Alexandra Leon, "Fulton Street is the Most Expensive Retail Stretch in Brooklyn, Report Says," DNAInfo, March 31, 2017, www .dnainfo.com/new-york/20170331/downtown-brooklyn/fulton-street-retail -prices-real-estate-board-rebny/.

28. 82nd Street Partnership, 2018 Annual Report, www.82ndstreet.org.

29. New York City Landmarks and Preservation Commission, "Jackson Heights Historic District," October 19, 1993.

30. Ines M. Miyares, "From Exclusionary Covenant to Ethnic Hyperdiversity in Jackson Heights, Queens," *Geographical Review* (October 2004), p. 470.

31. Sam Stein and Tarry Hum, "The Politics of a 'New Deal' for Roosevelt Avenue," in *Immigrant Crossroads Globalization, Incorporation, and Placemaking in Queens*, edited by Tarry Hum and others (Temple University Press, 2021), pp. 299–321.

32. Philip Kasinitz, Mohamad Bazzi, and Randal Doane, "Chapter 8: Jackson Heights," *Cityscape: A Journal of Policy Development and Research* 4 (1998), pp. 161–77.

33. Katie Honan, "Planned Business Improvement District Loses Support of Major Advocacy Group," *DNA Info*, July 25, 2014, www.dnainfo.com/new-york/20140725/jackson-heights/planned-business-improvement-district-loses-support-of-major-advocacy-group/.

34. Ibid.

35. Mount Vernon Triangle Business Improvement District, Bylaws, Article II, Amended and Restated June 21, 2012, www.mountvernontriangle.org/wp-content/uploads/documents/MVT%20CID%20Bylaws.pdf.

36. Dan Kerr, "Downtown Displaced: Gentrifying Mount Vernon Square, 1840–Present," *Street Sense Media*, October 2, 2019, www.streetsensemedia.org/article/downtown-displaced-gentrifying-mount-vernon-square-1840-present/#.YQrO5C2caqQ.

37. Mount Vernon Triangle Community Improvement District, "Fostering Connections Fueling Growth, Fiscal Year 2018 Annual Report," p. 1, www.mountvernontriangle.org/wp-content/uploads/2019/05/FY-2018-MVT-CID-Annual-Report-FINAL-SINGLE.pdf.

38. Debbi Wilgoren, "Barren City Tract Set for Rejuvenation: Efforts Target Mount Vernon Triangle," *Washington Post*, March 28, 2004, p. 2.

39. David Montgomery, "Visions of NoMa Renaissance Concern Area's Artistic Denizens, Who Fear Urban Planners May Paint Them Out of the Picture," *Washington Post*, March 12, 2000.

40. Dana Hedgpeth, "On Edge: Builders Gamble on Next Hot Spot," *Washington Post*, April 5, 2004.

41. Mount Vernon Triangle Community Improvement District, "Real History, Real Life: Mount Vernon Triangle CID Celebrates Past, Present and Future through Coaster Project," *Cision PR Newswire*, June 15, 2016, www.prnewswire.com/news-releases/real-history-real-life-mount-vernon-triangle-cid-celebrates-past-present-and-future-through-coaster-project-300285383.html.

42. Mount Vernon Triangle, "MVT Together: Fiscal Year 2019 Annual Report," p. 12, www.mountvernontriangle.org/wp-content/uploads/2020/08/FY-2019-MVT-CID-Annual-Report_DIGITAL.pdf.

43. Alan Neuhauser, "A D.C. Strip Club Reopens to a Changed Neighborhood—of High-End Condos and Artisanal Toast," *Washington Post*, June 25, 2018.

44. DC Law 13-213, subsection b; Nathaniel M. Lewis, "Grappling with Governance: The Emergence of Business Improvement Districts in a National Capital," *Urban Affairs Review* (August 27, 2010), pp. 180–217.

45. Mount Vernon Triangle, "Five-Year Renewal Business Plan for the Mount Vernon Triangle Community Improvement District," March 2019, https://dslbd.dc.gov.

46. Lewis, "Grappling with Governance," p. 202.

47. Mount Vernon Triangle Community Improvement District, "Fostering Growth," 2018.

48. Empower DC & Current Movement, "Gentrification as Public Policy: BIDs, Displacement and Development in DC" (video), October 29, 2020, www.empowerdc.org/gentrification_as_public_policy.

49. Georgia Constitution, Article IX, Section VII. Community Improvement Districts, law.justia.com/constitution/georgia/conart9.html.

50. Andrew I. Ewoh and Ulf Zimmerman, "Public-Private Collaborations: The Case of Atlanta Metro Community Improvement District Alliance," *Public Performance & Management Review* 33 (March 2010), pp. 395–412.

51. Evermore Community Improvement District, "2019 Annual Report," www.evermorecid.org/documents/2019%20Annual%20Report.pdf.

52. Lindsay Kuhn, Sarah Larson, and Carolyn Bourdeaux, "Georgia's Improvement Districts (CID)," The Center for State and Local Finance, Working Paper 19-08, Georgia State University (April 2019), pp. 1–107.

53. George Chidi, "Businesses Turn to CIDs to Improve Three Areas," *Atlanta Journal-Constitution*, June 21, 2006, p. 3J.

54. Steve Visser, "U.S. 78 Group Hopes New Name Spruces up Area; Evermore: Community Improvement District Leaders Say Change has a More Pleasant Sound and Could Help Boost Property Values along the Highway," *Atlanta Journal-Constitution*, March 19, 2007, p. 1J.

55. Shane Blatt, "Board Taps Two New Members: Evermore CID Looks to Move Forward. Greene, Garner Bring 'New Blood' to Bickering Members in Gwinnett," *Atlanta Journal-Constitution*, January 28, 2011, p. 2B.

56. Shane Blatt, "Gwinnet County: Evermore Recall Valid, Judge Rules," *Atlanta Journal-Constitution*, May 21, 2009, p. 2B.

57. Patrick Fox, "Deadlock Spells End for Director of Evermore CID: After Bitter Infighting, Tie Vote Seals Brooks' Fate," *Atlanta Journal-Constitution*, September 23, 2010, p. 5B.

58. Joel Anderson, "Evermore CID Seeks New Leader," *Atlanta Journal-Constitution*, May 31, 2011, p. 2B.

59. Shane Blatt, "Former Gwinnett Commissioner Takes Interim CID Post: Hill to Do Day-to-Day Duties, Help Evermore Seek New Director," *Atlanta Journal-Constitution*, October 29, 2010, p. 3B.

60. Kuhn, Larson, and Bourdeaux, "Georgia's Improvement," p. 61.

61. There are, as our cases show, exceptions. At certain moments, BIDs have worked with a broader group of stakeholders. And, indeed, in every city, one can find instances of innovative leadership pushing BIDs toward the role of "community building." In New York, some of the smaller community-based BIDs have served in these roles, as has been true in Philadelphia and in other cities as well. And even some of the larger corporate BIDs have invested in homeless services, education, and empowerment programs. However, there is nothing in BID law to ensure that social capital development be required; thus, this is far more likely in a CDC, where community engagement is legally mandated, than in a BID.

62. Archon Fung, "Saving Democracy from Ourselves: Democracy as a Tragedy of the Commons," in *Ideas That Matter: Democracy, Justice, Rights*, edited by Debra Satz and Annabelle Lever (Oxford University Press), pp. 9–35.

63. Rikki John Dean, "Beyond Radicalism and Resignation: The Competing Logics for Public Participation in Policy Decisions," *Policy & Politic 45* (April 2017), pp. 213–30.

64. Vivian Lowndes and Marie Paxton, "Can Agonism be Institutionalised? Can Institutions be Agonised? Prospects for Democratic Design," *British Journal of Politics and International Relations* 20 (July 2018), pp. 693–710.

65. Mary Uhl-Bien and Michael Arena, "Leadership for Organizational Adaptability: A Theoretical Synthesis and Integrative Framework," *Leadership Quarterly* 29 (2018), p. 92.

66. Michael Arena, "Adaptive Space: Shifting from Structural to Social Design," *Management and Business Review* 1 (Winter 2021), p. 86.

SIX

How Should Place Governance Support People Experiencing Homelessness?

ELENA MADISON

JOY MOSES

A mplified by the coronavirus pandemic, homelessness has burst into national and local media with hundreds of headlines. Images of people sleeping in parking lot spaces, in encampments in parks and on city sidewalks have shocked the nation. Yet, addressing this crisis and meeting the needs of our most vulnerable neighbors has been an ever-growing challenge for decades, and is a particularly thorny subject for the organizations tasked with stewarding the public realm. Place governance entities and their partners have long questioned what their responsibilities are—that is, if and how they should support people experiencing homelessness. In the end, many organizational leaders feel that the issue is too big and too multifaceted for any one single entity or approach to solve.

This chapter discusses the relationship between public space management organizations and people who experience homelessness, beginning with the systemic issues that contribute to homelessness and its emergence into the public realm. When examining the responses and acknowledged responsibilities of local governance structures to address this crisis, the questions of power and accountability discussed in this volume come to the forefront. To illustrate the wide range of reactions and strategies, the chapter looks at challenges and best practices that place governance organizations have applied in three public spaces in three very different cities: New York City, San Francisco, and Atlanta.

Understanding Homelessness in America

Homelessness is often seen but rarely understood. It impacts a wide diversity of people, but some groups are far more likely to be standing in lines waiting for shelter than others. It can be found in a broad range of community types but is more likely to be a severe problem in certain areas. Understanding the nature of homelessness is critical to understanding its relationship with public space, a relationship that shifted during the COVID-19 health crisis and economic recession.

Who Is Homeless?

The U.S. Department of Housing and Urban Development (HUD) collects data annually that helps define the homeless population. Nationally, 70 percent are individuals (people not living as part of a family with children).[1] Among this group of individuals, 70 percent are men.[2]

In recent years, the racial and ethnic dynamics of homelessness have been put under the microscope via expansions in data collection and analysis. Existing disparities mirror those in housing, employment, and other sectors. In 2020, 18 of every 10,000 people were homeless. Numbers are elevated among certain groups of color—52 of

10,000 Black people were homeless, as well as 45 of 10,000 American Indians, and 22 of 10,000 Hispanic people.[3]

Older adults can be found in the nation's shelters. In the 2010s, service providers reported continued growth in the size of this subpopulation.[4] In the five-year period from 2012 to 2017, the overall number of people in the nation's shelters decreased, while the sixty-two-and-older subpopulation increased by 60 percent.[5] Although older adults are underrepresented within homelessness, researchers project continued and significant growth in this age group over the next several years. Focusing on major cities, a recent study estimated that the sixty-five-and-older homeless population will more than double by 2030.[6]

Poor health is another defining feature of the unhoused. According to a 2019 California Policy Lab study, 84 percent of unsheltered people and 19 percent of sheltered people reporting at least one physical health condition.[7] Likewise, 78 percent of unsheltered people and 50 percent of sheltered people report a mental health issue.[8]

Those experiencing the greatest challenges are considered chronically homeless. This means they have a physical or mental disability and have experienced long-term or repeated bouts of homelessness. In 2020, only 27 percent of unhoused individuals fit within this definition.[9] These individuals facing the most significant barriers to self-sufficiency often are the most noticeable in public spaces. However, many unhoused people are not categorized as chronic, are first-time homeless (66 percent of individuals in shelter), and often self-resolve, finding their own ways out of literal homelessness.[10] The COVID-19 health crisis and economic recession may very well have impacted one or more of these dynamics, though, at the time of this writing, limited pandemic-era data is available.

Understanding the demographics of homelessness helps spotlight the humanity of unhoused people to prevent individuals from being reduced to a simple label: "homeless person." Instead, they are older adults experiencing medical conditions tied to aging, or people of color who often experience housing discrimination, as just two examples. Demographic information also is useful in identifying ways to meet the needs of people experiencing homelessness in public spaces. For instance, the presence of older adults and people with disabilities should inform decisions about how to structure public seating and restrooms, and the presence of Black people experiencing homelessness could spark discussion about how to make Black people more generally feel safe and welcome in a space.

The COVID-19 crisis increased housing instability and potentially shifted the picture of who is homeless in America, and data limitations may be hindering large-scale and subpopulation-specific interventions in ways that could impact both the unsheltered and the public spaces they may occupy.

Why Are People Homeless?

In various cities and towns in America, people can be found sleeping on sidewalks or roadsides and waiting in lines for basic necessities like shelter and food. These scenes have become so commonplace it is easy to forget they reflect two ongoing and intertwined crises.

THE HOUSING CRISIS   In general, housing in America is unaffordable to low-income people. The evidence, which has existed for decades, is extensive and growing.

Each year, the National Low Income Housing Coalition (NLIHC) calculates "housing wages," or the amount of income renters must earn to comfortably afford housing (spending no more than the recommended 30 percent of one's income on this line item). In 2020, the national housing wage was $23.96 per hour for a two-bedroom and $19.56 per hour for a one-bedroom.[11] Many jurisdictions have housing wages well above these national averages. For example, in San Francisco (the most expensive jurisdiction in the country), a renter must earn $64.21 per hour to be able to afford a two-bedroom apartment. At $7.25 an hour, the federal minimum wage is far below these numbers.

A major driver of high housing costs is a lack of sufficient housing stock for all types of renters. According to HUD, there are only sixty-nine affordable housing units for every 100 extremely low-income renter households.[12] Some areas of the country have even more dire needs than the national average. Advocates estimate that, as of 2021, the nation required nearly 7 million new affordable units to meet the need.[13]

Researchers have worked to document the connections between the affordable housing crisis and homelessness. Zillow's economic research team identified two critical points that define and differentiate regions. When renters in a community spend 22 percent (on average) of their income on rent, homelessness starts to go up.[14] Where renters spend 32 percent or more, homelessness escalates dramatically.

The COVID-19 crisis and recession surely contributed to this already existing storm of challenges. As 2021 rolled in, 29 percent of renter households told the Census Bureau that they had little to no confidence they would be able to pay the next month's rent.[15] Although not everyone who misses a rent payment will become homeless, researchers are predicting that COVID-related unemployment and evictions will increase homelessness, perhaps for multiple years into the future.[16]

THE PUBLIC SERVICES CRISIS The housing shortage is not the only shortage that exists among low-income people. America has a porous safety net and diminished public services systems that have serious implications for homelessness. A thorough analysis of the challenges could fill volumes, but there are a few areas that should be briefly highlighted when trying to understand homelessness in communities across the country.

The Unemployment Insurance (UI) system is broken. It disproportionately excludes certain categories of low-wage workers—those new to the labor force, inconsistently employed, undocumented, or whose incomes are too low to meet income requirements for the program.[17] Benefits are meager, providing only 36 percent of the average weekly earnings of production and nonsupervisory workers.[18] Current recession-related relief is temporarily altering the status quo, but in general, the system provides limited aid to workers who may have been struggling to pay the rent even before they lost employment.

Mental health service delivery is broken. Fifty-seven percent of adults with a mental illness in America are not receiving treatment.[19] Inadequate insurance and cost barriers are factors limiting access to those who seek treatment.[20] Further, those in low-income neighborhoods have less access to mental health treatment than those in higher-income neighborhoods.[21] The implications of these challenges are twofold. People with limited economic resources may not be able to get the help they need when experiencing early or mild symptoms. Conditions that may have responded to treatment could unnecessarily spiral out of control, impacting basic life functioning—including the ability to maintain employment, personal relationships, and housing. Homelessness can be the result. Once homeless, poverty also may be a barrier to getting sufficient mental health care to get back on one's feet.

The criminal justice system is broken. Even after vigorous and lengthy reform efforts, mass incarceration still exists and continues to disproportionately impact people of color. Exiting the system is difficult and loaded with pitfalls that include difficulties finding work and landlords willing to rent to a person with a criminal background. As many as 11 percent become homeless shortly after leaving prison.[22] Discharge planning and reentry programming currently are not keeping up with the need for supports and services.

These are not the only aspects of the social safety net that are frayed or failing, but challenges associated with criminal justice, mental health, and unemployment play some of the most significant roles in homelessness.

Public Spaces and People Experiencing Homelessness

The systemic failures discussed above led over 580,000 people into homelessness in 2020. But what brings people experiencing homelessness into public spaces?

Not Enough Beds

A little under half of individuals experiencing homelessness are unsheltered, spending nearly all their time in public spaces. In fact, the homeless services system typically does not have enough beds for everyone. On the night of the most recent nationwide Point-in-Time Count, the number of unhoused individuals exceeded the number of year-round shelter beds by nearly 202,000.[23]

COVID-19 only complicated service delivery. The CDC recommended social distancing, keeping beds/cots at least six feet apart. Following this guidance often meant fewer beds were available in existing facilities. Relief programs allowed for the use of motel and hotel rooms; but, through surveys of communities conducted by the National Alliance to End Homelessness, indicated that only a small fraction of people experiencing homelessness had access to these rooms. Survey respondents further estimated that 11 to 15 percent of people were unsheltered after they left the motel or hotel.[24]

Given pre-pandemic bed shortages, bed shifts occurring during the pandemic, and the likelihood that homelessness grew during the most recent recession, there is reason to be concerned that unsheltered numbers are rising because people have nowhere else to go.

Shelter Rules

Even when individuals are able to access shelters, many shelters function in ways that lead people into public spaces. For instance, many facilities require residents to leave during the day to allow for proper cleaning and to minimize amounts of required staffing. Even when shelters are open during the day, many do not have attached outdoor spaces. Nevertheless, many individuals want to go outside for the same reasons everyone else does—to move around, get exercise, breathe fresh air, interact with others, and take care of personal needs (for example, getting food, searching for work, participating in services).

Research suggests that some individuals also choose not to stay at a shelter due to burdensome rules, safety concerns, and other factors.

Thus, some people are in public spaces simply because they are avoiding available public services.

Location of Services

Services, including both public benefits and charitable assistance, often are located in central locations such as downtown areas, town squares, parks, and transportation hubs that may not be near shelters or other types of emergency housing. People who need those services will gravitate toward those areas.

The Social and Economic Benefits of Public Spaces for People Experiencing Homelessness

People experiencing homelessness—including those temporarily living in shelters, single-room occupancy units (SROs), emergency housing, and congregate housing—live in a heightened state of mutual dependency, where social relationships and a strong exchange economy are key to survival. Public spaces are where exchanges take place and where social ties are forged. More than perhaps anyone else, people experiencing homelessness rely on the public realm for their basic social, economic, and physical needs.

The daily needs—such as food, information, personal hygiene and health, sociability, and entertainment—that the general public satisfies indoors—in their homes, in restaurants, or places of work—all are found in the public realm for people experiencing homelessness. Food distribution or dumpstering opportunities mostly are found outdoors in public space, be it a parking lot, a back alley, or a sidewalk. Mobile restrooms and showers, sometimes with barbers and hairstyling, also have been made available outdoors. The same applies for income generation through day labor, can collection, panhandling, selling objects on the street, and miniloans. People experiencing homelessness spend much of their time in public space looking to connect with members of their networks, which is important for getting and sharing information and resources. The difficulty of making plans ahead of time, or of communicating without a mobile phone, make waiting in public space for chance encounters with specific individuals a necessity.

Multiple studies have shown that public spaces contribute to the sense of community and well-being we all experience.[25] This sense of community is "a feeling that members have of belonging, a feeling that members matter to one another and to the group, and a shared faith that members' needs will be met through their commitment to be together."[26] They also allow people to enjoy cultural and recreational activities free of charge, removing income barriers and enhancing city and neighborhood social benefits for those who otherwise would be excluded from them. These positive experiences are particularly important to the most vulnerable members of our communities—to the people who may otherwise feel excluded or "undesirable" because of age (often seniors and teens), income, social isolation, access to housing, mental or physical health challenges, and immigration status.[27] For people experiencing homelessness, public spaces offer an opportunity to feel normal and included—to reject stigma and isolation.

John Beard, the creator of the clubhouse model of mental health, goes even further, noting that "beyond any need for food or shelter, people [with mental illness] needed to feel needed. The need to be needed is a basic human experience."[28] The best public spaces thus not only are engaging and enjoyable for all users but also offer people opportunities to contribute through volunteerism, ambassadorship, maintenance, gardening, and so on.

The public realm provides both economic and social supports, partly through "trust agents." Trust agents are individuals who are sympathetic and helpful but are not agents of authority and are thus outside of the power relationships that govern interactions with marginalized groups. Trust agents are different from social workers, police officers, or park ambassadors, and their lack of connection to systems of control is what makes them unique. They could be the coffee shop or fast-food-chain employee who lets people sit inside their store without purchase during the overnight shift, the bodega owner who allows individuals to use their restroom, or the street cart vendor who may offer free coffee or the pastries left over at the end of the day. In addition to providing needed resources, these trusted individuals are a source of information, and sometimes their opinion or approval is valued more than that of a peer or a figure of authority.

The sudden disappearance of the subtle but meaningful support of trust agents during the lockdowns in the early days of the COVID pandemic was felt immediately in many cities and public spaces. While people experiencing homelessness were left with diminished resources, they also suddenly became more exposed and more visible. With many organizations shifting from in-office work to work from home, temporarily or permanently, the pedestrians that busied themselves on city sidewalks evaporated, along with many of the retail and food businesses that catered to them. Those that remained open, like Starbucks and McDonald's, no longer allowed customers to eat inside or use the restrooms, to prevent the spread of the disease. As a result, individuals experiencing homelessness saw increasing difficulty satisfying basic needs such as restroom use and access to drinking water. These challenges were documented in newspaper articles from New York City,[29] San Francisco,[30] and cities across the United States,[31] as well as in a survey conducted of a small number of street homeless individuals in New York City.[32]

Access to resources is precarious for people experiencing homelessness, which makes them susceptible to massive collective shocks and upheavals from events like natural disasters, major economic crashes, wars, terrorist attacks, and pandemics. For example, business closures and reduced pedestrian activity on city streets can impact people's ability to get cash through panhandling, which, in turn, affects access to food and shelter.[33] As Don Mitchell and Nik Heynen observe, "To meet their own needs, homeless and hungry people learn both to live in and reformulate a geography of survival—one that reconfigures their habitat so they may better inhabit the city."[34] Typically, public space is at the heart of this geography of survival; however, the disappearance of basic supports, and the trust agents that provide them, during times of crisis inadvertently changes this geography for people experiencing homelessness.

Evolving Approaches to Homelessness in Place Management

An ever-growing challenge for communities, homelessness has become a major area of concern for the organizations responsible for stewarding public spaces. While COVID-19 may have put the challenge into sharper focus, many place governance organizations have wrestled for years to balance the needs of vulnerable users with the demands for clean, safe, attractive, and actively populated public spaces. Organizations have had to question their own responsibility to unsheltered users as well as their competencies within the provision of needed services. The struggle for many has been both external, as it relates to interacting with these users, and internal, as it relates to their organizational mission, accountability, and purpose. In this context, key questions about who is responsible and who benefits from place governance—discussed in other chapters of this volume—become particularly pertinent.

Traditionally, the core mission of place governance organizations, including business improvement districts and parks conservancies, has been to address safety and maintenance issues within their designated territories and to attract specific types of users, such as students, office workers, or families with children. At their inception, most of these organizations were created as single-purpose entities, and these purposes are sometimes viewed as being incongruent with the needs of people experiencing homelessness.[35] In particular, their target audience may not want to share public spaces with people experiencing homelessness, resulting in a not-in-my-backyard dynamic. This will not only impact who is made to feel welcome in a public square or park, but it could affect where shelters and services are located.

As these organizations continue to grapple with the challenges of homelessness, they are developing a stronger understanding that public space management must be inclusive of the needs of people experiencing homelessness. However, the continuing expansion of this scope is a relatively recent phenomenon, and many place governance organizations find it difficult to address the complex issues associated with homelessness because of their funding and board structures, their general competencies, and the various rules and regulations governing parks and public spaces that are beyond their control. The result often is a mixed—or weak—response both across and within organizations.

Place governance organizations, along with urban professionals working to create new management entities, have long asserted that "clean and safe" is the first step in capable management in an almost Maslowian hierarchy of needs in the public realm. Before any programming, marketing, or capital campaigns could be successful, management entities need to ensure public spaces are attractive and comfortable. With the evolution of place management has come a growing belief that thoughtful physical and social design can accomplish this without visible and intrusive security. Safety and maintenance personnel often are described as "ambassadors" for the public space, whose role is to make people feel "hosted" and "welcomed." Following Jane Jacobs's well-known concept of "eyes on the street," there is, then, an expectation that lively public spaces will become self-policing to a large extent. In other words, the more people feel safe in a space the more users the space attracts, which, in turn, further increases the safety of the space.

The reality, however, is that many place governance organizations do actively police public spaces with their own security in coordination with local law enforcement. Individuals experiencing homelessness and other marginal people often are a major focus of these policing efforts. Place governance organizations are sometimes guided and funded by business interests that are proponents of quick-fix or punitive approaches to the presence of people experiencing homelessness in public space. These approaches have ranged from heavy policing and prosecution to ushering "undesirable" people away from designated areas to using "hostile architecture" that discourages certain people and behaviors to removing amenities from public areas altogether, making them unwelcoming to everyone. In addition, restrictions on behaviors—such as prohibitions on rummaging in trash receptacles, solicitation, using plastic material or tarpaulins on lawns, etc.—often are codified in park rules and regulations and disproportionately target marginalized groups.[36] Such approaches have been ineffective in resolving public space conflicts, detrimental to individuals experiencing homelessness, and oblivious to the spillover effects these actions have on other public spaces and users.[37]

A slightly more progressive approach taken by place governance organizations has been to allow the presence of a certain number of individuals experiencing homelessness in a strategy of "inclusion by dilution." This strategy suggests that in an active, busy public space a limited number of marginalized people can be "absorbed" by the general public and will not disrupt the functioning of the space. In busy, crowded places like New York's Washington Square Park or Bryant Park, one can observe college students and tourists sharing a bench or a table with individuals who may be experiencing homelessness. Intended to create a space for everyone, this approach seeks to reduce the prominence of people experiencing homelessness and socially discourage the behaviors that set them apart.

In all cases, these traditional efforts by place governance organizations have been directed predominantly at resolving visible public space conflicts, not at addressing the root causes of homelessness.[38] Place governance organizations have a sense that they lack the skills necessary to solve the issue, and that it is within the missions and scopes of other agencies to do so. The same could be said about planners, placemakers, designers, and other urban professionals who make recommendations and interact with other experts on a myriad of issues—

including education, economics, health, wellness, aging, ecology, culture and art, events and sports, labor and employment—but shy away when it comes to challenges related to homelessness. This is due in part to the mission and accountability mechanisms of such organizations but also to a perceived lack of competencies.

Today, place governance entities responsible for public spaces where homelessness is a challenge recognize that many of the traditional measures, punitive and otherwise, are expensive in addition to often being ineffective, harmful to individuals experiencing homelessness, and unpopular with the public. Forward-looking public space managers are seeking new strategies that "include regulating uses, managing conflicts between users, and coordinating interventions in the uses of public spaces to be inclusive of all, including people who are unsheltered and have no other feasible options."[39] The aim is not simply to balance the needs of different constituents but to actively contribute to low-barrier solutions that help get people into housing.

For example, many organizations have begun engaging disadvantaged members of the community, including people experiencing homelessness, as volunteers, advisers, and, sometimes, paid consultants or employees. Place governance entities have been building these engagement skills, learning from each other, and sharing best practices. For individuals experiencing homelessness, volunteer and workforce development opportunities in public space, through training and employment programs, have been extremely effective and beneficial. In addition to building confidence, skills, and paths to permanent employment, these opportunities satisfy that fundamental "need to be needed."

New York City has a long history of such programs like the Doe Fund's Ready, Willing and Able program, or the Horticultural Society's GreenTeam.[40] GreenTeam, for example, focuses on underserved communities and delivers workforce development training, horticultural care, and sanitation services through a partnership with the Association of Community Employment Programs for the

Homeless (ACE). Likewise, San Francisco's Street Teams program engages homeless and low-income men and women as volunteers working collaboratively on beautification projects.[41] Team members receive a non-cash stipend to help cover their basic needs while participating in this one-year transitional program into permanent housing and employment. These kinds of workforce development programs have become more widespread in recent years—a response to calls for inclusion and to the growing demand for peer specialists.

The recent social justice and anti-racism movement also has brought a vocal rejection of punitive approaches to homelessness. Communities now are actively working to remove or reduce the role of law enforcement in addressing conflicts in public space related to homelessness and mental illness. As cities search for best practices, many look to the CAHOOTS (Crisis Assistance Helping Out On The Streets) model of 911 alternative in Eugene, Oregon.[42] The initiative, launched in 1989, provides mental health first response for crises involving mental illness, homelessness, and addiction. In New York City, where recent crisis intervention teams of police with specialized training did not perform well, new mental health teams based on the CAHOOTS model, which do not include police, are being piloted.[43] Other cities, such as Los Angeles and San Francisco, are exploring similar initiatives.

In addition, there is growing support and funding for facilities that can help people orient themselves and enter the continuum of care. Respite centers, navigation centers, and low-barrier shelters have been gaining momentum (while also provoking NIMBY-ism). The use of hotels as temporary shelters during the pandemic has brought on debates, but also a recognition of the need for supportive services to accompany temporary housing or shelter.

While promising new models like these for place governance organizations to assist in addressing homelessness at a systemic level have emerged in recent years, they are still in their infancy. The coronavirus pandemic presented major setbacks to these efforts as well as to the more traditional goals of place governance organizations, like bringing people downtown. The following section explores how place governance actors in three American cities are grappling with these evolving challenges.

Supporting People Experiencing Homelessness through Place Governance: Lessons from San Francisco, Atlanta, and New York City

In considering the current practices of place governance organizations looking to address the complicated needs of people experiencing homelessness in public space, we sought to identify some of the new approaches producing the best results. The following discussion is based on multistakeholder, place-specific roundtable conversations in three major cities—San Francisco, New York City, and Atlanta—and is focused on a distinct central public space in each: the Times Square area of Midtown Manhattan, the Civic Center and adjacent public spaces in San Francisco, and Woodruff Park and surrounding areas in downtown Atlanta.

Each of the three places included in this exploration have a long history of attracting and sometimes failing to properly support people experiencing homelessness and other vulnerable users. All three are managed by organizations that have used place-based strategies to address other planning, design, and management challenges, including developing adequate programming, attracting a variety of users, and establishing responsive governance structures.

Participants in each roundtable included representatives of these management organizations, social service organizations working in the area, people with lived experience of homelessness, and municipal representatives from a variety of agencies, including homeless and social services, economic development, and, in some cases, local elected officials.

In this chapter, we provide background on each area before summarizing lessons from across the roundtable engagements.

Civic Center, San Francisco, California

San Francisco's challenges with homelessness are some of the most significant in the nation. The city ranks seventh in overall homeless population size and seventh when homelessness is considered as a share of the general population. Compared to the rest of the country, an unusually large share of this population are unsheltered—64 percent. People are living in encampments or on their own in various parts of the city, particularly downtown.

San Francisco's Civic Center includes three linked public spaces: Civic Center Plaza, UN Plaza, and Fulton Street between the Asian Art Museum and the San Francisco Public Library. A variety of city departments and agencies are actively involved in the Civic Center through services and facilities, including the Asian Arts Museum and the Public Library. The spaces are under the management of the Civic Center Community Benefits District and the adjacent Tenderloin Community Benefits District.

In 2016, the City of San Francisco created the Civic Center Commons Initiative, a strategic multi-partner effort to transform daily experiences in the public spaces of the area and create a unified public commons. The initiative focused on bringing positive and inclusive activities to the spaces while engaging and supporting a variety of stakeholders, including individuals experiencing homelessness and facing other personal struggles in the public space. Many of the stakeholders working on the Civic Center Commons participated in the discussion and shared their experience and impressions over the last three years.

The efforts in the Civic Center have been directed toward creating a safe and meaningful shared experience that integrates all space users, including downtown office workers, visitors, residents, and sheltered and unsheltered people spending time downtown. However, with the COVID-19 pandemic, positive trends toward better integration, stronger engagement, appropriate services, and workforce development were interrupted and even completely disrupted. Furthermore, downtown was largely "hollowed out" because office workers were gone, giving the impression—at the time of this writing—that the Civic Center is vacant, dangerous, and populated only by people experiencing homelessness. In addition, negative behavior trends that had been less visible and often self-policed before the pandemic, such as drug use and selling, have become more overt and potentially widespread, compromising the feeling of safety and belonging for all public space users. The needs of people suffering addiction and mental health problems have become more urgent and more visible, as well.[44]

Woodruff Park, Atlanta, Georgia

Of the cities in which we held roundtables, Atlanta has the fewest people experiencing homelessness, both in total and per capita. It also has the lowest housing wage, potentially making it easier for residents to avoid falling into homelessness and less expensive to rehouse those who do. Unlike San Francisco, the vast majority (71 percent) of people experiencing homelessness in Atlanta are sheltered at night, and prior to the COVID-19 health crisis and economic recession, unsheltered and overall homelessness were dramatically trending downward. From 2010 to 2019, the city cut the number of people without housing by 54 percent.

Public spaces in downtown Atlanta are managed and governed by the Atlanta Downtown Improvement District (ADID), a public-private partnership that strives to create a livable environment. ADID was founded by and shares leadership with Central Atlanta Progress (CAP), a community development organization with a long history of providing leadership, programs, and services to preserve and strengthen the economic vitality of downtown Atlanta. Since 2016, ADID, CAP, and the city of Atlanta have worked together to build and revitalize downtown's signature Woodruff Park. These partners have worked on updating and implementing a programming and management strategy that gives consideration to existing and potential park users, with a renewed emphasis on social wellness and the need for expanded arts and culture offerings. The park's 2020 strategic plan has a strong focus on social impact and inclusion with a strategic goal to make it a safe and equitable space where all users feel included, comfortable, and able to enjoy the space and activities. The park has a history as a downtown place with a dedicated audience of users who spend much of their day in the space. Many of these regulars are experiencing homelessness or struggling with precarious, institutionally regimented housing arrangements that require them to spend most of their day outside. Rather than ignore these users or confront them with hostile tactics and policing, recent placemaking efforts focused on a dual strategy of physical improvements and strengthening park management for social impact.

In 2018, ADID began working with a full-time case manager from a partner social service agency to integrate social service provision into daily park operations. Rather than covering a wide geographic area, this social work focused on a hub where potential clients already congregated to facilitate the multiple trust-building interactions necessary to ensure that people feel comfortable seeking and accepting help.

While this approach was proving successful, the coronavirus pandemic significantly changed the situation in the park. Like in other public spaces, the slow, incremental progress made over years of integrating all public space users while focusing on the needs of the most vulnerable has been set back. The pandemic has exposed homelessness in a very visible way in every space downtown, in part because downtown Atlanta has a concentration of resources, including social service providers, shelters, transportation, and food opportunities. While there is not an officially recorded increase, stakeholders report that people experiencing homelessness or living in temporary housing have become much more visible.[45]

Times Square, New York City, New York

New York City faces significant affordability challenges. The housing wage is well above the national average and, compared to all other jurisdictions in the United States, it has by far the largest number of people experiencing homelessness (nearly 78,000 in 2020). Even before the 2020–2021 recession, overall counts had been on the rise, increasing by 40 percent over the last decade.

Due to legal precedent, all residents of New York City have a right to shelter, and according to city reports, 95 percent of people experiencing homelessness are sheltered at night. However, this still leaves a large number of people with limited places to go during the day.

When it comes to understanding both challenges and solutions related to the inclusion of vulnerable people in public space, no place has been a stronger or more visible icon than Times Square. Known as New York's town square and as the crossroads of the world, in the past, this area has epitomized the failure of cities to address vital social issues and had been an infamous symbol of urban decline. Today, Times Square is an example of transformation and rebirth, but also of the collaborative efforts of many stakeholders to solve problems. The management of Times Square is the responsibility of the Times Square Alliance, a business improvement district created in 1992. The Times Square district covers most of the territory from 40th Street to 53rd Street between 6th and 8th Avenues, as well as Restaurant Row (46th Street between 8th and 9th Avenues), yet the Alliance has a strong impact beyond Midtown Manhattan, including nationally and internationally. The Alliance describes itself as but one player in the transformational efforts of the place, "one with eyes on the street and an understanding of the local community's needs."

Since the BID was established, Times Square has been a place where major public space conflicts have played out, including public debates over safety, free speech, public nudity, hawking, and vehicular traffic. The now famous pedestrian plazas at Times Square were carved out of the busy streets first as a temporary experiment in 2009; since then, the spaces have evolved into a multimillion-dollar public destination that attracts an unparalleled density and diversity of users and businesses.

Times Square's struggles take the challenges faced by other public spaces to the extreme. The successes and failures of this legendary place put well-known problems and debates in American society into the sharpest relief possible, while continuing to draw the attention of the world. With this in mind, the Times Square Alliance has made deliberate efforts to share the lessons it has learned and to stay open to new ideas. The Alliance has focused on a compassionate health-driven approach to people experiencing homelessness, emotional trouble, or addiction in the space, seeking to offer a path to health and recovery rather than displacement or arrest. This approach developed through long-term partnerships with a number of social service providers. These include the city's Assertive Community Treatment (ACT) outreach teams and Breaking Ground, a social service organization offering supportive housing paired with wraparound services to people experiencing street homelessness.[46]

Common Challenges

While each roundtable was steeped in the specific context of its city and public space, participants identified several shared challenges related to addressing the needs of unsheltered people in the public realm.

Lack of a Coordinated Strategy

Place governance entities and social service providers alike are looking for city-wide coordination with municipal policies that acknowledge the current conditions and landscape and allocate sufficient resources to address the new normal.

As it stands, place governance organizations struggle with coordination between their activities, social service organizations, and city agencies. For example, public spaces in downtown Atlanta are governed by different jurisdictions, with state parks, city parks, and business districts each having different rules and approaches to addressing conflicts. The state parks are very restrictive about the uses they allow and are swift to enforce regulations and restrict access. City parks, on the other hand, have limited capacity for hands-on management and thus can offer little support. Various providers of homeless infrastructure, such as shelters and temporary and emergency housing, each have different rules, hours of operation, barriers for access, etc. In the public sector, different pieces of the homeless infrastructure are driven by different agencies at various levels of government, which creates confusion and discord. Meanwhile, outreach to people experiencing homelessness is driven by complaints instead of a place-based strategy for impact. There is a clear continuum of care but no strategy with regard to the public realm.

In New York City, roundtable stakeholders similarly noted that city agencies and nonprofit organizations are unable to maintain sufficiently good communication to allow them to address problems collectively, while the restrictiveness of existing city bureaucratic structures and funding mechanisms inhibit innovation. Meanwhile, in San Francisco, homeless service providers reported ongoing challenges with building relationships and effective collaborations with BIDs and retailers.

In all cases, stakeholders expect specific policies and actions to address homelessness to be designed with all the partners working together, but with the city in a leading role, providing funding, coordination, and strategic support.

Insufficient Funding and Resources

Cities need resources to address homelessness. In both New York and San Francisco in particular, roundtable participants reported that social service workers are burned out and underpaid.

All the roundtable cities have street outreach programs that are hampered by an inability to provide sufficient aid to unhoused people. While workers can make effective contact, they often are unable to connect people to housing (with limited subsidies and permanent supportive housing being available) or jobs (with no appropriate programs that have open slots). Roundtable participants suggested these street outreach programs should be equipped with greater power to actually help people. They also stressed that they should involve people with lived experience as well as trained professionals such as physical and mental healthcare workers.

In San Francisco, nonprofit leaders also found it difficult to identify dedicated funding streams for public space management, including for the Urban Alchemy workforce described later. The status quo makes it difficult to scale up models that engage people with lived experience in efforts to integrate unhoused people and manage public spaces. Moreover, contracting with a municipality can be difficult for nonprofits in San Francisco and other cities. Funds may end abruptly and often are delayed, threatening the jobs of low-income workers, including those people with lived experience.

The Coronavirus Pandemic

During the pandemic, many downtowns saw an increase in the visibility of people experiencing homelessness, although at the time of this writing actual counts are not available to confirm increases. Downtowns are suffering from a significant drop in pedestrian activity because of COVID-19, as well as a sharp decline in office workers on site. All the roundtable participants who represented place governance organizations operating in downtowns were bracing for this major challenge. In Atlanta, for example, downtown organizations expressed concern about the near- and medium-term economic outlook for downtown. They anticipate that bringing office workers back after the pandemic will be a challenge, and that challenge is related to the image of downtown as a safe and dynamic place to be.

The COVID-19 pandemic also caused a real loss of community spaces and of community ties for people experiencing homelessness, forcing them to shelter in place in public space. People lost many of the supports that had been available to them before, such as friendly businesses and community facilities like libraries to use a restroom, get water, relax indoors, or access the internet. Any positive trends toward resolving conflicts in public space while offering supports to the most vulnerable were interrupted and, in some cases, completely undone in a period of just a few months.

Promising Practices

While each roundtable group expressed many common challenges, each one also described unique and innovative practices across a wide range of issues, from inclusive approaches to placemaking to addressing mental health conditions to new kinds of outreach.

Creating Places for People Experiencing Homelessness

Like all other people, those experiencing homelessness should have alternatives other than public space available to them. Most people are in public spaces by choice; they are deliberately seeking fresh air, a meeting spot, or exercise. People experiencing homelessness, by contrast, often have no other choice. For this reason, some advocates and service providers feel that anything that encourages people experiencing homelessness to remain outdoors rather than seek shelter is counter productive and defeatist. Stakeholders noted that some facilities (shelters and COVID-19-related hotel placements) had rules that forced residents outside during the day, but advocacy and collaborative problem solving has led to solutions that allow people to spend some daytime hours in the places they sleep at night.

However, everyone needs outdoor spaces and informal social connections to thrive, especially people in highly condensed forms of housing, like homeless shelters or SRO units. One of the San Francisco providers was working toward making these spaces not only available on site but also beautiful and practical. All people can appreciate comfortable places to sit, beautiful trees and foliage, and places to walk their dogs.

Public spaces also can become a connection point for delivering services such as food, health care, and hygiene facilities, and public space managers can coordinate with public and nonprofit sector entities toward these ends. Roundtable participants in New York City, for example, were particularly interested in opening a drop-in or welcome center in one of Times Square's vacant storefronts or food kiosks. It could be a place to make connections with providers offering such services as mental and physical health care, housing assistance, and employment help. Such a location also could help meet hygiene needs, offering restrooms and places to shower. San Francisco maintains handwashing stations and staffed Pit Stops, which are clean and safe restrooms with running water and hand towels, in various neighborhoods throughout the city. Nonprofit organizations also offer mobile shower facilities in some neighborhoods.

Providing Programming for All Users

The task of engaging people experiencing homelessness through programming and public activities is sometimes perceived as daunting, or even unnecessary, based on the idea that individuals experiencing homelessness "have other needs." However, all the roundtable cities were grappling with the concept of ensuring a sense of community in public spaces that include unhoused people.

The staff at Woodruff Park in Atlanta developed programs with the explicit goal of integrating diverse audiences and fostering interactions. The stakeholders from New York City have experimented with "Friendship Benches," where community members can sit down and discuss their challenges and problems with a friendly neighbor volunteering to lend an ear. In San Francisco, creative partnerships resulted in an installation by the Exploratorium, a local museum that explores the world through science, art, and human perception. "Middle Ground: Considering Ourselves and Others," which opened in the Civic Center in 2019, explores the lives of different types of citizens and their interconnections with one another, including unhoused people.

Some social service providers also were exploring ways to engage community trust agents, described above, in helping connect individuals to services and to provide helpful support and encouragement.

Managing Conflict and Outreach

In San Francisco and Atlanta, place management organizations are experimenting with new ways to manage conflicts that arise in public space, and to connect people experiencing homelessness to services and shelter in the process. Multiple members of San Francisco's round-table praised the work of Urban Alchemy, which "utilizes the trans-formative power of love, passion, respect, and a sense of belonging to reshape the lives of society's most vulnerable members, into society's most valued members."[47] It employs people with various types of lived experience related to homelessness in jobs that help maintain and manage public spaces, including the Civic Center. For instance, they serve as attendants at Pit Stops, remove litter from sidewalks and other public spaces, and maintain the cleanliness of train station elevators. Urban Alchemy workers frequently interact with people experiencing homelessness and have been able to assist with conflicts and distur-bances involving unhoused people in public spaces. Service providers believe these workers' life experiences translate into skills that allow them to understand and manage such events in ways that are better than the approaches of law enforcement and others.

Meanwhile, in Atlanta, place management organizations are test-ing a Social Impact Safety Team (A.S.I.S.T.), a mobile response team that includes social workers, a social service specialist, and safety ad-vocates. ADID created and funded this effort in-house, instead of con-tinuing to rely on contracting with other service providers as they had in the past. ADID also has a partnership with Atlanta's new Gate-way Center, a low-barrier shelter that is the "gateway" to support services and housing opportunities. This partnership allows A.S.I.S.T. to access shelter beds and services during extended hours, guaran-teeing admission. Individuals referred by A.S.I.S.T. can enter the continuum of care without the need for other intermediaries.

Homing in on Severe Mental Health and Addiction Issues

Many cities are grappling with the double and triple morbidities as-sociated with severe mental illness that often lead to homelessness. Only a small percentage of people experiencing homelessness are also experiencing mental illness, but they are one of the most visible groups in public space as well as super-users of services. For this reason, they often need specialized, intentional support to succeed.

Comprehensive solutions for people with mental health and addiction issues were stressed by New York's roundtable participants. For example, the clubhouse model developed by Fountain House is a non-residential, drop-in program that stresses community, peer support, and individual strength building to support successful integration into communities.

Assertive Community Treatment teams also have been employed in New York City neighborhoods, including Times Square. They are mobile, multidisciplinary teams that offer mental health treatment and other services to people with severe mental illness. However, roundtable participants pointed out that the efficacy of these teams, particularly with people experiencing homelessness and mental health crisis, is not always satisfactory. In addition, the municipality is exploring alternatives to law enforcement intervention, such as having mental health professionals respond to 911 calls.

Changing Perceptions through Advocacy

In Atlanta, CAP and ADID are working with local elected officials and others to educate downtown business owners and residents about the challenges of homelessness to reduce stigma and eliminate negative stereotypes. Communication and education are making audiences aware of what is available for people experiencing homelessness and how to get them help by, for example, calling the homelessness response team instead of the police. Community organizations in New York City were, similarly, pursuing advocacy and other strategies to raise awareness.

Atlanta's public space managers are taking this advocacy one step further by explicitly including addressing homelessness as part of their mission. The new strategic plan for Woodruff Park is focused on social impacts and contains a social services and equity plan as a unique element of the overall park strategy. The plan also is seeking to build and sustain the delicate balance of welcoming unhoused people while inviting a variety of other users to enjoy the same space.

Final Thoughts

Ideally, homelessness would be rare, quickly addressed, and leave no one sleeping out in the cold. This requires a "Housing First" approach, which expeditiously moves people into permanent housing, paired with necessary services such as mental health care, employment assistance, and aging in place supports. A Housing First approach demands that affordable housing availability be drastically expanded. Given the prevalence of homelessness among individuals, this must include units that reach that population. Solutions that have disappeared from cities in recent decades must be revived and improved, such as SRO units. And sufficient temporary housing options like shelter must be readily available to ensure everyone has a place to sleep at night. Studies have shown that, when successfully implemented, Housing First works even for those facing substantial challenges—it keeps them housed and improves their participation in services.

Beyond these fundamentals, urban leaders also must center certain overarching principles specifically related to place governance. Addressing the needs of people experiencing homelessness in public space is not only a crisis-response task. Instead, it should be approached as a place-based community-building effort that includes and offers special supports to vulnerable groups.

As place governance organizations develop relationships with social service providers, municipal entities should integrate their efforts into their broader framework of municipal policies and resources. If they succeed, public spaces could become gateways into a robust continuum of care and lasting housing solutions. As yet, however, efforts to address homelessness often lack a citywide strategy that incorporates both social service providers and place managers—as well as the resources and cross-sector coordination—to make that dream a reality.

For now, with homelessness on the rise and conflicts in public space growing, place governance entities must, themselves, look to models like those noted above to ensure that design, programs, and interventions in public space serve the needs and interests of all users. While satisfying everyone's needs is not an easy task, these organizations are uniquely placed to build new partnerships with service providers and municipalities so they can, together, undertake the complex work needed to help lift people out of homelessness.

NOTES

1. U.S. Department of Housing and Urban Development (HUD), *2020 Annual Homeless Assessment Report (AHAR) to Congress: Part 1—Point-in-Time Estimates of Homelessness* (2021).

2. Ibid.

3. National Alliance to End Homelessness, "State of Homelessness: 2021 Edition" (2021).

4. HUD, "Annual Homeless Assessment Report to Congress: Part 2—Estimates of Homelessness in the United States" (2010–2018).

5. HUD, *AHAR Part 2.*

6. Dennis Culhane and others, "The Emerging Crisis of Aged Homelessness: Could Housing Solutions Be Funded by Avoidance of Excess Shelter, Hospital, and Nursing Home Costs?," Actionable Intelligence for Social Policy (2019), www.aisp.upenn.edu/wp-content/uploads/2019/01/Emerging-Crisis-of-Aged-Homelessness-1.pdf.

7. Janey Rountree, Nathan Hess, and Austin Lyke, *Health Conditions among Unsheltered Adults in the U.S.* (California Policy Lab, 2019).

8. Rountree, *Health Conditions among Unsheltered Adults in the U.S.*

9. HUD, *2020 AHAR: Part 1* (2021).

10. HUD, *2018 AHAR: Part 2* (2020).

11. National Low Income Housing Coalition, "Out of Reach: The High Cost of Housing" (2020).

12. U.S. Department of Housing and Urban Development, "Worst Case Housing Needs: 2019 Report to Congress" (2020).

13. National Low Income Housing Coalition, "The Gap: A Shortage of Affordable Homes" (2021).

14. Chris Glynn and Alexander Casey, "Priced Out: Homelessness Rises Faster where Rent Exceeds a Third of Income" (Zillow Research, 2018).

15. U.S. Census Bureau, "Week 22 Household Pulse Survey: January 6–18" (2021).

16. See Daniel Flaming and others, "Locked Out: Unemployment and Homelessness in the Covid Economy" (Economic Roundtable, 2021); Community Solutions, "Analysis on Unemployment Projects 40–45% Increase in Homelessness this Year," *Community Solutions* (blog), May 11, 2020.

17. Annelies Goger, Tracy Loh, and Caroline George, "Unemployment Insurance is Failing Workers During COVID-19. Here's How to Strengthen It" (Brookings, 2020).

18. Goger, Loh, and George, "Unemployment Insurance is Failing Workers During COVID-19."

19. Mental Health America, "The State of Mental Health in America: 2020" (2019).

20. Ibid.

21. Janet Cummings and others, "Geographic Access to Specialty Mental Health Care across High- and Low-Income US Communities," *JAMA Psychiatry* 74 (May 2017), pp. 476–84.

22. Stephen Metraux, Dana Hunt, and Will Yetvin, "Criminal Justice Reentry and Homelessness," Center for Evidence-Based Solutions to Homelessness, 2020.

23. HUD, *2020 AHAR: Part 1.*

24. National Alliance to End Homelessness, "Voices from the Field: COVID-19 and Recession Surveys, Interviews, and Data," 2020–2021, endhomelessness.org/voices.

25. William Davidson and Patrick Cotter, "The Relationship between Sense of Community and Subjective Well-Being: A First Look," *Journal of Community Psychology* 19 (July 1991), pp. 246–53; Emily Talen, "Measuring the Public Realm: A Preliminary Assessment of the Link Between Public Space and Sense of Community," *Journal of Architectural and Planning Research* 17 (Winter 2000), pp. 344–60.

26. David Chavis and others, "Sense of Community through Brunswik's Lens: A First Look," *Journal of Community Psychology* 14 (January 1986), pp. 24–40.

27. Stephen Carr and others, *Public Space* (Cambridge University Press, 1992).

28. Alan Doyle, Julius Lanoil, and Kenneth Dudek, *Fountain House* (Columbia University Press, 2013).

29. Reuven Blau, "No Bathroom Relief in Sight for Thousands Living on the Streets," The City (blog), August 13, 2020, www.thecity.nyc/2020/8/13/21365521/nyc-homeless-bathroom-penn-station-subways-manhattan.

30. Brian Howey, "SF to Add Water Outlets in Neighborhoods with Large Homeless Populations," San Francisco Public Press (blog), January 14, 2021, www.sfpublicpress.org/sf-to-add-water-outlets-in-neighborhoods-with-large -homeless-populations/.

31. Elizabeth Brico, "Lack of Access to Clean Water is Putting Homeless People at Risk Even as Cities Reopen Amid COVID-19," The Appeal (blog), March 29, 2020, https://theappeal.org/lack-of-access-to-clean-water-is -%20putting-homeless-people-at-risk-even-as-cities-%20reopen-amid -covid-19/.

32. Human.nyc, "Homeless in the Summer of COVID-19" (2020), www .human.nyc/summer-survey.

33. Spencer Ross and Sommer Kapitan, "No Spare Change: How Charities, Buskers and Beggars Aren't Feeling so Festive in Our Cashless Society," The Conversation (blog), December 17, 2020, https://theconversation.com/no -spare-change-how-charities-buskers-and-beggars-arent-feeling-so-festive -in-our-cashless-society-151024.

34. Don Mitchell and Nik Heynen, "The Geography of Survival and the Right to the City: Speculations on Surveillance, Legal Innovation, and the Criminalization of Intervention," *Urban Geography* 30 (May 2013), pp. 611–32.

35. Göktug Morçöl and Ulf Zimmermann, "Metropolitan Governance and Business Improvement Districts," *International Journal of Public Administration* 29 (August 2006), pp. 5–29.

36. David Madden, "Revisiting the End of Public Space: Assembling the Public in an Urban Park," *City & Community* 9, no. 2 (June 2010).

37. Arnold Ventures, *Inclusive Public Space Management* (2020), https:// craftmediabucket.s3.amazonaws.com/uploads/AV-homelessness-public-space .pdf.

38. Ibid.

39. Ibid.

40. The Doe Fund, "Ready, Willing, and Able," www.doe.org/programs /ready-willing-able/; The Horticulture Society of New York, www.thehort.org /programs/greenteam/.

41. Downtown Streets Team, www.streetsteam.org/index.

42. White Bird Clinic, "What Is Cahoots?," https://whitebirdclinic.org /what-is-cahoots/.

43. City of New York, "New York City Announces New Mental Health Teams to Respond to Mental Health Crises," November 10, 2020, www1.nyc .gov/office-of-the-mayor/news/773-20/new-york-city-new-mental-health -teams-respond-mental-health-crises.

44. Participants in the roundtable conversation about the Civic Center's place-based efforts and the challenges with addressing the needs of people experiencing homelessness included social service providers from Downtown Streets Team and Urban Alchemy; place managers from the Studio for Public Spaces at the Exploratorium and the City of San Francisco's Office of Economic and Workforce Development; public sector service providers from the city's Healthy Streets Operation Center (HSOC); operators of nearby shelters and navigation centers from Episcopal Community Services; and policy researchers from the Benioff Homelessness and Housing Initiative (BHHI).

45. The discussion about addressing the needs of people experiencing homelessness while integrating all users and resolving conflicts in the Woodruff Park area included the park manager from ADID and the leadership of its new Atlanta Social Impact Safety Team (A.S.I.S.T.); the executive leadership of CAP; shelter operators from Gateway Center; and a downtown elected official.

46. The conversation about the daily struggles to address the needs of vulnerable people in New York's Times Square area included place managers from the Times Square Alliance; social service providers from Fountain House New York; supportive services and housing providers from Jericho Project; and a professor and advocate from the NYU Silver School of Social Work.

47. San Francisco and other cities are engaged in an ongoing debate about the role of community ambassadors in public spaces. For an introduction to the conversation, see www.msn.com/en-us/news/us/breed-poured-millions -into-tenderloin-community-ambassadors-and-police-has-it-helped/ar -AAShilP.

SEVEN

What Can the United States Learn from the Rest of the World about the Stewardship of Place?

NANCY KWAK

Cities around the world today are beset with problems of unequal development and spatial inequality. While the details of American suburban sprawl and urban decline might be unique to this country, the broader struggle over deeply unequal, segregated cities and regions is, unfortunately, one experienced around the world. Whether in the spreading rustbelts across shrinking industrial cities or in the mega-cities and informal communities of the Global South, inequality is played out at the level of neighborhood and street—and it is visible everywhere. Racial conflicts and class divisions are jarringly familiar across cities with very different histories and social contexts; gentrification, eviction, and redevelopment all have become part of a shared vocabulary of cities.

At the root of these struggles over physical spaces and the right to the city are questions of governance that are local yet also global: How should governments, residents, business interests, nonprofit organizations, and others work together in ways that produce more meaningful, just, and prosperous connections between people and places?

Global examples chart some clear lessons for U.S. cities. First, experiences with business improvement districts and neighborhood associations in Johannesburg, Singapore, and Tokyo illustrate the critical balance that needs to be achieved between three of the most important stakeholders: governments, business and property interests, and citizens and residents. As extremes in private-led (Johannesburg), state-led (Singapore), and community-led (Tokyo) place governance, these three cities offer critical insights.

Second, megaprojects can expand their stakeholders to include the voices of a larger "public," especially in the case of projects that directly address conditions of ecological and climate crisis in the city. Seoul's Cheonggyecheon project is one of the most well-known recent megaprojects that focuses on urban ecology and climate change response. The river restoration project also provides a clear example of some of the scales of "local" and "public" engagement necessary in placemaking.

Third, innovative participatory budgeting in Brazil points to the advantages of inclusive, community-oriented financing while also highlighting some of the risks of overly local policymaking; the case is especially interesting and important because it is the first of its kind in the world, and widely studied and weighed.

Finally, Berlin and Rotterdam's experiences transforming "empty" urban spaces into vibrant public spaces offer some key lessons on how cities might interact with local residents and move the city forward together with more ecologically sound, community-engaged places. These two cases also bring forward two very different kinds of vacancy—one in the wake of deindustrialization and massive political change (the fall of the Berlin Wall), and the second in an interstitial, neglected space between two neighborhoods.

Although American policymakers and local government officials typically look for model solutions within the United States, this chapter proposes consideration of innovative approaches from around the world. Comparative study can be instructive, as issues like community governance, spatial inequality, and public-private balance often come into sharper relief when seen in less familiar surroundings. For both inspiration and analytical insight, then, it is useful to widen the view.

Public-Private Balance: Business Improvement Districts and Neighborhood Associations

Public-private partnerships have existed in different forms for many years, but their explosive growth in popularity and application in the 1980s led urban theorist David Harvey to argue that, for advanced capitalist nations, the "managerial" city of the 1960s had given way to the "entrepreneurial city" of the 1970s and 1980s—one where cities focused on economic development and local employment over the provision of services, facilities, and benefits.[1] Various cities adopted business improvement areas or districts, beginning first in 1971 in the Toronto neighborhood of Bloor West Village and followed soon after in 1975 by New Orleans, before picking up momentum across the United States. By the 1990s, BIDs were found in Johannesburg, Pretoria, and Cape Town (there called "city improvement districts") in South Africa. In the twenty-first century, cities in Britain, Germany, New Zealand, Australia, Austria, Belgium, Denmark, France, Japan, Netherlands, Norway, Portugal, Spain, Sweden, and Singapore all followed suit.[2]

For American cities in the 1970s, 1980s, and 1990s, BIDs offered the possibility of private investment in a context of capital flight and decline. BIDs were meant to address problems that had been several decades in the making. After World War II, federal housing policies incentivized upwardly mobile white families to move out of central cities and into white suburbs, forming what HUD secretary George Romney called a "high-income white noose" around the central city. In the increasingly abandoned urban core, a new "inner city" came into existence—a segregated site of disinvestment that was deliberately deprived of the same opportunities that helped white suburbs thrive. Given that the federal government looked generally unwilling or unable to solve the urban crisis, many leaders turned to private investment to restore economic health to the city. BIDs seemed like one such solution, directing private investment to the improvement of urban neighborhoods while arguably distributing costs more fairly among all business interests that might profit from collective improvements. (Several prior chapters in this volume offer a nuanced assessment of U.S. cases.) While cities inside and outside the United States wrestled with their own particular blend of urban crises, the BID model, nonetheless, spread because leaders and business interests found utility in the broader principle of public-private investment and because many outside the United States saw American cities—New York City in particular—as a model for achieving global city status.[3] Looking today from the viewpoint of the United States, these global applications now offer a rich repository of data and experience for American leaders to look at and learn from.

In South African cities like Johannesburg, city improvement districts (CIDs) were deployed in response to racial and class conflicts akin to those found in American cities. As in the United States, wealthy white residents suburbanized to the north and less affluent white families to the west, leaving Black residents in central cities and peripheral townships to struggle with rapidly spreading urban blight.[4] To add to Johannesburg's troubles, decline in mining and manufacturing industries joined with office vacancies starting in the 1970s, and landlord disinvestment in housing maintenance in the 1990s further fueled urban decline in the central city.

In this context, CIDs became a way for businesses to bring a certain kind of security to the fore, linking public safety concerns to investment protection starting in the mid-1990s. While there was some local variation, CIDs across the Johannesburg metropolitan region clearly prioritized spending on private policing and security, as 71 percent of the Central Business District's 2001 CID budget and 54 percent of suburban Sandton's went to security services.[5] Those CIDs that did attend to social issues did so mostly in cosmetic ways, and business leaders stated frankly in interviews that "CIDs are more about controlling and regulating space for economic purposes than solving social problems or promoting social policies."[6]

Given this limited definition of "public" in the public-private partnership, the case of Johannesburg demonstrates the importance of balancing business-led CIDs with robust public sector engagement in urban revitalization programs at the broader scale. CIDs are not fundamentally motivated to take on these larger aims, and they more often negate rather than support anti-apartheid principles like "one city, one tax base" through "top up" services organized for only some parts of the city. Equally troubling, CIDs justify their existence by portraying the public sector as weak or incompetent—images that can become self-fulfilling as they undermine faith in the public sector.

If Johannesburg is an example of the need for stronger, state-managed social policies to balance BIDs, Singapore provides an opposing model, one where the public sector holds most of the power and not only directs BIDs but creates them. In Singapore, BIDs first began as an initiative of the Urban Renewal Authority (URA)—a powerful planning body within the central government. The URA tested place management in Marina Bay and eventually institutionalized this work in a new agency in 2011, the Place Management Department, and in a new forum, the Place Management Coordinating Forum, to encourage more "place-based" initiatives. The names of both groups were telling: These were not placemaking bodies but, rather, place management systems. In 2012, with funding from the URA and "voluntary contributions from stakeholders," the first BID (Singapore River One) brought together stakeholders (business operators and landlords) in Clark Quay, Robertson Quay, and Boat Quay to "harmonize" attractions, increase appeal to local and foreign consumers, and to "resolve problems" like "rowdiness and sleaze."[7] By 2017, the city-state progressed to a pilot BID program where interested groups might apply to the URA to become a BID; if accepted, the BID would receive government funding in the form of a dollar-for-dollar match up to $500,000 (SGD) annually. Funds would be used to "clean up" areas and to provide more character.

Eventually, some BIDs also were permitted to rent out public land to raise funds—a practice that has since become a way to deploy arts and culture for local and international visitors' consumption. This is a common strategy used by governments to provide greater financial security to BIDs. Japanese BIDs, called Area Management Organizations (AMOs), for instance, permit rental of public spaces to stabilize AMOs and reduce direct government subsidy. Like AMOs, then, Singaporean BIDs rent out public roads converted to pedestrian use for events and for retail use. Unlike Japanese AMOs, however, Singaporean BIDs do not incorporate significant input from resident groups and continue to rely heavily on government funding.

Why are BIDs so top-down in Singapore? Part of the reason is that the state has chosen to target neighborhoods typically more commercial in character and that serve tourists and international residents more than the local population. (The majority of the latter live in public housing estates, not in the urban core.) As one report summed up, "Overall, placemaking in Singapore appears to remain a mainly government pursuit."[8] The broader lesson of Singapore is that if governments want to foster more authentic placemaking practices, they must become more comfortable with truly democratic city-making processes. Given that the People's Action Party historically has seized control of all kinds of public space, including the clearance of hawker stands and even the regulation of open void decks in public housing estates, it should come as no surprise that the state also must produce community culture for "public" consumption. Cities in the United States would do well to observe the costs of overregulation. Communities of artists, vibrant political engagement, informal and spontaneous gatherings, and layered diverse use are all important ways that people build a sense of connection with space. And, put bluntly, shared place governance cannot happen if communities have not been allowed to build meaningful connections in the first place.

Both the Johannesburg and Singapore cases demonstrate the problems of imbalance in public-private partnerships and the importance of strengthening the position of resident communities vis-à-vis state and business actors. While most urban neighborhoods and downtowns are multiuse rather than solely commercial or residential, governance structures do not always give equal weight to commercial and residential needs. Is there a more positive example of community-engaged, community-led place governance, then, where resident communities hold some power and where governments and business interests find some measure of balance with them?

One example of greater community and residential participation can be found in the Yanaka neighborhood in central Tokyo. There, citizens have been notably successful at devising an alternate form of community governance that invents and protects local uses of streets, houses, and public spaces. Japanese neighborhood associations (*chonaikai* or *jichikai*) are a helpful example of residential organization, one that is intentionally representative of residential needs over commercial ones. While neighborhood associations are arguably equally imbalanced, they point out the possibilities for other kinds of governance structures that might more meaningfully bring together both commerce and residents. The Japanese example demonstrates that residential groups have as much organizational capability and potential as commercial interests.

Chonaikai or *jichikai* were disbanded briefly during the American occupation period and reemerged informally thereafter, without the sanction of the government. Neighborhood associations gained traction in the 1970s and 1980s as a way for communities to push back against large-scale redevelopment projects. The Yanaka neighborhood association, for one, reemerged in the 1990s to work with a new group of sympathetic faculty and students from Tokyo University to organize and defend small houses, narrow roads, and public spaces from real estate developers. They did so by promoting knowledge of local history and celebrating local residents, artists, and creative use of public spaces.

To be clear, this coalition was not always successful. In two instances of resistance to large-scale condominium development, the neighborhood association succeeded in influencing one developer and failed to affect the other. Nonetheless, this kind of community involvement in placemaking and place governance illustrates both the potential of these engagements as well as the incredible labor and effort required to sustain them. As André Sorensen explains: "The power to create community space emerges from dialogue and building shared understandings, and will be unlikely to long outlive them. This contingency imparts a positive imperative of continuous engagement, but carries with it the threat of exhaustion or burnout of key actors. On the other hand, with this strategy neither ownership nor the state is necessary to transform neighborhood streets into meaningful and vibrant community spaces."[9]

In this way, community-led place governance is at once strong and fragile. How might U.S. cities learn from these experiences and sustain community-engaged place governance, then? Local governments might provide resources to stabilize and institutionalize the ongoing production of local culture. In Yanaka, neighborhood associations celebrated local history, artistry, creativity, and character, and this sort of placemaking played a key role in how residents valued and felt connected to their community. Government actors also might facilitate negotiations with developers, keeping in mind their multiple constituents and remembering that truly vibrant community spaces add real value to streets, houses, and parks.

Megaprojects and Citizen Participation

While BIDs operate at the level of the district and neighborhood, megaprojects can be even larger, more complex multistakeholder affairs. Governments can use large projects to think of placemaking at the scale of the city, pursuing a branding or rebranding of their urban identity through monumental designs: Whether in Marunouchi (Tokyo), La Défense (Paris), or the failed airport project in Mexico City, city officials pursue global ranking and elusive status through such projects.[10]

At the same time, all megaprojects, even at their largest, have to be built at the level of the neighborhood and street—spaces with competing local claims and needs. To succeed, states must successfully incorporate major stakeholders, including business owners and investors either in the path of development or hoping to benefit from new construction, and residents and resident groups who have established communities in the space, often over many years. Citizens can play vital roles in determining how, where, and when a megaproject will be built, as well as in daily decisions over use after completion. The Cheonggyecheon Restoration Project in Seoul, South Korea, offers a particularly rich case study of the possibilities and limits of one megaproject in more equitably and meaningfully incorporating diverse stakeholders in the organization and use of one urban space.

Cheonggyecheon was an important stream running through northern Seoul, and one that had historical importance for the city of Hanyang during the Joseon Dynasty. Under the Japanese empire, however, poor urban dwellers set up shanties along its banks, and after the Korean War (1950–1953), masses of refugees transformed the area into a public health concern as the waterways became severely polluted. In the following decades, public officials viewed the water as a liability and built roadways over the stream from 1955 to 1961. Traffic increased, and in 1976, the construction of a large, elevated expressway transformed the area into a modern commercial and shopping area. Light industry and the production of consumer goods grew apace as the neighborhood became a critical part of South Korean export-oriented industrialization. By the end of the century, however, the region had slumped again as the same expressway showed the effects of decades of poor maintenance and the surrounding communities struggled with traffic, air pollution, and soil and water contamination. In the race for Seoul mayor in 2001, former Hyundai CEO Lee Myung-bak articulated a plan for a dramatic transformation of the region and a large-scale restoration of the original stream—a vision that played a strong role in inspiring voters to put Lee into office.

This part of the story is well-known and brings together crowd-pleasing elements of ecological restoration, green public spaces, community-serving economic redevelopment, and aspirational language about world city status. What is more interesting for the purposes of this chapter, however, is the way the Seoul Metropolitan Government (SMG) negotiated with soon-to-be displaced tenant-merchants and commercial interests while soliciting general public participation and compliance.

Restoration was planned via three organizations. First, the Cheonggyecheon Restoration Project Headquarters included public officials, urban planners, and administrators; second, the Seoul Development Institute brought in city researchers, specialists, and experts; and third, the Cheonggyecheon Restoration Citizen's Committee (CRCC) brought in over a hundred "famous professors, journalists, pastors, and professionals" to manage public opinion and to represent the voices of citizens, including merchants.[11]

Notably, the elite group of community representatives chosen for the CRCC did not initially include everyday residents, union representatives, local tenant-merchants, or others who were likely to derail the project. While landowners would stand to benefit from this public investment in government-owned land, the same could not be said for local tenant-merchants, many of whom rightly feared displacement and who enjoyed no benefit from rising property values. Some of these merchants had worked in the area for multiple generations and adamantly opposed the restoration project on the basis of community as well as personal investment. This was not a small or marginal number of people: By municipal estimates, some 60,000 shops, 220,000 merchants, and over 3,000 street vendors would need to relocate because of the project.[12]

Because of vociferous merchant protests and marches, however, the CRCC had no choice but to acknowledge these stakeholders, and eventually created the aptly named the Public Opinion Subcommittee to serve as a mediator between city officials and merchants. Over 4,000 meetings were held in which merchants negotiated with the SMG to get key concessions, including the creation of a specialty shopping district and shopping complex for those shop owners interested in relocating.[13] SMG refused all cash compensations but did agree to convert part of the Dongdaemun Stadium for street vendors to use as a folk flea market, and to provide free vocational training through a counseling center for street vendors.

These concessions and the mediating structure of the Public Opinion Subcommittee should not be interpreted as a truly collaborative system of governance but as a more traditional negotiation between residents and city government. Inclusion of citizen groups (whether elite professionals, local merchants, or everyday Seoulites) never meant they would be able to stop the project. Instead, public officials, it could be argued, used the CRCC to pressure community members to comply. A 2017 study echoed some of the paternalistic tone in its assessment of the role of citizen groups:

> Most conflicts surrounding urban development projects tend to evolve into a deadlock from mere disagreements between the city government and the stakeholders. This time, by involving citizen groups favourable to the restoration in governance as early as possible, [the Seoul Metropolitan Government [(SMG)] would be largely immune from the common criticism that citizen participation was insufficient. SMG took the high ground, being able to defend its actions with the opposition. With this role, SMG was able to effectively manage conflicts.[14]

The political use of citizen participation showed Lee's awareness of the importance of buy-in from the city and perhaps even the nation as a whole. The project needed to appear inclusive even as it moved inexorably forward. An openly strong-state approach could not have accomplished what Lee wanted, either in terms of suppressing opposition or building public goodwill toward a public space for all urban dwellers. Relatively inclusive governance also was necessary to accrue the personal political benefits of the project. Just as much as citizens needed to play a visible role in planning the space, business interests needed to be invested without directing the process (as was the case with other controversial urban redevelopment projects).

While not an example of participatory planning, the Cheonggyecheon restoration project does raise the important question of which "community" must be served by a megaproject. Clearly, there were winners and losers. Relocated and evicted merchants paid the price. Of the 1,045 merchants who availed themselves of the remotely located Garden Five Mall relocation site (only 10 percent of the total number of merchants), only 100 merchants remained at the mall by 2016 because of weak sales.[15] Meanwhile, property values adjacent to the restoration site skyrocketed in value, stimulating new redevelopment programs that continue to trigger displacement. Profits went to some obvious beneficiaries: Lee would leverage his successes to become president of South Korea in 2008.

The project did improve quality of life for many Seoul residents, and the site is even now being continually remade with active local use. For instance, planners may not have anticipated how important the site would become for Korean diasporic communities who long to see remnants of the old Seoul they left. Moreover, the site is integrated into the urban landscape in a way that makes it accessible and attractive to locals at the scale of the city. Of the 180 million visitors in the first decade of its existence, only 7 million were foreigners, according to the Seoul Metropolitan Facilities Management Corporation. While the SMG continues to promote the space through media coverage and pop-up events, in practical terms the stream provides a pleasant walk from the center of the city to a popular shopping area (Dongdaemun), and it has helped revitalize the northern part of the city.

From a sustainability perspective, the positive results of the project are unambiguous. The 10.84-kilometer-long public space has prompted an 18.4 percent increase in public transportation use over vehicular transit, with a corresponding drop in small-particle air pollution. The stream has increased biodiversity by 639 percent in terms of plant, aquatic, insect, mammalian, and amphibian presence, and it has reduced the urban heat island effect.[16]

These costs and benefits highlight the important question of what it means to govern "locally" in the context of a megaproject. According to one World Bank blogger and visitor of the restoration project, Koreans had devised "local innovations to find a local solution to a specific problem in a local context."[17] Yet, "local" in this instance included all of the urban dwellers who benefited from this amenity without bearing the cost of displacement and economic hardship. For U.S. cities building large-scale public amenities—especially much-needed amenities that improve urban ecology, the heat burden, flooding, water management, or any other aspects of the climate crisis—it may be that "public" and "local" governance must be thought of at different scales.

Put simply, not all publics can win all the time. Even at the micro-scale of a single neighborhood or street, it is hard to imagine policies that perfectly benefit all. Instead, the Cheonggyecheon project demonstrates the potential benefits of a governance structure that allows different stakeholders to regularly share concerns and desires with project leaders, and to pursue a sustained conversation about why decisions are made for bigger publics or for longer-term interests that affect more residents. This sort of governance system brings communication and learning into what otherwise might be conflictual processes, and helps local stakeholders understand—if not necessarily agree with—the decisions that are ultimately made.

Learning happens in both directions. Leaders learn what residents and community members value most, while the latter learn why projects still might be beneficial or necessary despite the costs to themselves. While one can only speculate about what might have been, it could be that a planning process focused more on mutual education may have resulted in greater acceptance even among displaced merchants in Seoul.

Participatory Budgeting

Placemaking projects are important sites of experimentation, and they often change the way citizens think about places as well as their role in shaping them. To build momentum from individual projects, more and more cities are experimenting with participatory budgeting—a practice that institutionalizes collaborative governance and creates opportunities for community-led placemaking. If placemaking is the process by which people make meaning in space, then it makes sense that one of the ways communities build place is by being able to decide what specific physical spaces should look like, what resources should go where, and what public amenities, roads, and sanitation should be installed.

Participatory budgets bring residents directly into government functions instead of relying on an outside structure to bridge the gaps between public officials, residents, and business interests. The local dominates. People living in neighborhoods discuss what they would like their streets to look like, what infrastructure is missing, and what ought to be changed in their shared public spaces. The community with inadequate street maintenance can explain why their needs ought to be attended to before neighboring communities' concerns with a lack of public parks, for instance. This kind of public discussion about the distribution of resources and hierarchy of needs builds a stronger sense of collective local identity as the city decides together which issues ought to be addressed and in what priority or order. In this way, participatory budgets give groups a sense of ownership over specific places and empower them to change that place in ways that are meaningful to them. In other words, participatory budgeting has a placemaking dimension in addition to the more obvious aspects of shared governance and equitable distribution of resources.

Participatory budgeting first began in Porto Alegre, Brazil, in 1988, and it has since been used in cities in countries like Ecuador, Peru, Argentina, Uruguay, Chile, Colombia, France, Spain, Italy, Germany, the UK, Senegal, Cameroon, the Congo, Madagascar, South Korea, China, and India, as well as the United States.[18] In Porto Alegre, the practice began simply. The democratic socialist *Partido dos Trabalhadores* (PT) decided the most effective and efficient way to solve problems of segregation between the wealthy core and the peripheral *vilas* was to transform the process of determining urban policy itself. Instead of reproducing inequality through a clientelist state, the PT dismantled the system of patronage-based neighborhood associations and corrupt backroom deals.[19] In their place, the PT put together sixteen clusters of neighborhoods into "budget regions" that then determined infrastructural needs and priorities through open assemblies. Once each budget region had settled on its priorities, they would elect two representatives to a municipal budget council that would then determine which departments would implement which tasks and with how much money. The city assembly would draw up the budget law and approve each year's proposed spending plan.

Porto Alegre's participatory budget had a powerful impact on urban infrastructure and placemaking, improving basic urban services like clean water, sanitation, and roads in poorer neighborhoods and involving residents in critical decisions about housing, education, and sports, while also giving hitherto atomized neighborhoods a glimpse of the larger regional community. The participatory budget worked remarkably well at addressing local needs and creating more buy-in to democratic institutions. It also improved accountability to local actors and generally drove more resources to indigent and neglected communities.

There were costs and missteps, too. Because participatory budgeting as a process emphasized the needs at the local scale, large-scale and long-term projects with regional priorities got less political attention and support. A neighborhood was more likely to raise the problem of a broken local sewer system than the question of sustainable

regional water planning, for instance. Shifts in national and state
government funding systems brought serious fiscal challenges, too.
With less revenue in city coffers, it became much more difficult to
actually implement the plans agreed upon through this process. At the
same time, political leadership changed, with strong advocates for participatory budgeting leaving and the incoming mayor proposing a
policy of *Governança Solidária Local*, which argued that the government could not single-handedly address the needs of indigent communities, and that it required a "network of co-responsibility" with
communities and the private sector.[20]

The new model made critical changes in the mechanism of governance: Neighborhoods would no longer gather in assemblies to determine the priorities for their budget region. Instead, neighborhoods
competed with each other to secure as many resources as possible for
their community. Federal programs to prepare the city for the World
Cup in 2010 highlighted the role of businesses and invested in infrastructure that prioritized vehicular access over public transportation,
and that resulted in the relocation of poor families from center to
periphery. Worst of all, the rate of completed participatory budget
projects dropped from 82 percent completion from 1994 to 2004, to
42 percent from 2005 to 2016—an indication that the success of participatory budgeting depended entirely on a sustained commitment
to shared governance by all levels of government.[21]

Despite these weaknesses in the Porto Alegre experiment, other
cities still found—and continue to find—the participatory budgeting
model compelling because of the way it brings underrepresented
voices to the table and directs public investments to underserved
neighborhoods. At the same time, the case of Porto Alegre offers
some lessons learned. For one, it highlights the critical and irreplace-
able role of sustained government commitment to shared governance. Second, participatory budgeting can slip into competition
between communities and can sacrifice larger goals of sustainability
and city-making if safeguards are not put into place. Third, successful placemaking can result in the displacement of the politically

weakest residents. American anti-eviction activists understand this last danger all too well.

Digital tools may address at least some of these shortcomings in the future. As seen in Lisbon, Portugal; New South Wales, Australia; Pune, India; and various cities in Brazil and Germany, an online system of proposal submission has the potential to greatly expand participation in the United States as well. Hamburg and Belo Horizonte use digital mapping and budgeting programs to educate the public, and online discussions, chats, and texted policy updates have been shown to facilitate public engagement in cities like Malaga, Spain, and South Kivu in the Congo. In Belo Horizonte, e-voting is expanding the number of participants across a fairly large and dispersed urban population.[22] U.S. cities like New York have likewise adopted digital voting to ensure a more truly democratic participation, and other U.S. cities, counties, and school districts continue to develop local adaptations.

Placemaking in "Empty" Spaces

All the examples thus far have focused on deliberate actions to make or remake space. This section turns to those spaces that are "empty," whether because they are unplanned by public officials, unnoticed or unwanted by business interests, or because they are interstitial spaces between neighborhoods and unseen until recently by residents and government alike. Examples, from Berlin, Germany, and Rotterdam, the Netherlands, demonstrate that unplanned places can already be or can become rich sites of meaning and community—of placemaking.

The Gleisdreieck area in Berlin is a site that for many years seemed to have no use or meaning to the average passerby. The railyard area was ostensibly the responsibility of the *Deutsch Reichsbahn* (West German Railways), but its proximity to the east meant that passenger and freight train service was halted after 1945 and the site left mostly

unused. Gleisdreieck, like other politically in-between spaces of the
Cold War, became an urban wasteland. Native and nonnative trees
and vegetation, animals, and insects grew at their own pace, and biodiversity proliferated.[23] The land became a source of quiet for the few
individuals who used the park, and part of the appeal was its medita-
tive rather than recreational nature. Painter Tom Drake Bennett spoke
of the isolation in choosing the space for his walks: "One could have
gone to Viktoria Park, but that was often too crowded. Gleisdreieck
was much quieter, apart from the prostitutes and the drug addicts . . .
The wasteland was a 'void' in the city of Berlin. It was beautiful,
because it was quiet . . . It was kind of no-go area, with no real en-
trance. Gleisdreieck was a secret among certain people."[24]

By the time debates erupted over the possible erection of an expressway in the 1970s, the site had bloomed into a rich hybrid of wilderness and human use. Planned development triggered immediate
controversy between ecologists, conservationists, urban planners,
landscape planners, public officials, and residents in neighboring
Kreuzberg and Schöneberg (two areas with little in the way of green
space or planned parks). When the Berlin Wall fell in 1989 and opened
up more green space for the first time to West Berliners, residents had
to decide what they wanted to do about this and other "wilderness"
sites scattered across the city.

Because different publics imagined what at first appeared to be conflicting futures for this space, the planning process was necessarily
complex. Open community planning began with walking tours, planning workshops, and 1,600 surveys sent to neighbors living within a
twenty-minute walk from the site—all organized and run by the city.
In the competitive design process, thirty-two working groups included
stakeholders like the three directly affected district governments,
the railway company, and the developers who would finance most
of the construction. City government and citizens worked closely together on a users' advisory board, including some activists who had
fought against the "car-friendly city" for nearly half a century by the
time the park's redesign was complete. During a "planning week-

end," nearby residents attended forums and looked at design exhibits, meeting competing design firms and jury members.[25]

Eventually, a *Konzept der vier Naturen*, or Four Natures Approach, emerged, with a more fully developed appreciation for non-landscaped, nonagriculture land—an ethos that "wild urban nature in urban wasteland is fundamentally valuable and noteworthy."[26] This desire to preserve place—albeit one created by nature as much as humans—drove a new interest in preserving the "openness and ambivalence" of urban wastelands.[27] At the same time, demands for community gardens from community organizations like AG Gleisdreieck also found a home in the new park, creating a space that was split into two parts, east and west. The Ostpark kept its untamed environment and the western side catered more to planned entertainment and sports; the former preserved walkable open space in a moment of intense housing pressure while the latter provided desirable recreational space. The park also included new ideas for children's education (the Experiencing Nature pilot project.)

In the end, the park is appealing to so many Berliners because the city engaged a diverse array of community stakeholders, leading to a far better design. Biodiversity, community gardening, parkland preservation, multigenerational use, and historical knowledge all could have fallen by the wayside without this sort of considered approach—and the city would have been poorer for it. Again, artist Tom Drake Bennett's comments about the space help explain the enduring meaning of the site for at least some Berliners:

> I think people like the park because of its connections to the past. The objects are very important: the railway tracks, the bumpers and so on, they form its character, its identity. You can connect to its history. . . . In the course of time . . . the railway bumpers and signals will disappear due to the weather, changing the character of the park. The connection to history will no longer be so clear. Today we still have these magnificent relics from the past, beautiful sculptures and objects, and these

lead us into the past. In Germany and Berlin we have a special relationship to history: The deportation of Jews, the trains which for example departed from Anhalter Station and transported them over this area, represent a tragic chapter of our past.[28]

The second example of remaking "empty" space also comes from Europe—this time from Rotterdam. Rotterdam is faced with a climate change problem that is familiar to the many American cities living in spaces protected by levees, which currently includes over one-third of American urban communities of 50,000+ people. Rotterdam is vulnerable to flooding because of sea-level rise and increasingly unpredictable rainfall. All evidence points to the need for multilevel coordinated planning at the municipal, regional/provincial, and national levels if the city is to be better prepared to cope with the cataclysmic effects of natural disasters. For Rotterdam, the tangle of provincial and national actions is made even more complex by the fact that the Rhine and Meuse rivers are managed to some degree by international commissions.

Because the highest levels of government and international planning are engaged in problems of climate change, the first important step in a new vision of water-sensitive urban planning came during the 2nd International Architecture Biennale Rotterdam under the 2005 theme, The Flood. The envisioning project—the Rotterdam Water City 2035—proposed a combined solution to the "water challenge" and the "urban challenge," separating clean and wastewater and storing seasonal rainfall while also addressing upper-class suburban flight and inner-city decline. Water policy could revive the attractiveness of the central areas for suburbanites, the project suggested.

In 2007, the Rotterdam Climate Initiative continued this line of thinking by bringing together local city government with the Rotterdam port authority, a regional environmental protection agency, and private business interests through an organization called Deltalinqs. The Climate Initiative provided a space for all stakeholders to share ideas for future action, one of which ended up being a public roof park (*Roofpark Vierhavenstrip*). One year later, the city added a Rotterdam Climate Proof program with the goal of protecting the city against flooding and the heat island effect by 2025—all while also improving daily life, particularly in the inner city, city harbours, and "deprived neighborhoods."[29] Institutionally, these efforts came together under what became known as the Sustainability and Climate Adaptation Offices—administrative offices that coordinated work between city departments and regional and national government groups, including water boards, business interests, residents, community organizations, and researchers both in the Netherlands and abroad.

While the Rotterdam and Berlin projects share an interest in building public spaces that address ecological needs, it is fair to say Rotterdam took a much more top-down approach to planning. Government officials led this work, seeking input without building a truly participatory system with all stakeholders. The result was a more predictable design outcome, exemplifying the kind of multipurpose infrastructure the Climate Initiative envisioned. Situated between Agniesebuurt and the center of the city, planners saw the *waterplein* transforming what was essentially a vacant space between various tall buildings—a square in name only—to a vibrant community resource and a lure to bring suburbanites back to the city as residents and visitors. The catchment would save rainwater in three pools during the winter, and in the summer, it would dry out to become a recreational sports facility with bleacher seating and a skating park.[30] The cost was not small at 4.5 million euros, and the process of shared governance resulted in some confusion over who would maintain the site—the city or the water boards.[31] While the Dutch planning process officially engaged the communities surrounding the *waterplein* using standard representative leadership groups and, indirectly, by following the *Stadsvisie* (City Vision), *Omgevingsvisie* (Environmental Vision), and Vision for Public Space (all three of which involved Rotterdam residents' input), most of the design of this space occurred through official planning bodies.[32] Public needs and public interest were invoked, but officials spent less time on placemaking as a planning process.

As American cities scramble to copy the example of New York's High Line to alchemically transform urban wastelands into world city status, there are at least two critical lessons embedded in these international cases for American cities. First, the Gleisdreieck case demonstrates that peripheral, less regulated, or "wild" spaces have assets that might not be immediately visible to outsiders.[33] Community-led placemaking can be seen as a way to preserve the value of these "wild" spaces and to build on their strengths; local knowledge can prevent needless waste and the destruction of valuable local assets. Berlin's specific community engagement strategies also were thoughtfully executed and might be equally useful in other places, whether it be the process of surveying, offering walking tours, or otherwise offering multiple points of conversation and mutual engagement by developers, planners, designers, residents, and community organizations. Second, promising technical innovations like Rotterdam's *waterplein* can be more widely applied beyond interstitial or marginal land only if joined with a more inclusive planning process. As one reporter noted about the potential applicability of overseas models like the *waterplein* to Texas cities: "Many of these solutions make sense when given tabula rasa to build from scratch, but they would be difficult to implement within the existing city fabric without a serious land acquisition program."[34]

Participatory placemaking, in other words, needs to be as much a part of the planning process as the outcome. This insight is traveling around the world as sites like the *Parisian Petite Ceinture* are now treated by the municipal planning agency, *Atelier Parisien d'Urbanisme*, as an invaluable source of biodiversity and belonging for groups marginalized in the formal city.[35] Informal urban greenspaces have meaning to local communities as potential places of recreation, including children's play, air purification, food production and agriculture, biodiversity, nature conservation, calm, and beauty, and as an alternative to restrictive parks and formal space. Researchers have found that, for residents in places like Sapporo and Brisbane, informal urban greenspaces are an everyday part of life and are valued for their proximity and relatively unmonitored and unregulated usability and as sources of aesthetic pleasure.[36] Only in the small minority of sites perceived as unclean or littered did residents reject informal urban greenspaces, and even then, simple adjustments—the removal of physical barriers like fences cordoning off lots, the provision to residents of maps of local spaces, the most rudimentary of maintenance such as litter removal—all transformed marginal spaces into usable, meaningful ones.[37] One study of green urban wasteland in Polish cities assembled a "wasteland toolkit" that suggested planners and public officials take account of users and stakeholders of "empty spaces" by interviewing and mapping, and that open design and tactical urbanism be considered as ways to retain spontaneity.[38] All these ideas make good sense and have possible application in U.S. cities.

Conclusion

Global examples are instructive for American cities experiencing similar challenges but also opportunities for development and place-making that yield widespread social and economic benefits. No ideal model is ever complete, and even failed attempts at equitable place governance have important lessons embedded in them. Within the experiences of Johannesburg, Singapore, Tokyo, Seoul, Puerto Alegre, Berlin, and Rotterdam, practitioners and policymakers will find practical tactics that might be adapted to suit American community organizations, city governments, and business and landowners.

Besides expanding the practical toolkit, these cases also offer different ways to think about place governance more broadly. To review: First, cities, businesses, and community organizations need to pursue balance with each other in setting up a planning and governing process. Dominant local business leadership in urban rehabilitation programs can exacerbate problems of social inequality in the long run (Johannesburg), but the opposite extreme—heavy state-managed placemaking—can lead to consumer-oriented uses of public spaces devoid of real connections to communities (Singapore). Furthermore, community organizations can shape urban planning and determine the future of their physical neighborhood, but devoted residents and steady access to resources are necessary to sustain these efforts (Japan). Second, the Seoul megaproject shows the importance of considering stakeholders at multiple scales, including the local, the national, and even international levels. When it comes to making large-scale urban places that have meaning for all residents and that address climate change, it is important to think carefully about who the "public" is. Third, the case of Porto Alegre demonstrates the power and potential of participatory budgeting to bring a wider array of participants and stakeholders into the governance process. At the same time, the Brazilian city shows the importance of maintaining large-scale and long-term planning and governance alongside hyperlocal participation. Fourth, and finally, the Berlin and Rotterdam experiences building green places in "empty" or "edge" spaces demonstrates that informal uses are just as important as formal ones. Spaces can be remade to be greener, but they can be remade even better when local stakeholders are consulted and taken seriously.

With Black Lives Matter and the coronavirus pandemic opening up more frank conversations about racial and spatial inequality in the United States, and with communities, businesses, and governments actively seeking more inclusive practices of place governance, American leaders do not need to rely only upon themselves for answers. Climate change will bring cities together in new ways in the next decades, and the United States has much to gain in continuing to look around the globe for creative, if imperfect, models and instructive examples.

NOTES

1. David Harvey, "From Managerialism to Entrepreneurialism: The Transformation in Urban Governance in Late Capitalism," *Geografiska Annaler Series B, Human Geography* 71, no. 1 (1989), pp. 3–17.

2. Lorlene Hoyt, *The Business Improvement District: An Internationally Diffused Approach for Revitalization* (Washington, DC: International Downtown Association, 2004), pp. 1–65.

3. S. Didier, E. Peyroux, and M. Morange, "The Spreading of the City Improvement District Model in Johannesburg and Cape Town: Urban Regeneration and the Neoliberal Agenda in South Africa," *International Journal of Urban and Regional Research* 36, no. 5 (2012), pp. 915–35.

4. Karina Landman and Willem Badenhorst, "Gated Communities and Spatial Transformation in Greater Johannesburg," in *Changing Space, Changing City: Johannesburg after Apartheid—Open Access Selection*, edited by Philip Harrison, Gotz Graeme, Todes Alison, and Wray Chris (Wits University Press, 2014), pp. 215–29.

5. Elizabeth Peyroux, "City Improvement Districts in Johannesburg: An Examination of the Local Variations of the BID Model," in *Business Improvement Districts*, edited by R. Pütz (Verlag, 2008), p. 148.

6. Didier, Peyroux, and Morange, "The Spreading of the City Improvement District Model," p. 930.

7. Ken Lee and Alison Lee, *Place Management in Japan and Singapore: Benefits, Opportunities and Challenges* (Singapore: Centre for Livable Cities Publications, 2020), p. 7.

8. Yulia Pak, "Creative Placemaking: A Policy and a Practice of Urban Regeneration in Singapore: Negotiating Power Relations and Forging Partnerships in Civic Society," Asia Research Institute Working Paper Series 268, September 2018, p. 16.

9. André Sorensen, "Neighborhood Streets as Meaningful Spaces: Claiming Rights to Shared Spaces in Tokyo," *City & Society* 21 (2009), p. 224.

10. N. C. Hanakata and A. Gasco, "The *Grand Projet* Politics of an Urban Age: Urban Megaprojects in Asia and Europe," *Palgrave Communications* 4, no. 86 (2018); Ananya Roy and Aihwa Ong, editors, *Worlding Cities: Asian Experiments and the Art of Being Global* (Chichester, West Sussex: Wiley-Blackwell, 2011).

11. T. J. Lah, "The Dilemma of Cheonggyecheon Restoration in Seoul," 2012, p. 4, http://prospernet.ias.unu.edu/wp-content/uploads/2012/09/SPC-learning-case-2_final.pdf.

12. Chehyun Ryu and Youngsang Kwon, "How Do Mega Projects Alter the City to Be More Sustainable? Spatial Changes Following the Seoul Cheonggyecheon Restoration Project in South Korea," *Sustainability* 8, no. 11 (2016), p. 1178.

13. Chang Yi and Yoon-Joo Jung, *Role of Governance in Urban Transformation of Seoul: Best Practices* (The Seoul Institute, 2017).

14. Ibid.

15. Ryu and Kwon, "How Do Mega Projects Alter the City," p. 1177.

16. Alexander Robinson and Myvonwynn Hopton, *Cheonggyecheon Stream Restoration Project* (Landscape Architecture Foundation, 2011).

17. Sujoyini Mandal, "Seoul Goes Local in Development," *Sustainable Cities*, World Bank blog, 2013, https://blogs.worldbank.org/sustainablecities/seoul -goes-local-development.

18. Y. Sintomer, C. Herzberg, G. Allegretti, and A. Röcke, "Learning from the South: Participatory Budgeting Worldwide," 2010, www.buergerhaushalt .org/sites/default/files/downloads/LearningfromtheSouth-ParticipatoryBud getingWorldwide-Study_0.pdf.

19. Rebecca Abers, "From Clientelism to Cooperation: Local Government, Participatory Policy, and Civic Organizing in Porto Alegre, Brazil," *Politics and Society* 26, no. 4 (1998), pp. 511–38.

20. Rebecca Abers, Robin King, Daniely Votto, and Igor Brandão, "Porto Alegre: Participatory Budgeting and the Challenge of Sustaining Transformative Change," World Resources Institute, 2018.

21. Ibid.

22. Carsten Herzberg, Yves Sintomer, and Giovanni Allegretti, *Learning from the South: Participatory Budgeting Worldwide—An Invitation to Global Cooperation*, Engagement Global/*Servicestelle Kommunen in der Einen Welt*, 2013, pp. 12–13.

23. Noël van Dooren, "*Park am Gleisdreieck*, a Dialectical Narrative," *Journal of Landscape Architecture* 14, no. 1 (2019), pp. 30–43.

24. Andra Lichtenstein and Flavia Alice Mameli, editors, *Gleisdreieck/ Parklife Berlin* (Germany: transcript, 2015), p. 55.

25. Katherine Burgess, "Community Participation in Parks Development: Two Examples from Berlin," *Smart Cities Dive*, 2014, www.smartcitiesdive.com /ex/sustainablecitiescollective/community-participation parksdevelopment two-examples-berlin/1027166/.

26. Ingo Kowarik, "Gleisdreieck: How Urban Wilderness Became Possible in the New Park," in *Gleisdreieck/Parklife Berlin*, edited by A. Lichtenstein and F. A. Mameli (Transcript-Verlag, 2015), p. 220.

27. Ibid.

28. Lichtenstein and Mameli, *Gleisdreieck/Parklife Berlin*, p. 55.

29. Katharina Hölscher, "Capacities for Transformative Climate Governance: A Conceptual Framework," in *Transformative Climate Governance: A Capacities Perspective to Systematise, Evaluate and Guide Climate Action*, edited by Katharina Hölscher and N. Frantzeskaki (London: Palgrave Macmillan: 2020), pp. 49–96.

30. David Bravo, "'Water Square' in Benthemplein," *Centre de Cultura Contemporania de Barcelona*, June 12, 2020, www.publicspace.org/works/-/project /h034-water-square-in-benthemplein.

31. Rutger van der Brugge and Rutger de Graaf, "Linking Water Policy Innovation and Urban Renewal: The Case of Rotterdam, the Netherlands," *Water Policy* 12 (2010), p. 396.

32. Katherine Peinhardt, "Resilience through Placemaking: Public Spaces in Rotterdam's Climate Adaptation Approach," Discussion Paper 1 (2021), Bonn: Deutsches Institut für Entwicklungspolitik.

33. Carla Corbin, "Vacancy and the Landscape: Cultural Context and Design Response," *Landscape Journal* 22 (2003), pp. 12–24.

34. Jack Murphy, "What Austin Can Teach Houston about Flood Control," *Houston Chronicle*, April 6, 2017.

35. Jennifer Foster, "Hiding in Plain View: Vacancy and Prospect in Paris' Petite Ceinture," *Cities* 40, no. B (2014), pp. 124–32.

36. Christophe D. Rupprecht, Jason A. Byrne, Hirofumi Ueda, and Alex Lo, "'It's Real, Not Fake like a Park': Residents' Perception and Use of Informal Urban Green-Space in Brisbane, Australia and Sapporo, Japan," *Landscape and Urban Planning* 143 (2015), pp. 205–18.

37. Ibid.

38. Ryszard Nejman, Maciej Łepkowski, Anna Wilczyńska, and Beata Gawryszewska, "The Right to Wild. Green Urban Wasteland in the Context of Urban Planning," *Urban Development Issues* 59, no. 1 (2018), pp. 43–53.

EIGHT

Frontiers of Place Governance

TRACY HADDEN LOH
NATE STORRING

When confronted with the failure of municipal government to contend with the growing complexity of metropolitan regions, in 1961, urban thinker and activist Jane Jacobs observed, "The invention required is not a device for coordination at the generalized top, but rather an invention to make coordination possible where the need is most acute—in specific unique localities."[1]

Jacobs imagined a city of "administrative districts" that could be shared across all municipal functions and in which city officials would collaborate on cross-functional teams to deliver coordinated services to each unique urban place. Every district would be overseen by a chief administrator as versed in the nuance of their jurisdiction as in the tools at their disposal.

Of course, the last half century of American urban history had something else in store for place governance. Rather than an expansion in the scale and complexity of metropolitan government, municipalities were decimated by the unfurling "urban crisis" coupled with reduced federal funding. An alphabet soup of place governance organizations arose—CDCs, EDCs, BIDs, CLTs, URAs, and so on—operating outside of but in coordination with the public sector. Contrary to Jacobs's vision, the result was an even gaudier "crazy quilt" of overlapping jurisdictions, which often has lacked any greater capacity for coordination than the labyrinthine public bureaucracies she observed in the late 1950s. Perhaps the one saving grace of these organizations within Jacobs's schema is that they do often possess as deep an expertise in the specific places they work as they do in the services they provide.

In the meantime, however, income inequality and polarization has deepened while patterns of racial segregation that were prevalent even before the rise of neoliberalism have persisted, coasting on the momentum of generations of *de jure* discrimination. As we have explored throughout this book, place governance has coevolved alongside these developments; it is both a symptom of late-twentieth-century American political economy and a constitutive part of it. However, when understood as a coherent, integrated regime rather than a collection of unrelated endeavors or the chaotic detritus left over from a once-powerful public sector, place governance also could hold the seeds of a more effective, equitable approach to managing our neighborhoods and public spaces.

This final chapter summarizes some of the most important takeaways from the previous seven chapters, and highlights promising stories from the field that demonstrate how place governance can evolve to meet our most pressing urban challenges today. After a summary of the state of place governance, we return to three key questions that inspired this book and that practitioners and policymakers will have to answer to fulfill the potential of place governance: To whom is it accountable? Who holds the power? And who benefits?

The Necessary Messiness of Place Governance

The story of the public sector in place governance today often is told as a battle between an inequitable and intractable status quo versus a return to a mythical time when a benevolent government managed places with an even hand and a generous pocketbook. However, neither side of this narrative holds up upon close inspection. The government management of districts and public spaces has never been so fair or effective, and while the status quo is, indeed, rife with inequity, it is less static than it appears.

While the level of complexity may be new, the patchwork of governance in American cities has roots that stretch back to the colonial era. Contemporary academic discourse on issues of place governance frequently frames the rise of business improvement districts and countless other place-based nonprofit organizations in the latter half of the twentieth century as government abdicating its "natural" responsibilities. However, as Alexander von Hoffman reveals in his history of place governance in the United States, the early-twentieth-century government consolidation of responsibility over sub-metropolitan places through new authorities and expanded public agencies has been the exception rather than the rule. Historically, the most economically valuable areas of cities relied on growth coalitions of local governments, landowners, and wealthy residents for their development, redevelopment, and management, creating *de facto* forms of place governance in the process. Meanwhile, poor and marginalized neighborhoods were left almost entirely to their own devices and developed informal place governance arrangements to meet their own needs—at least until the growth coalition decided that land could be used more "productively," too.

Even at its height, public sector-only place governance in the United States has not always led to fair or positive outcomes. One only needs to turn to *The Color of Law*, Richard Rothstein's comprehensive history of *de jure* racism in the United States, to find the many ways that government at every level has enforced and reinforced a regime of segregated inequality in American cities.[2] From race-based and land-use zoning to discriminatory suburban home loans and public housing to slum clearance and urban renewal, many place-based government decisions since the Civil War have contributed to our present-day status quo of systemic racism. Even the idea that the responsibility for keeping public spaces "clean and safe" was once the jurisdiction of a responsible public sector seems quaint as our society reconsiders the institution of policing itself in light of its violence against young Black men, people with disabilities, and others. Likewise, many cities grapple with generations of uneven public investment in parks, streets, schools, and other public amenities in communities of color that predate the neoliberal retreat from so-called big government. Consider, for example, the Trust for Public Land's finding that over 100 million Americans do not live within a ten-minute walk of a park, a result of biases during a prior era of park-building as well as ongoing injustices.[3] Given this history, perhaps it is time to reconsider the simplistic narrative of privatization and look ahead with what we have at hand today, instead of looking back nostalgically at an imagined past.

Today's place governance is messy. As Sheila Foster and Juliet Musso explore in chapters 3 and 4, place governance has developed into a multiplicity of arrangements between the public, private, and civic sectors, as well as unincorporated community groups, all with their own unique dimensions of power. What is more, if we closely examine any one model—BIDs, say—we find even more diversity, particularly in terms of their community outcomes, as Jill Gross demonstrates in chapter 5. On one hand, this range of organizations can be viewed as hyperlocal "laboratories of democracy," always reinventing themselves; on the other hand, they can be seen, instead, as capricious regimes that lead to wild inequalities and divergent impacts from place to place. Both visions have some truth to them.

This diversity becomes complexity when we examine how these many different organizations function as an ecosystem at the hyperlocal level. Musso's example of the interactions between neighborhood councils, BIDs, and community land trusts around the issue of homelessness in Los Angeles, for example, demonstrates how these organizations participate in a fractious and opaque extension of local politics. Even organizations that claim simply to offer a set of services mount campaigns and counter-campaigns, develop strong and weak relationships, and court stakeholders with multiple roles and allegiances—all of which influences municipal decisionmaking, for better or worse. Meanwhile, in chapter 6, Elena Madison and Joy Moses observe that some of the most promising street-level responses to addressing homelessness and mental health in public space involve complicated partnerships between place management organizations, social service providers, and city agencies. In fact, they argue, the missing link in improving the ability to connect people to shelter and services may involve matching the complex patchwork of organizations in a place with a proportionately sophisticated level of coordination—particularly across scales.

For all its difficulty, does this messiness have value? As Jacobs cautions, researchers and decisionmakers should carefully differentiate between genuine disorder and their own discomfort with complexity. While fragmentation, duplication, and overlapping missions and jurisdictions may seem inefficient, often the economies of scale projected by those who would consolidate and simplify these arrangements turn out to be mirages. As Nobel-winning economist Elinor Ostrom discovered in her studies of public services like water distribution and policing, collections of small departments almost always outperformed large departments in terms of a simple ratio of service value to cost. As Ostrom summarizes, "We demonstrated that complexity is not the same as chaos in regard to metropolitan governance."[4]

There is, however, a legitimate critique of how systematically difficult it is to appropriately resource place governance when it is outsourced to nongovernmental organizations (NGOs) and thus not directly accounted for in a public budget. On the one hand, this outsourcing has made it possible to raise new revenue and deliver services at the place level with efficiency and innovation in jurisdictions where the public sector is troubled by stagnation, inflexibility, inertia, or corruption. On the other hand, this layering becomes a method of concealing from ourselves the true cost of place governance. It is a mechanism for the public sector to abdicate its responsibility to earn or generate accountability at the most local level and instead extract it from struggling nonprofits often with only nominal or minor support.

The city of Minneapolis's Community Participation Program is illustrative of this. The murder of George Floyd by a city employee in the Powderhorn Park neighborhood on May 25, 2020, became a clarion call (for some) to address systemic inequities in policing and in government at large. But in terms of place governance, the city of Minneapolis's own Neighborhoods 2020 process (which predated Floyd's death) was already supposed to "redefine the roles and expectations of neighborhood organizations . . . to make Minneapolis' network of 70 neighborhood organizations, the City's neighborhood-based engagement structure, more equitable and effective."[5] The baseline structure was an example of a seemingly fair and equal system that instead fortified existing inequalities: Every neighborhood group received $20,000, regardless of impact or need. The Neighborhoods 2020 process imposed more requirements on neighborhood groups to receive funding from the city, many of which were intended to build racial equity into the work of the groups. However, as Tabitha Montgomery, the executive director of the Powderhorn Park Neighborhood Association observed, the functional outcome is a demand to "do more work and better work for the same money, which just doubles down on existing inequities." It does not change the status quo that, in the words of Montgomery, "most communities need the same things; but we have decided that only some places should have what they need."

The incremental changes of Neighborhoods 2020 show the limits of local democracy. In a democracy, governing is a political act rather than a pragmatic one. It is focused first and foremost on voter perception and behavior, which sometimes align with public needs and sometimes do not. Thus, we see the public sector struggling with the core task of delivering services to voters while there are enormous unmet human needs among those most likely to be disenfranchised. Furthermore, there is tremendous inertia in the sector, and it is not at all unusual for structures, once established, to stay in place for a century. This inertia creates an enormous bias in favor of legacy structures and stakeholders that results in inefficiency and serves as a barrier to change, even without incentive or malice.

These limitations are not the only reason the future of place governance does not lie solely with the public sector. At the end of the day, good governance is relational, not transactional. What is needed is a system that fosters an ethics of care in the management of urban places.[6] Effectively caring for a public space, a neighborhood, or a downtown district is more like raising a child than designing and building a product. The complex, evolving nature of place requires a level of attention, observation, iteration, and even affection that may be best provided by a person or team dedicated primarily to its success, backed up by public systems that make good "parenting" possible.

What might this more robust, supportive place governance regime look like? Let us return to some of the key questions that motivated this collection in the first place to find out.

To Whom Is Place Governance Accountable?

Throughout this book, many of the authors have raised questions about the accountability of existing place governance organizations. How can we ensure that the users most likely to be excluded not only have a voice in place governance but receive genuine power and benefits from this regime?

The organizations that operate as part of a city's place governance ecosystem do not operate in a vacuum. On the contrary, many of the most important decisions these organizations could make are in fact made for them by authorizing legislation created at a higher level such as the city or state. This legislation, then, offers an important lever for elected officials, the general public, and others to impose greater accountability on place governance entities. However, even in the absence of a legal mandate, place governance entities also can impose greater accountability upon themselves through bylaws, equity and inclusion initiatives, and other strategies.

Authorizing Legislation: The Foundation of Place Governance

The spectrum of place governance explored in this book includes informal groups of people in proximity engaged in collaboration, formally incorporated entities that operate in a specific legal framework that structures the collaboration, and special districts that combine some of the attributes of a local government with particular rules for a defined geography. Both nonprofit corporations and special districts are formal structures that provide scaffolding to build sustainability and scalability for place governance. In the United States, the legal formation of corporations, the act of incorporation, is governed by state law within a basic framework provided by federal law. States authorize different corporate structures and impose varying requirements on those structures, typically leaving a great deal of discretion to the organizers of any corporate entity regarding membership and bylaws. State authorizing legislation is also required for special districts, and this power is, according to John Ratliff, "among the most significant ways in which state law allows for the differential treatment of places."[7]

For example, every state and the District of Columbia in the United States has some form of authorizing statute to permit the creation of business improvement districts, but state-level authorizations vary significantly in the forms of revenue used to support the districts (for example, taxes on property, businesses, or hospitality/tourism consumption); the process to establish a BID; requirements, restrictions, and appointment power for board of directors seats; and reporting, oversight, and other accountability structures within the bylaws. As a result, there is significant variance in the functioning and governance of BIDs between states. For example, BIDs in Washington, DC, are required to create five-year business plans with measurable goals and submit these plans for certification and registration with the executive branch, a process that includes public hearings at both the neighborhood level and the Council of the District of Columbia. Beyond BIDs, these same variations in governance practices across states and structures exist in every form of place governance.

As discussed at length in this book and elsewhere, accountability of place governance entities is a widespread and well-founded source of criticism. John Ratliff noted that many of these entities "perform key public functions but are not well understood by the public, and many fail to adhere to modern standards of government budgeting or spending transparency," and that "public confusion is particularly acute in places where multiple entities exercise similar or overlapping authorities," including with the general-purpose local government.

Accountability in place governance most often takes the form of requiring periodic, regular reporting and public oversight of the activities and expenditures of place governance organizations. However, daily accountability for place governance rests with the governing bodies of these entities, the structures and decisions of which test the limits of inclusion. In some states, authorizing legislation for place governance specifies or restricts the membership of the board of directors to particular stakeholders; for example, property owners within a BID. Therefore, reform of authorizing legislation at the state level also can be an opportunity to revisit assumptions about accountability and inclusion, especially for place governance entities. States can and should exercise the authority to enact reforms that improve place governance accountability, such as Florida's 2018 Uniform Special District Accountability Act, which imposed on special districts financial reporting standards comparable to those of municipalities and counties where either authorizing legislation or the bylaws position the board of directors in an influential role.[8]

Accountability in Practice

Writing or rewriting authorizing legislation requires significant political will, which takes time and effort to mobilize. But place governance organizations that want to achieve greater equity and inclusion
in their structure and their outcomes need not wait for that day to
come. Each place governance entity has significant wiggle room
to create bespoke decisionmaking mechanisms, bylaws, and initiatives
that can be used for good or ill. Some organizations use these structures and activities as a way to assert and consolidate control. Others
use them as an opportunity to build in the kind of balance of power
and transparency that can support the buy-in of a diverse coalition of
stakeholders. As we have seen throughout this book, this kind of tactical accountability is not strictly altruistic, either; it enhances the stability and efficacy of place governance organizations by fostering
goodwill, useful relationships, and a sense of popular legitimacy.

Consider the origin story of the North Westwood Neighborhood
Council in Los Angeles. As discussed in chapter 4 of this book, the
city of Los Angeles has a neighborhood council system with directly
elected council members serving on advisory bodies that function-
ally possess significant decisionmaking power in local land-use and
transportation issues and are supported by public funds. The democratic ideal underlying the neighborhood council system is that it
creates a mechanism for residents to have a voice in local issues, as a
forum for Ostrom's "cheap talk" that is needed to solve hairy and
hyperlocal problems. In reality, there are a range of place stakeholders—
such as individuals experiencing homelessness, business owners, workers, renters, students, and immigrants who do not possess citizenship
status—who may find themselves poorly served by a system designed
to empower "residents."

In Westwood, a coalition of UCLA students, business owners, and
Persian immigrants dissatisfied with the status quo—a neighborhood
council controlled by homeowners—petitioned the city for a ballot
initiative to create the North Westwood Neighborhood Council

under a new set of bylaws by splitting the prior jurisdiction of the Westwood Neighborhood Council. These new bylaws, approved by Westwood voters in 2019, define a council of nineteen members and formally specify shares of representation for homeowners, renters, local businesses and workers, and various college and university stakeholders, among others.[9]

While almost Seussian in its nominal distinction between Westwood and North Westwood, what this story illustrates is that the exact same structure (a neighborhood council and its bylaws) can be used to promote accountability and inclusion or to assert exclusion and control. Faced with this paradox, some leaders have concluded that the solution is to abolish place governance. For example, the city of Seattle under Mayor Ed Murray dissolved its formal relationship with its neighborhood district councils in 2016 and replaced it with a new system for community involvement that is less place-based.[10] Are these recent reforms throwing the baby out with the bathwater? Should we conclude that if everywhere cannot have powerful place governance then nowhere should have it? This is a genuine conundrum created by the fundamentally problematic context of extreme segregation and inequality for hyperlocal place governance.

Stephen R. Miller cut to the heart of the matter when he identified place governance as not a symptom of, but a viable alternative to, both the kind of "secession" from the city by micro-municipalities that employ defensive incorporation to hoard resources and municipalities that underinvest in marginalized neighborhoods. Miller's key insight was the layering of multiple governance entities to create "legal neighborhoods," in a "loose affiliation of tools operating simultaneously."[11] Many neighborhoods are already well on their way to establishing such legal neighborhoods; for example in North Westwood, where in addition to the neighborhood council, the commercial corridor is organized into the Westwood Business Improvement District. Perhaps someday there will also be a "friends" group for the local park or a community investment trust for local real estate. This additional organizing and these additional structures can help limit what Katherine Levine Einstein and her co-authors described as the potential for "capture by small, advantaged groups with intense preferences"[12] or, as Ellen Shiau and her co-authors caution, those who are "reactive to pocketbook issues."[13] This bears a notable similarity to Ostrom's polycentric governance, and the research of both Miller and Ostrom find considerable evidence that these arrangements, while messy, can be effective statecraft.

Are legal neighborhoods just an attempt to cure a hangover with another drink? Or an even more frantic attempt to hide from ourselves the true cost of place governance? American activists and organizers concerned with "empowerment and self-determination for oppressed communities"[14] have been highly critical of the "nonprofit industrial complex" composed of not-for-profit corporations operated for charitable purposes in compliance with the Internal Revenue Service's definition of 501(c)(3) tax status.[15] Among other critiques, such organizations are limited in the political and lobbying activities they may engage in. With politics at the heart of place governance, as with all scales of governance, it is understandable how such a restriction creates a disingenuous mismatch between nonprofit corporate governance constraints and the mission of empowered, self-determined communities.

One solution is that the viability of "legal neighborhoods," and the future of place governance, requires a diverse, flexible mix of structures and models beyond the familiar 501(c)(3) rather than the abdication of hyperlocal civic organizing altogether. However, the tax protections extended by 501(c)(3) status also apply to donors to such organizations. Individuals and foundations engaged in philanthropy, as well as the public sector, will have to both think bigger and account differently in order to provide the stable funding necessary for a truly diverse array of community-based organizations to achieve their missions.

Still, individual place governance organizations can and should strive to improve their own internal accountability structures, as in North Westwood. One major issue that complicates such efforts, though, is the tendency of these organizations toward mission creep. Certainly, one reason for this creep is the growth pressures facing organizations like BIDs or economic development corporations. Public and private backers expect returns, staff strive to cover their own operating costs, and organizational leadership and powerful stakeholders pursue their political, financial, and personal ambitions.

However, another underappreciated reason for mission creep is the web-like complexity of the many issues facing communities. As Juliet Musso argues in chapter 4, the legal structures that enable a BID define its services as a "club" or "toll" good, in which those who pay have exclusive access to a good or service, such as commercial property owners paying for a "clean and safe" shopping environment. However, in practice, the club analogy does not hold up. The impact of BIDs, which operate in the public realm, is not as exclusive as intended. Public spaces are the frontlines of so many urban issues, from policing to affordability to climate change. Every public space is the jurisdiction of multiple city agencies and defined by the spillovers of countless private decisions. When place governance organizations try to take on a narrowly defined corner of public space management, like the traditional BID scope of maintenance and security, they often end up tugging on threads that unravel clear divisions of responsibilities, outcomes, and stakeholders. How do efforts to improve "safety" handle political expression in public space or the desire of teenagers to socialize outdoors? How does "cleanliness" respond to cultural traditions that gentrifiers find untidy, disruptive, or threatening?

These thorny questions are one way that place governance organizations wind up broadening their scopes, expanding their areas of control and influence, or building partnerships with complementary organizations. And this dynamic holds true for place governance organizations with less connection to the exchange value of property. Whether it is the health center, cultural institution, and universities that banded together to found the Cortex Innovation Community in St. Louis or social service provider HOPE Atlanta partnering with Central Atlanta Progress to place a social worker in a downtown park, engaging with the intricate web of place often prompts organizations to broaden their viewpoint.

But the more a place governance organization's scope grows, the greater the expectations for representation and accountability. Whether through ambition or necessity, as these organizations approach what Juliet Musso describes as "general purpose quasi-governments," a gap often grows between their narrow set of official stakeholders and the broad range of users that, in fact, hold a stake in their operations. If underlying governance assumptions stay the same as an organization's scope grows and the context in which they operate continues to evolve, it is no surprise that tensions tend to build up and explode into moments of crisis and transformation, as Jill Gross observes in chapter 5. These explosive changes could be avoided with a more proactive approach to accountability. Even in jurisdictions with strong regulations on place governance organizations, public consultation and public sector intervention often take place only in response to proposals or missteps by the organization.

Oversight bodies could change this dynamic by mandating, incentivizing, or financially supporting the kind of early, frequent, and inclusive community engagement that generates trust and alignment between a place governance organization and its full range of stakeholders. However, organizations also could enshrine this kind of deep engagement in their missions, bylaws, policies, and strategies. Either way, as Gross puts it, we could then rely on place governance organizations as consistent "community builders" rather than "breakers" or "erasers."

Who Holds the Power?

In June 2021, Joel Caston was elected to local office. He was also in jail.

The District of Columbia has a system of advisory neighborhood commissions (ANCs), composed of nonpartisan elected representatives from single-member districts (SMDs), each of which includes approximately 2,000 residents. Each commission includes anywhere from two to twelve SMDs.[16] The 7F07 SMD was created after redistricting in 2011 and includes both the DC Jail, the Harriet Tubman Women's Shelter, and the former DC General Family Homeless Shelter. Prior to Caston's election, this SMD seat had never been filled.

Neighbors who live near the DC Jail (but not within the 7F07 SMD) organized and advocated for the DC Department of Corrections to facilitate outreach to inmates at the jail, informing them of the existence of the SMD seat and the opportunity to serve in it. The coronavirus pandemic had already motivated the District to transfer all ANC operations to virtual platforms and to offer universal mail-in voting for the first time. These procedural reforms reduced some of the barriers to participation that had previously kept the SMD seat empty. However, both the advocacy of Neighbors for Justice and the cooperation of the DC Department of Corrections were catalyzing ingredients in the process. In a new landmark for inclusion, Joel Caston now represents well over 1,000 residents of the District of Columbia, and may well be the only incarcerated elected official actively serving in the United States.[17]

Caston's story illustrates that structural limits to inclusion can be procedural (for example, how votes are collected in an election), technical (for example, access to meetings), or logistical (for example, cost of activities or times and places of elections and meetings). However, these limits can be transcended. Existing models that appear broken and obstacles as substantial as the bars on a cell window can be reformed and overcome with new technologies, collaborations, and structures to rebalance who holds the power in place governance arrangements.

Although power is often simplified into a question of formal mechanisms like board representation, as Juliet Musso argues in chapter 4, there are multiple dimensions of power at play in place governance, including what an organization is legally authorized to do, what it has the capacity to do, and what it has the legitimacy to do. If policymakers and practitioners seek to broaden the range of stake-holders who hold power, they will need to understand all of these dimensions and devise interventions that rewire who gets a say in each.

Since the examination of formal structures is well represented in this volume, we want, instead, to turn to an issue of power that has not yet been discussed in full: the importance of organizational capacity.

Capacity Is Power

While democratic mechanisms such as boards, memberships, or public meetings play an important role in good governance, the reality is that the vast majority of day-to-day decisions are made by an organization's staff members. These decisions often happen informally and are constrained as much by available staff time, expense, and professional and interpersonal incentives as they are by formal governance structures. To that end, it is important to consider how creative ways to increase capacity also can empower place governance organizations that have limited resources.

Throughout this book, we have heard a lot about economies of scale. However, as noted in chapter 1, Ostrom and others have demonstrated that, in governance, there are real diseconomies of scale as well, which is one of the explanations for the persistence of something so messy as place governance. Consolidations of governance that were undertaken in the name of efficiency have, at times, ended up costing more and becoming more cumbersome than the mélange that was there before. Take, for example, the amalgamation of the six municipalities that once made up Metropolitan Toronto, undertaken in the 1990s by the Ontario provincial government (over the protests of a local referendum) ostensibly for the sake of efficiency. Some studies later found that even though redundancies were eliminated, the amalgamated city cost more to run than the independent municipalities, perhaps because of the increased need for coordination and localization.[18]

There is a Goldilocks problem when it comes to place. What is too small, what is too big, and what is just right? It is not clear that there is a universal answer to this that translates across structures or regional contexts. An alternative way to think about it is to expand the question of size beyond one dimension. Across the place governance landscape, innovative, flexible, scalable models that combine elements of disaggregation with some aspects of consolidation are emerging. The general idea is to achieve economies of scale with the scarcest, most expensive resources while not cutting the root of place. These hybrid models have the potential to allow place governance organizations to do more and to reach more people and places.

The Main Streets movement in the United States is a national-scale, long-standing example of this. Individual Main Street programs are stood up by places, facilitated by a recommended structure and set of principles for practice provided by Main Street America, formerly known as the National Main Street Center. In addition to these start-up resources, Main Street America provides multiple forums for Main Streets to collaborate, sharing tips and tricks to support each other—"cheap talk" that is valuable, indeed. Many Main Street programs also are federated at the state level in partnership with state government, as another obvious scale at which sharing information and grant resources makes sense.

The District of Columbia, as both a city and a functional (if not constitutional) state, is an interesting case study for the Main Street model. The District has twenty-six Main Street programs serving distinct commercial corridors in neighborhoods across the city, each of which was selected through a one-time request for proposals (RFP) process. But the fiscal reality is that the grant funding provided by the District of Columbia is not enough to pay for any Main Street's staff and operations, even the leanest among them. Main Street programs leverage the District's grant funding by raising additional funds from the communities they serve. However, this means that neighborhoods that do not have disposable local wealth are at a disadvantage. Moreover, the unusually close geographic proximity of the District's main streets creates an environment in which the places may view each other as competitors when it comes to attracting resources.

District Bridges has grown since 2005 from a small nonprofit operating a single one-day festival in one neighborhood to a multineighborhood collaboration helping to address some of these capacity issues. It currently operates seven Main Street programs, taking advantage of proximity to achieve Goldilocks economies of scale by sharing internal capacity across the programs while still supporting a full-time, laser-focused Main Street manager for each corridor. This internal capacity is both costly and challenging to fundraise for, and includes fundraising itself, as well as accounting, administration, reporting and data collection, institutional knowledge, relationships, and redundant systems. By sharing these resources, District Bridges gains the ability to think along longer timelines and to shift from a reactive to a proactive stance both in working with partners and serving stakeholders. It enables programs to "buddy up" and channel economies of scale into outcomes that include more places, and to work alongside Main Street America on larger problems too big for individual small businesses or Main Streets to solve on their own but that occur over and over again across contexts.

Capacity is power. While many organizations still lack sufficient financial resources or mechanisms to increase their capacity, support systems that share resources like Main Street America and District Bridges provide one path toward redistributing power with the tools we have today.

Who Benefits?

Throughout this book, the chapter authors explore the question of how the benefits and costs of place governance are distributed among its stakeholders from multiple angles—from the types of partnerships that structure place governance actors to the hyperlocal politics of BID boards to the particular kinds of exclusion faced by people experiencing homelessness.

Perhaps the greatest imbalance of outcomes in terms of sheer scale, however, is between those communities that have place governance structures and the millions of people and thousands of neighborhoods that have little access to systems of place governance at all. While so much has changed since the nineteenth century, it is still true that many neighborhoods—particularly those occupied by low-income people and people of color—are left to their own devices, inventing makeshift forms of problem-solving and decisionmaking with few resources. To move beyond this outdated and inequitable model, practitioners and policymakers will need to collaborate closely with these communities to invent and scale new forms of shared ownership and resources.

Reinventing Ownership to Include More People

Property ownership still plays an outsize role in this hyperlocal part of our democracy. While the requirement of owning land to participate in democratic institutions in the United States has receded, at least in principle, this inequitable tradition persists at the hyperlocal level. Perhaps the most ubiquitous place governance entities in the United States—BIDs and common interest communities (which house nearly 74 million Americans)—generally favor property owners by law.[19] The enabling legislation for business improvement districts in most states, for example, stipulates that the majority of seats on their boards of directors must be held by commercial property owners.

The result is that these models of place governance tend to be most attuned to the exchange value of the land they steward rather than the use value. Commercial tenants and residential renters generally have significantly less influence, while workers, frequent users, and people experiencing homelessness typically have even less. At best, some forward-looking, property-oriented place governance organizations may offer tokenistic board positions or consult these other constituencies in a nonbinding way, but ultimately, their enabling legislation generally prevents them from doing anything more radically inclusive. As Elinor Ostrom reminds us, we should not discount the value of this kind of informal coordination, but formal governance structures should be paddling in the same direction.

Partly as a result of this landowner bias, displacement, exclusion, and perceptions of cultural gentrification are persistent problems in U.S. cities. In residential areas that are already expensive, organized residents stymie efforts to improve affordability through public housing or development of any kind. On the frontiers of gentrification in hot-market cities, commercial and residential landowners organize to protect and increase their property values, exacerbating direct and indirect displacement. Even beyond these strictly economic contexts, when non-landowners are excluded from place governance, their many diverse use values are ignored. Homogenous places mark a loss not only for these disenfranchised communities but also for the city as a whole.

If state governments will not update enabling legislation that favors landowners, then another way to approach this problem is to change the nature of ownership itself. As Sheila Foster and Juliet Musso explore in their chapters, this speaks to the growing popularity of structures like community land trusts, which take land off the market and create diverse, collaborative decisionmaking structures for its use.

Mercy Corps's East Portland Community Investment Trust (CIT) is a novel model that engages in the market dynamics of real estate as opposed to taking property off the market. Mercy Corps, an international humanitarian and development organization, is based in Portland, Oregon, and has long maintained a domestic arm, Mercy Corps Northwest, to serve their home region. Both routine evaluation of their existing programs as well as changing economic conditions in the Portland region raised awareness within Mercy Corps that a new domestic solution for asset development was needed, especially for residents who rent their homes. After an extensive human-centered design process targeting majority-renter communities in Portland and a lengthy financial product design and feasibility study, the CIT was born.[20]

Mercy Corps, through a subsidiary LLC, established the CIT pilot project and acquired Plaza 122 in December of 2014, a 1960s-era shopping center on the far eastern side of Portland in dire condition and foreclosure. Once 44 percent vacant, after renovation and lease-up, the property is now 95 percent occupied and has generated positive cash flow for the nearly four years since the community investment launched. The initial purchase was financed by a commercial bank with base equity for the down payment and capital to address deferred maintenance provided by Mercy Corps and two impact investors, who are now being paid back through revenue raised by selling shares of ownership to community investors, who each invest between $10 and $100 per month after completing a financial education course called "From Owing to Owning." The shares transfer both equity (and any equity growth) to investors, as well as pay an annual dividend, which has averaged 9.0 percent over four rounds. Community investors can sell their shares and withdraw at any time, a critical flexibility that distinguishes the CIT from many other real estate investment models. In addition, the CIT, through a letter of credit with a local bank, guarantees community investors and protects them from loss—they cannot lose their principal. As of mid-2021, the East Portland CIT Corporation (a state-registered C-corp) had 220 investors, with the capacity ultimately to include 300 to 500, and a deeply distressed real estate asset in the community has been fully rehabilitated and revitalized, becoming an activated neighborhood hub and center for businesses, many owned by immigrants, and nonprofits.

In addition to creating a shared model of investment and ownership, this initiative demonstrates the less tangible value of changing how people feel about their places. The economic and social disruptions of suburbanization, globalization, digitalization, and, most recently, the coronavirus pandemic all have directly challenged and threatened that value and revealed the consequences of its diminishment and loss: widespread social distrust and extreme income inequality. The question for those in local government attempting to sustain and operate an apparatus that stewards prosperity and well-being is whether it is possible, and necessary, to protect, nurture, and capture that value. While tangible benefit to investors in the CIT in the form of both short- and long-term financial returns is obvious, the experience of participating also has changed perceptions and behavior. In the 2021 annual survey of investors, 65 percent of investors reported becoming more involved in their community, and 33 percent reported an improved credit score. In a survey of 191 participants at baseline, 55 percent of them said they "always" voted. In aggregate across resubscription surveys, 64 percent reported voting in the last election, suggesting an increase in voter participation.

The CIT is just one of several innovative community ownership models for commercial real estate currently being piloted in neighborhoods across the United States.[21] With the pandemic accelerating the failure of old commercial real estate business models, their fall may create space for the rise of marginalized people and small businesses who want to be enfranchised through ownership.

Expanding Financing to Include More Places

One of the biggest limits to broadening the benefits of place governance is funding, particularly funding mechanisms that give organizations financial stability for the long haul, like the property assessments levied by a BID. However, American place governance innovators are creating new models for financing that are breaking down these barriers in some places.

In April 2001, a Black Cincinnati teenager named Timothy Thomas was shot and killed by a police officer in the Over-the-Rhine neighborhood. After Thomas's death, the subsequent three days of protests and riots were enough to convince the city's public and private sector leadership that they had a crisis on their hands. Among other reforms, key elected and private sector players collaborated to provide place management and nonprofit real estate investment to Over-the-Rhine via the Cincinnati Center City Development Corporation (3CDC), in parallel to Downtown Cincinnati Inc (DCI), a BID that had been managing the adjacent downtown area since 1994.

At its founding in 2003, 3CDC possessed three distinct supports that have made it one of the best-resourced and most impactful mission-driven developers in the United States.[22] The most obvious and least innovative of these supports was that 3CDC is a private non-profit entity, whose operations and capital budget were originally funded by corporate contributions from Cincinnati-based companies,[23] several of whom are in the *Fortune 500*, and whose leadership compose 3CDC's board of directors. These companies do not derive any direct profit from 3CDC's development activities, putting 3CDC in the somewhat unusual position of harnessing the flexibility and resources of a private company in service of a charitable purpose.

The public sector, however, also has played a critical role in supporting and shaping 3CDC. After Thomas's death, public, private, and civic leaders lobbied the Ohio state legislature to pass legislation enabling tax increment financing districts. At the time, the Ohio authorizing legislation that ultimately passed was notable in that the maximum district size was relatively large (300 acres) compared to other states (it has since been reduced). Then councilmember (later mayor) John Cranley leveraged this flexibility to create two parallel TIF districts (see figure 8-1) that linked downtown Cincinnati and Over-the-Rhine, an unusual structure that created a formal link between the prosperity of downtown and the future of an adjacent disinvested neighborhood. The city council made these TIF district proceeds available to eligible projects within the district boundaries.

In addition, 3CDC has leveraged its location in a qualifying Census tract and Over-the-Rhine's remarkable collection of Italianate architecture to secure multi-millions of dollars of federal New Markets and historic preservation tax credits over dozens of projects. Combined with local TIF proceeds, these public subsidies provide the second of three key supports in the structure.

The third key support structured into 3CDC is the ongoing management of income-producing assets. One of the very first tasks 3CDC was charged with was a make-over for Fountain Square in the heart of downtown Cincinnati, including rebuilding and then managing the

FIGURE 8-1. Innovative Use of TIF Districts in Cincinnati

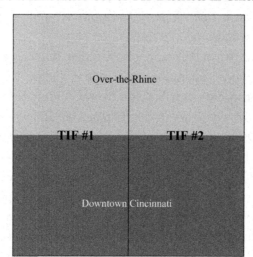

municipal underground parking garage that is beneath the square. 3CDC then raised slightly under $10 million in equity to borrow almost $40 million in public and private debt to pay for an approximately $50 million transformation of Fountain Square into a lively civic space.[24] Increased parking revenues from both a rise in demand and sensible pricing (something that can be challenging for the public sector to do) are enough to pay for the debt service on the project. In later years, 3CDC has repeated this income-generating model with other parking assets connected to public spaces, as well as renovations of retail storefronts. Today, 3CDC is as much an asset manager as it is a developer, with an unusually sustainable operating model that is not reliant on ongoing new money from the public or private sectors.

The lesson of the 3CDC model is not that revitalization must be led by the private sector, or simply that beginning with traditional public space placemaking can yield tremendous value (though this latter point is clearly true). Rather, this story illustrates that from crisis came a new will to collaborate across multiple once-firm boundaries: the private and public sectors; downtown and Over-the-Rhine; civic spaces and commercial real estate. This collaboration, not corporate boards or festival marketplaces, is the powerful heartbeat of transformative placemaking.

What happened in Cincinnati after Timothy Thomas died was a radical act of rebounding. Leaders across sectors stopped pointing fingers or waiting and, instead, took responsibility for creating and resourcing solutions. John Cranley literally drew new borders, crossing the boundaries that divide neighborhoods and creating new connections between them. And 3CDC leveraged capital assets into operating dollars in a strategic cycle of borrowing, investment, and growth. In this story, we once again see a familiar tool—in this case, TIF districts—being used to share the fruits of growth rather than to hoard them.

In recent years, the collaboration between downtown Cincinnati and Over-the-Rhine has deepened. Most recently, the boards of 3CDC and Downtown Cincinnati, Inc., which oversaw the Special Improvement District in the city's central business district, coordinated a merger of the two organizations, which went into effect on January 1, 2019. The combination of these two entities yielded sufficient economies of scale at the management level to save, conservatively, half a million dollars in expenses a year, the equivalent of over 15 percent of DCI's annual operating budget.

The story of downtown Cincinnati and Over-the-Rhine reveals the true cost of place governance—DCI's annual operating expenses were over $3 million, and 3CDC's annual operating budget (which now includes operating DCI) was roughly $17 million in 2021. In the shared prosperity of downtown and Over-the-Rhine, we also see a reframing of the relationship between racial and class equity and economic growth—often assumed to be a trade-off—into a joint endeavor. The prosperity of downtown and Over-the-Rhine, threatened by police violence and riots, is instead delivered through nonprofit equitable development. When more people and places benefit, the net result is greater prosperity all around: a transition from scarcity to abundance.

Conclusion

While this book contains countless useful case studies on the innovations and shortcomings of place governance organizations today, if
readers take away one thing, we hope it is this: Despite the diverse
ways place governance plays out on the ground, we should understand
it as one coherent regime. When we cut through the fragmented and
overlapping arenas of action and study, what we find is that neighborhood councils, business improvement districts, land trusts, "friends"
groups, and even the innovative arrangements we have yet to name
are all collaborative, cross-sectoral arrangements designed to shape
the economic, physical, social, and civic dynamics of specific places.
They share DNA in their missions, their governance, their strategies,
and the ways they are overseen by government.

When seen in this light, we hope practitioners and policymakers
can appreciate the full range of possibilities for change available to
them. When practitioners encounter a challenge or opportunity in
their day-to-day work, they need not look only to other organizations
operating under the same acronym to find a new approach. Across the
stories of place innovators related in this chapter, we have seen there
are already many tools available—even some that may have a reputa-
tion in some circles as tools of hoarding—that can increase the reach,
capacity, and accountability of place governance.

However, even the canniest practitioner still will meet limits of resources, capacity, coordination, and authority they cannot break
through alone. That is why we hope that policymakers, too, will benefit from this more holistic perspective on the ecosystem of place governance organizations that shape our cities and towns today. While
the public sector may not be responsible for directly managing as many
places as it once was, it has a vital and unfulfilled role to play in
strengthening, expanding, and regulating that ecosystem.

Twenty-first-century place governance came into being primarily
because of the perception of politicians and policymakers that outsourcing some public sector responsibilities would reduce government

spending while maintaining a reasonable level of service. As we have seen, though, often these arrangements hide and diffuse their true costs. Instead, what if the greatest value of place governance lay in its efficacy rather than its efficiency? As many of the stories throughout this book demonstrate, when we invest adequately in place governance, hyperlocal organizations can become more responsive, effective, and fair than any overarching government agency could ever hope to be.

But place governance organizations need a clear scope defined by authorizing legislation. Where this legislation exists, as it does for BIDs, it can be refined, and where it does not exist, as is the case for CITs, it can be created. Place governance organizations require dedicated operating funding—ideally not in the form of money floods and droughts and, ideally, from sources and mechanisms that do not undercut or conflict with their mission and key constituencies. Place governance organizations need effective relationships with complementary organizations operating in the same area, and with city and state agencies that can connect the frontlines of issues like homelessness to long-term and large-scale strategies and programs. Finally, place governance organizations need a sense of democratic legitimacy, an emergent quality that comes from the fit between scope and accountability and from sustained efforts at building trust.

In short, if excellence in place governance is to become the rule rather than the exception, politicians and policymakers must set their sights on cultivating a place governance ecosystem that is accountable, coordinated, fairly and adequately funded, and representative of all users. While our current decentralized system provides hyperlocal actors with some decisionmaking autonomy, a truly effective polycentric system requires thoughtfully nested levels of decisionmaking as well as strategies to resolve conflicts, recognize systemic inequalities, and update the rules of the game. Right now, these very elements are the Achilles heel of American place governance.

Where to start? Policymakers could begin by conducting a simple audit of existing legislation, jurisdictions, and relationships. Most state and local governments do not even know *what they already know* about place governance. The various flavors of place-based organizations are regulated by different agencies and levels of government, and different agencies hold relationships with different nongovernment actors without coordination. And to our knowledge, most cities and states do not even have a comprehensive map of every overlapping place governance jurisdiction. Without this basic knowledge, it is hard to imagine developing the kind of policy necessary to contend with place governance as a unified regime.

We should put in the time and effort. In some communities, place governance has not been positive for everyone, and in others, it barely exists at all. However, in many cities and towns around the United States, place governance organizations are making communities more lively, welcoming, beautiful, and meaningful. They are inventing new and more inclusive models of participation and ownership. They are collaborating with the private, public, and civic sectors to address wicked problems like homelessness.

Our place governance ecosystem can give more communities the tools they need to uplift themselves—if we invest in it and care for it.

NOTES

1. Jane Jacobs, *The Death and Life of Great American Cities* (New York: Random House, 1961), p. 418.

2. Richard Rothstein, *The Color of Law: A Forgotten History of How Our Government Segregated America* (New York: Liveright, 2017).

3. See The Trust for Public Land, "The ParkScore® Index: Methodology and FAQ," www.tpl.org/parkscore/about.

4. Elinor Ostrom, "Beyond Markets and States: Polycentric Governance of Complex Economic Systems," *American Economic Review* 100 (June 2010), p. 644.

5. See City of Minneapolis, "Neighborhoods 2020," www2.minneapolismn .gov/government/departments/ncr/neighborhood-programs/neighborhoods -2020/.

6. Lynda H. Schneekloth and Robert G. Shibley, *Placemaking: The Art and Practice of Building Communities* (Hoboken, NJ: Wiley, 1995), p. 103. Coined by feminist psychologist and ethicist Carol Gilligan, "ethics of care" is an approach to defining right and wrong that emphasizes relationships over self-

reliance, standing in contrast to the "ethics of rights" common in the male-dominated field of ethics at the time. Applying this lens to the design and management of public places, Schneekloth and Shibley describe placemaking as "public housework," with all the connotations that may come with the phrase. "The term *public housework* reveals the tension between celebrating what can be liberating, caring work," they write, "and recognizing its denigration within the dominant culture and its potential as a form of subjugation" (p. 103). On a more hopeful note, they add, "Perhaps one of the reasons for the denigration of both housework and caring in our culture is that such work is an act of subversion with the power to transform oppressive circumstances. The public housework of placemaking has the potential to be a liberating and critical practice of care" (p. 108).

7. John D. Ratliff, "State resilience and recovery: Strategies to reduce inequality and promote prosperity by creating better places," The Brookings Institution, September 15, 2021, www.brookings.edu/research/state-resilience-and-recovery-strategies-to-reduce-inequality-and-promote-prosperity-by-creating-better-places/.

8. Ibid.

9. See Los Angeles Department of Neighborhood Empowerment, "North Westwood Neighborhood Council Bylaws," 2018, https://empowerla.org/wp-content/uploads/2019/10/NWWNC-Approved-Bylaws-091818.pdf.

10. Daniel Beekman, "Seattle's New Involvement Commission: More Voices or Less Pushback?," *Seattle Times*, December 12, 2016, www.seattletimes.com/seattle-news/politics/seattles-new-involvement-commission-more-voices-or-less-pushback/.

11. In this paper, Miller coins the phrase "legal neighborhood" to describe a "de facto" entity that "emerges in the overlay of legal and political tools that empower the neighborhood." These tools include district-based (as opposed to at-large) council elections; hyperlocal political representation, such as neighborhood councils; neighborhood associations and other place-based nonprofit entities; TIFs; BIDs; zoning overlays; schools/school districts; community-based courts; historic districts; and community benefit agreements. Stephen R. Miller, "Legal Neighborhoods," *Harvard Environmental Law Review* 37 (2013), pp. 105–66.

12. Katherine Levine Einstein, David M. Glick, and Maxwell Palmer, *Neighborhood Defenders: Participatory Politics and America's Housing Crisis* (Cambridge University Press, 2020), p. 32.

13. Ellen Shiau, Juliet Musso, and Jefferey M. Sellers, "City Fragmentation and Neighborhood Connections: The Political Dynamics of Community Revitalization in Los Angeles," in *Urban Neighborhoods in a New Era:*

Revitalization Politics in the Postindustrial City, edited by Clarence N. Stone and Robert P. Stoker (University of Chicago Press, 2015), p. 141.

14. Adjoa Florência Jones de Almeida, "Radical Social Change: Searching for a New Foundation," in *The Revolution Will Not Be Funded: Beyond the Non-Profit Industrial Complex,* edited by INCITE! Women of Color Against Violence (Duke University Press, 2017), p. 192.

15. Andrea Smith, "Introduction: The Revolution Will Not Be Funded," in *The Revolution Will Not Be Funded: Beyond the Non-Profit Industrial Complex,* edited by INCITE! Women of Color Against Violence (Duke University Press, 2017), p. 8.

16. See D.C. Office of Advisory Neighborhood Commissions, "About Advisory Neighborhood Commissions," https://anc.dc.gov/page/about-ancs.

17. Martin Austermuhle, "'I May Be Incarcerated, but My Voice Still Matters': Resident at D.C. Jail Wins Local Election," dcist, June 16, 2021, https://dcist.com/story/21/06/16/dc-jail-incarcerated-joel-caston-wins-anc -election-ward7/.

18. Matthew Lesch, "Legacies of the Megacity: Toronto's Amalgamation 20 Years Later," IMFG Forum, Institute on Municipal Finance and Governance, 2018, https://tspace.library.utoronto.ca/bitstream/1807/90239/3/imfg _forum_9_legaciesofthemegacity_lesch_August_21_2018.pdf.

19. See Foundation for Community Association Research, https:// foundation.caionline.org/.

20. The Community Investment Trust Case Study, "A New Form of Real Estate Investment Can Help Low-Income People Build Assets and Resilience," Community Investment Trust, http://investcit.com/Content/resources /EPCIT%20Case%20Study%20MC%20White%20Paper%20Updated%20 073120.pdf.

21. Tracy Hadden Loh and Hanna Love, "The Emerging Solidarity Economy: A Primer on Community Ownership of Commercial Real Estate," the Brookings Institution, July 19, 2021, www.brookings.edu/essay/the-emerging -solidarity-economy-a-primer-on-community-ownership-of-real-estate/.

22. A detailed case study describing 3CDC is available from Bruce Katz, Karen L. Black, and Luise Noring, *Cincinnati's Over-the-Rhine: A Private-Led Model for Revitalizing Urban Neighborhoods* (Drexel University Nowak Metro Finance Lab City, 2019), https://drexel.edu/~/media/Files/nowak-lab /NowakLab_3CDC_CityCase_web.ashx.

23. In the intervening years, 3CDC has developed several other equity funding sources, including below-market developer fees and asset management fees. Today, corporate contributions account for approximately 14% of the organization's annual revenue.

24. Bruce Katz et al.

Contributors

SHEILA R. FOSTER is the Scott K. Ginsburg Professor of Urban Law and Policy at Georgetown, where she holds a joint appointment with the Law Center and the McCourt School of Public Policy. Her work focuses on property law and land use, environmental justice, and local government law. She is the coauthor of *Co-Cities: Innovative Transitions Toward Just and Self-Sustaining Communities* (2022). You can learn more about her at sheilarfoster.com.

JILL SIMONE GROSS is a professor of urban policy and planning at Hunter College of the City University of New York and the director of the graduate program in urban policy and leadership. Her work explores urban and regional governance, and her published works include the co-edited *Constructing Metropolitan Space: Actors Policies and Processes of Rescaling in World Metropolises* (2019).

ALEXANDER VON HOFFMAN is a senior fellow at the Joint Center for Housing Studies and lecturer at the Graduate School of Design of Harvard University. An urban historian, he has written many works on housing and community development, including *House by House, Block by Block: The Rebirth of America's Urban Neighborhoods* (2004).

NANCY KWAK is an associate professor of urban history at UC San Diego. She is the author of *A World of Homeowners: American Power and the Politics of Housing Aid*, and she writes histories of housing policy for US cities as well as comparative and global studies of affordable housing, gentrification, and urban informality.

TRACY HADDEN LOH is a fellow with the Anne T. and Robert M. Bass Center for Transformative Placemaking at Brookings Metro, where she integrates her interests in commercial real estate, infrastructure, racial justice, and governance. She serves on the boards of the Washington Metropolitan Area Transit Authority and Greater Greater Washington.

ELENA MADISON is the director of projects at Project for Public Spaces. She has over two decades of experience leading community-based placemaking processes in public spaces across the United States and abroad. In addition to place visioning and implementation, her practice also focuses on co-creating social environments that support diverse users, including people experiencing homelessness.

JOY MOSES is the director of the Homelessness Research Institute at the National Alliance to End Homelessness. For over twenty years, she has worked to reduce poverty and advance racial justice via public policy. Joy has extensively published on these topics, including various white papers and articles.

JULIET MUSSO is an associate professor of public policy and management at the Sol Price School of Public Policy, University of Southern California. She has published extensively on neighborhood governance, urban revitalization, and intergovernmental finance and service provision.

NATE STORRING is the co-executive director of Project for Public Spaces. Storring's writing and projects explore participatory approaches to urban planning, policy, design, and stewardship. In 2016, he co-edited *Vital Little Plans: The Short Works of Jane Jacobs* with urban historian Samuel Zipp.

JENNIFER S. VEY is a senior fellow and the director of the Anne T. and Robert M. Bass Center at Brookings Metro, where she researches and writes on the relationship between place, placemaking, and inclusive economic development. Jennifer co-edited *Re-tooling for Growth: Building a 21st Century Economy in America's Older Industrial Areas* (2008).

Index